W9-DET-888

Improving Employee Health and Well-Being

A volume in
Stress and Quality of Working Life
Ana Maria Rossi, Pamela L. Perrewé, James Campbell Quick,
and James A. Meurs, *Series Editor*

Improving Employee Health and Well-Being

edited by

Ana Maria Rossi
International Stress Management Association

James A. Meurs
University of Calgary

Pamela L. Perrewé
Florida State University

INFORMATION AGE PUBLISHING, INC.
Charlotte, NC • www.infoagepub.com

Library of Congress Cataloging-in-Publication Data

Improving employee health and well-being / edited by Ana Maria Rossi, International Stress Management Association, James A. Meurs, University of Calgary, Pamela L. Perrewe, Florida State University.
    pages cm – (Stress and quality of working life)
 ISBN 978-1-62396-517-4 (pbk.) – ISBN 978-1-62396-518-1 (hardcover) – ISBN 978-1-62396-519-8 (ebook) 1. Job stress. 2. Quality of work life. 3. Employee health promotion. 4. Industrial psychiatry. 5. Psychology, Industrial. I. Rossi, Ana Maria. II. Meurs, James A. III. Perrewe, Pamela L.
 HF5548.85.I47 2014
 658.3'82–dc23

                                                    2013040774

Printed in the United States of America

CONTENTS

SECTION I

THE ROLE OF THE INDIVIDUAL
IN ORGANIZATIONAL STRESS AND WELL-BEING

SECTION II

EXAMINING THE SOCIAL ASPECTS OF OCCUPATIONAL STRESS

SECTION III

THE ROLE OF PREVENTION AND INTERVENTION IN THE QUALITY OF WORKING LIFE

FOREWORD

In the fourth volume of the series *Stress and Quality of Working Life*, we are pleased to present our book of readings entitled *Improving Employee Health and Well-Being*. We have assembled a multi-disciplinary group of experts, who provide an in-depth examination of improving employee health and well-being. This book takes international perspectives on occupational stress and employee well-being. It begins with six chapters that focus on employee psychological and physiological strain, as well as some individual differences that play a significant role in coping with and managing experienced stress. The next two chapters attend to the larger societal role of occupational stress. The final group of chapters in the book examines organizational interventions and preventative stress management in organizations. These twelve chapters explore both fundamental knowledge about occupational stress and new developments within the rapidly growing field of research. We hope that this book heightens your awareness of the role of job stress and that it offers some practical insight for organizations.

We divide our book into three major sections. The first section, *The Role of the Individual in Organizational Stress and Well-Being*, includes six chapters. In the first chapter, Rosen and Ganster examine the role of workplace politics on experienced psychological and physiological strain. In the second chapter, Tetrick and Haimann assess organizational demands and resources as to their effect on presenteeism and health. The third chapter, by Di Lascio, considers quality of working life through employees' sense and meaning. The fourth chapter, by Silva, Goulart, Lopes, Costa, and Guido, studies how to assess stress from an important group of individuals: nursing students. The fifth chapter, by Leon and Halbesleben, examines individual

Improving Emploee Health and Well-Being, pages vii–viii
Copyright © 2014 by Information Age Publishing
All rights of reproduction in any form reserved.

resilience as a way to improve employee well-being. The final chapter in this section is by Cocchiara, Gavin, Gavin, and Quick, who discuss what we can learn from stress responses from the opposite sex.

The second section, *Examining the Social Aspects of Occupational Stress*, includes two chapters. Leite explores the quality of life through the lens of Taylorism, and Bliacheris examines quality of life in public administration via socio-environmental responsibility.

In the third and final section, *The Role of Prevention and Intervention in the Quality of Working Life*, we have four chapters investigating different aspects of this important phenomenon. In Chapter 9, Kelloway, Calnan, Mullen, and Teed take a risk management approach to curbing workplace violence. Chapter 10, by Ogata and Simurro, examines how to encourage behavioral changes through integrative corporate-sponsored programs. In the next chapter, Hatzenberger and Carlotto look at the quality of life and self-care in civil servants. Finally, the last chapter, but Hurrell and Sauter, is an overview of job stress prevention approaches that superbly summaries this section.

A large number of preeminent organizational scientists have contributed their pioneering research to our book's examination of topics such as job stress prevention, workplace demands, physiological reactions to job stress, and socio-environmental considerations. We hope you enjoy the fourth volume in this series, *Stress and Quality of Working Life: Improving Employee Health and Well-Being.*

Ana Maria Rossi
James A. Meurs
Pamela L. Perrewé
Editors

PREFACE

Work overload, resulting in long work days, in addition to the fear of being dismissed, is among the main stressors for Brazilian workers. In Brazil, 70% of the economically active population is affected by the high strain level. Lack of information and awareness regarding the stress level has further compounded the situation.

Excess strain has become so widespread in today's society that it is no longer just a threat to quality of life, but a threat to life itself. For this reason, it is important to understand the level it can achieve and develop strategies that can help to improve quality of life. According to estimates, the cost of occupational stress in Brazil is 3.5% of the GDP/year. In the United States, the estimate is 300 billion U.S. dollars annually according to the American Institute of Stress (AIS).

Proper diagnosis and relevant information are essential so that both employers and employees can be aware of stressors and take effective measures to manage stress. Although quality of life is everyone's responsibility, companies could definitely benefit from the implementation of preventive actions, avoiding a high price to be paid due to absenteeism, sick leaves, reduction in productivity, and low work quality.

Books and meetings aiming at promoting a more in-depth debate cooperate for the clarification of forms of prevention and treatment. Our purpose with this book is to provide readers with tools through important information on stress and the ways of dealing with day-to-day demands and frustrations, because corporate pressures are expected to increase. Here we offer the experience and knowledge of some of the greatest world

Improving Emploee Health and Well-Being, pages ix–x
Copyright © 2014 by Information Age Publishing
All rights of reproduction in any form reserved.

experts in this field. And remember—if you have no control over what affects you, change the way you react to the situation. I wish you good reading and health!

—**Ana Maria Rossi, PhD**
President of ISMA-BR

SECTION I

THE ROLE OF THE INDIVIDUAL
IN ORGANIZATIONAL STRESS AND WELL-BEING

CHAPTER 1

WORKPLACE POLITICS AND WELL-BEING

An Allostatic Load Perspective

Christopher C. Rosen
University of Arkansas

Daniel C. Ganster
Colorado State University

ABSTRACT

Workplace politics has often been described as a source of employee stress. The current chapter draws from the allostatic load model, which is currently the dominant theoretical perspective in stress physiology, to present a framework for explaining how exposure to workplace politics affects employee well-being over time. In addition to describing the influences of politics on indicators of well-being, we draw from popular theories of work stress an individual difference (i.e., political skill) and coping activity (i.e., political behavior) that may serve to limit the extent to which exposure to a political context has an influence on well-being. The effect of political behavior and political skill moderates the effect of organizational politics on well-being. Following the presentation of our model and related propositions, we discuss the implications of our model and identify directions for future research.

Improving Emploee Health and Well-Being, pages 3–23
Copyright © 2014 by Information Age Publishing

3

Over the past 40 years, research examining workplace politics has flourished. The large body of research that has emerged has provided consistent evidence that exposure to workplace politics has deleterious effects on employee outcomes, including job performance, work attitudes, and well-being (see Chang, Rosen, & Levy, 2009). During the same time period, a number of empirical and theoretical advances in the work stress literature have served to enhance our understanding of how exposure to stressors at work affects employee well-being. For example, theories in the work stress literature have evolved to explain specific conditions (e.g., high job demands and uncertainty) that are likely to elicit a stress response from employees, as well as factors (e.g., high levels of control and coping resources) that are likely to mitigate these influences (Hobfoll, 2001; Karasek & Theorell, 1990). Similarly, organizational scholars have made advances in understanding the role of physiological reactivity in explaining underlying processes that link exposure to work stressors to worker well-being (Ganster & Rosen, in press). Drawing from these vast literatures, we develop a framework (see Figure 1.1) that (a) explains how exposure to workplace politics affects employee health and well-being over time and (b) identifies factors that serve to mitigate these influences.

We begin this chapter with a brief review of the workplace politics literature, with a focus on describing the key constructs that have emerged in recent decades. We then define work stress and discuss relevant theoretical frameworks (i.e., job-demands control [JDC] theory and the allostatic load [AL] model) that we use to inform the development of the proposed model in which employee political behavior and political skill collectively influence how employees are affected by workplace politics. Following the presentation of our model, we provide recommendations and identify directions for future research.

ORGANIZATIONAL POLITICS

Within the organizational politics literature, three distinct, but related, streams of research have emerged. The first stream considers politics from the observer's perspective, with a focus on understanding how employees respond to their *perceptions of organizational politics*. The second stream derives from the study of *political behaviors* of employees and how this set of activities is used to promote or protect employee self-interests. Finally, a growing body of research has considered employee political skill, which references an individual difference that influences how employees perceive and respond to the social context of work. Each of these constructs is discussed in detail below.

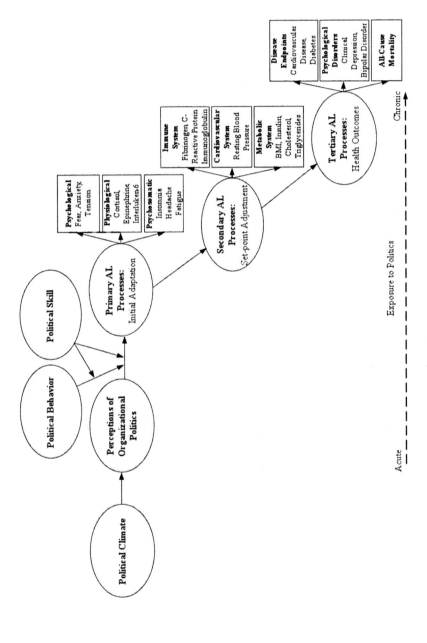

Figure 1.1 Integrative model linking organizational politics to employee well-being.

Perceptions of Organizational Politics

The majority of studies that have investigated workplace politics have focused on understanding antecedents and outcomes of employee *perceptions* of organizational politics (Chang et al., 2009). Perceptions of organizational politics refers to employees' perceptions of the extent to which their coworkers engage in self-serving behaviors (e.g., basing personnel decisions on favoritism rather than merit, taking credit for the work of others, backstabbing, strong-armed influence tactics, ostracism of competitors, impression management, and other influence tactics) that are not formally sanctioned by the organization (Ferris, Russ, & Fandt, 1989; Rosen, Levy, & Hall, 2006). These activities have been described as occurring without regard for, or even at the expense of, organizational goals (Valle & Witt, 2001), and researchers have suggested that perceptions of organizational politics reflect an important dimension of the context in which work is embedded (Levy & Williams, 2004).

Political Behavior

Research on political behavior has emerged somewhat independently of the perceptions of organizational politics literature. In contrast to perceptions of organizational politics, which is taken from the observer's perspective, political behavior refers to the activities of actors. Specifically, political behavior has been defined as a set of informal activities aimed at protecting or promoting self-interest by influencing the thinking, perceptions, or behaviors of others (Ferris & Judge, 1991; Kipnis, Schmidt, & Wilkinson, 1980; Mayes & Ganster, 1988). Political behaviors include both reactive (e.g., passing the buck, stalling, scapegoating) and proactive (e.g., ingratiation, upward appeals, and coalition building) behaviors. The latter category of political behavior is aimed at influencing others or accumulating power and is, therefore, related to one's sense of control over the work environment (Ganster, Rosen, & Mayes, 2011). Overall, accumulating evidence suggests that this set of activities is positively related to a number of work outcomes associated with power and influence, including salary, promotions, and other desirable career outcomes (see Higgins, Judge, & Ferris, 2003).

Political Skill

Political skill refers to the ability of employees to "understand others at work and to use such knowledge to influence others to act in ways that enhance one's personal and/or organizational objectives" (Ahearn, Ferris,

Hochwarter, Douglas, & Ammeter, 2004, p. 311). Extending this definition, political skill has been described as a pattern of social competencies (e.g., social astuteness, interpersonal influence, networking ability, and an ability to project sincerity) that provides individuals with an ability to (a) assess social cues, (b) match behavior to fit situations, and (c) attain goals using interpersonal influence (Ferris et al., 2005). Perrewé and colleagues (Perrewé et al., 2005) have suggested that politically skilled employees enjoy a greater sense of control over their work environment. Specifically, owing to their network centrality, politically skilled employees are thought to have greater access to important information at work, which may enhance one's *perceived* sense of control. Perrewé et al. (2005) also argued that their ability to influence others in their social networks provides politically skilled employees with *actual* control over events at work. Thus, Perrewé et al. (2005) argued that political skill serves as a coping resource that has the potential to mitigate the influence of job demands on employee outcomes, a suggestion that has been substantiated in recent studies (Brouer, Ferris, Hochwarter, Laird, & Gillmore, 2006; Rosen & Levy, 2013).

WORK STRESS

Consistent with Ganster and Rosen (in press), we define work stress as the *process by which workplace psychological experiences and demands produce both short-term and long-term changes in mental and physical health*. In the context of this definition, the term *stressor* refers to environmental events (both chronic and acute) that trigger psychological, physiological, and behavioral responses, which are often referred to as *strains* (Ganster & Perrewé, 2011). A number of theories have emerged to explain how and why exposure to psychosocial work stressors (i.e., events and work characteristics that affect individuals through a psychological process, rather than one that it is directly physical) relates to the experience of strain. Following, we review three theoretical perspectives from the work stress literature (i.e., the JDC model, resource theories, and the AL model) that are relevant to our discussion of how workplace politics relates to health outcomes.

Job Demands-Control Theory

Karasek's (1979) job demands-control (JDC) model has been the single most influential model in the work stress literature. Job demands have traditionally been defined as task requirements at work and include factors such as role conflict, workload, and time pressure (Karasek & Theorell, 1990). Control includes both the worker's authority to make decisions and the breadth of skills that are used. According to the JDC model, the effect of work on both mental and physical well-being is a function of these two factors. The JDC model has stimulated many large-scale studies in the psychology and management literature (Ganster & Perrewé, 2011). At the same time, however, the JDC model has focused researchers on a rather small set of constructs. This is especially the case with the job demands, which is operationalized almost exclusively using a small set of measures that mostly capture workload elements but exclude many others (e.g., negative interpersonal interactions and job insecurity). The control construct has also been treated in different ways, sometimes reflecting behavioral control (or autonomy) and other times combining control with skill and creativity levels of the job.

More recently, job control has come to be seen as one of several resources that can either buffer the effects of demands on well-being or have their own direct effects. The job demands-resources (JDR) model (Demerouti, Bakker, Nachreiner, & Schaufeli, 2001), for example, defines control as a resource but suggests that other resources can be found in physical, psychological, social, or organizational spheres. A more extensive set of resources is proposed in conservation of resources (COR) theory (Hobfoll, 2001), which identifies 74 resources that describe "a comprehensive set that appears to have validity in many Western contexts" (Hobfoll, 2001, p. 341). According to COR theory, people are driven to obtain, preserve, and regain resources and stress results from the loss of resources, the perceived threat of such loss, or when the anticipated return of additional resources is not realized from one's investment of resources. In addition, COR suggests that individual differences serve as resources that affect how individuals react to stressors, such that some people may be better at limiting their loss of resources when confronted with workplace demands (Grandey & Cropanzano, 1999).

The Allostatic Load Model

The allostatic load (AL) model evolved from the work of Selye (1955), who argued that the human body goes through three stages (i.e., alarm, resistance, and exhaustion) when confronted with an environmental threat. The concept of *allostasis* is the process through which the body achieves *stability through change*. Specifically, allostasis refers to physiological response systems that supplement the basic homeostatic systems and respond to environmental stressors, both current and anticipated ones. A distinguishing feature of the AL model is its suggestion that regulatory systems (e.g., the hypothalamic-pituitary-adrenal axis) operate around set-points that can be reset if exposure to chronic demands continually pushes them beyond their normal ranges. In addition, the AL model suggests that the central nervous system plays a critical role by using prior knowledge and experience to anticipate the need for physiological adaptation.

Allostasis, then, refers to the adjustment of various systems (e.g., the metabolic, cardiovascular, neuroendocrine, and immune systems) in order to cope with actual, perceived, or anticipated challenges to homeostatic systems. *Allostatic state* refers to chronic over-activation of allostatic regulatory systems, as well as changes to set points, and *allostatic load* refers to the "wear and tear" on the body after it has been in a repeated or sustained state of allostatic adaptation. Although adaptive in the short term, chronic over-activation of primary allostatic processes (e.g., sympathetic-adrenal-medullary and hypothalamic-pituitary-adrenal axes) can damage the complex of interconnected systems and leave the organism vulnerable to stress-related diseases.

Thus, an important feature of the AL model is that it suggests that multiple adaptation systems interact with each other in complex ways, and there is a temporal sequence to these processes that involves three cascading phases. The first stage of AL regulation involves *primary mediators* that operate in the acute phase and consist of stress hormones (e.g., epinephrine and cortisol) and inflammation-related cytokines (e.g., interleukin-6). These processes embody responses traditionally associated with the "fight or flight response" and are triggered in the central nervous system where threats are encoded. When these primary mediators are activated repeatedly, such as when exposure to stress is chronic, this can adversely affect the integrity of the allostatic mechanisms themselves, which may lead to a set of *secondary outcomes* in which a broader array of biological systems adjusts their normal operating ranges (set-points) in response to dysregulations in the production of primary mediators. At this stage, secondary indicators associated with metabolic (e.g., cholesterol and triglycerides), cardiovascular (e.g., blood pressure), and immune (e.g., fibrinogen, c-reactive protein) system functioning begin to show subclinical perturbations. The continuation of secondary dysregulations over time has the potential to lead to the *tertiary phase* of *allostatic overload*, which is characterized by disease endpoints including physiological, mental, and mortality-related outcomes.

Accumulating empirical research has begun to provide evidence for the three phases of the AL model, and there is evidence, albeit limited, that suggests that overstimulation of primary mediators is associated with dysregulation in secondary mediators and then with tertiary outcomes (see Juster, McEwen, & Lupien, 2010). This evidence is based largely on research that has examined how well composite AL indexes of primary and secondary AL mediators predict disease endpoints, cognitive and physical functioning, and mortality (Seeman, McEwen, Rowe, & Singer, 2001; Seeman, Singer, Rowe, Horwitz, & McEwen, 1997). Given the complexity of the systems involved, there is also some ambiguity regarding how best to operationalize various AL outcomes. AL, however, generally operationalized as some combination of primary and/or secondary mediators, does seem to be implicated in the progression of disease, declines in cognitive functioning in older age, and mortality, so it is of interest to explore predictors of AL itself. Moreover, recent studies have provided support for the AL model in organizational contexts, indicating that work stress (e.g., combinations of demands and control) is associated with various AL formulations (Bellingrath, Weigl, & Kudielka, 2009; Li, Zhang, Sun, Ke, Dong, & Wang, 2007). Together, this research suggests that the AL model is appropriate for explaining how exposure to workplace stressors, such as organizational politics, affects psychological and physiological well-being over time (Ganster & Rosen, in press).

WORKPLACE POLITICS AND EMPLOYEE HEALTH

Drawing from the preceding review, we present a model that explains how perceived politics, political behavior, and political skill combine to influence employee mental and physical health (Figure 1.1). This model serves to integrate the literature and extends existing research on the topic by describing how the influence of politics on well-being are contingent upon whether exposure to politics at work is acute versus chronic. In addition, this model identifies specific behaviors (e.g., political activities) and personal resources (e.g., political skill) that have the potential to neutralize the effects of workplace politics on employee outcomes. Finally, drawing from the AL perspective, our model identifies the various types of health outcomes that are likely to result from short- versus long-term exposure to the stress associated with workplace politics.

Linking Perceived Politics to Stress

The focal relationship in our model is the path that links perceived politics to employee well-being. Perceptions of organizational politics reflect one operationalization of workplace politics, and we acknowledge that there may be other ways of defining and measuring workplace politics (e.g., by assessing politics at the group level of analysis or through aggregation of individuals' behaviors within groups). However, there is likely to be a high degree of correspondence between the objective political climate (i.e., the frequency with which employees engage in political behavior) and employee perceptions of this phenomenon (Ferris et al., 1989; Perrewé, Rosen, & Maslach, 2012). Moreover, operationalizing politics in terms of employee perceptions of the immediate work environment is consistent with stress theories that suggest that the experience of stress is subjective

(Schuler, 1980), such that how employees perceive, appraise, and respond to stressors rests in the eye of the beholder (Folkman & Lazarus, 1990). This is especially true for psychosocial stressors, such as workplace politics, which affect individuals through a psychological stress process, as opposed to a directly physical one. Thus, our model specifies that employee perceptions of organizational politics mediate the effects of the political climate on well-being (Perrewé et al., 2012).

Perceptions of politics have been identified as hindrance stressors that act as a constraint that impedes employees from achieving professional goals (Chang et al., 2009). Moreover, theorists have speculated that politics place demands on employees by putting pressure on them to engage in political activities to (a) defend themselves, (b) get ahead, or (c) compete for limited resources. In addition, workplace politics have been linked to higher levels of interpersonal conflict (Vigoda, 2002), an aversive stimulus that places demands on employees' coping resources. Above all, however, it has been suggested that workplace politics are associated with high levels of ambiguity and uncertainty, as politics obscure reward standards in organizations (Rosen et al., 2006) and weaken linkages between performance and desired rewards (Hall, Hochwarter, Ferris, & Bowen, 2004). For example, in highly political work contexts, employees tend to receive rewards for engaging in influence tactics (e.g., impression management), being members of powerful coalitions, and taking credit for the work of others (Harrell-Cook, Ferris, & Dulebohn, 1999; Treadway, Hochwarter, Kacmar, & Ferris, 2005). However, the rules to the political game are likely to change as power bases shift and alliances are formed between individuals and across departments (Hall et al., 2004), which ultimately generates a great deal of uncertainty regarding which behaviors will lead to optimal career outcomes. Thus, uncertainty associated with high levels of politics, as well as changing and inconsistent reward standards, are likely to be associated with diminished feelings of control and authority, both of which represent key components of the JDC model. However, the extent to which exposure to politics affects various health outcomes is likely to depend on whether exposure to politics is an acute versus chronic aspect of one's work environment.

Acute influences. When politics reflect a more acute aspect of the work context, such that exposure is more event-based (e.g., a single instance of being undermined by a coworker), the AL model suggests that employees will demonstrate a range of emotional, physiological, and psychosomatic symptoms that are of short duration and that fluctuate with the presence of the stressor. Specifically, when politics are present, employees are likely to experience dysregulations reflected by changes in primary AL mediators (e.g., disruption to the diurnal cycle of cortisol output); when individuals are no longer exposed to acute forms of politics, psychological and physiological systems are likely to return to baseline with no changes affecting pre-existing points. This proposition has been corroborated by studies that have utilized within-person designs (e.g., diary and experience sampling studies) to assess momentary relationships between exposure to acute psychosocial stressors at work and a wide range of affective and physiological outcomes (Ilies, Johnson, Judge, & Keeney, 2011; Totterdell, Wood, & Wall, 2006). Moreover, the majority of studies that have explicitly considered the effects of politics on well-being have focused on primary indicators, providing consistent evidence that employee perceptions of politics are associated with a number of affect-laden work attitudes and emotions (Chang et al., 2009; Rosen, Harris, & Kacmar, 2009).

Given the evidence from within-person studies, as well as research that has provided consistent evidence for a relationship between perceived politics and affective outcomes, we posit that acute exposure to workplace politics elicits short-term changes in primary AL mediators involved in initial adaptation to stressors. These short-term fluctuations will be reflected by changes in psychological (e.g., fear, anxiety, and tension), physiological (e.g., increased heart rate, the release of cortisol and epinephrine), and psychosomatic (e.g., sleep disturbance, headache, and fatigue) indicators.

Proposition 1: *Acute exposure to organizational politics is associated with short-term activation of primary AL mediators, reflected by a variety of indicators, including heightened levels of anxiety and tension, somatic complaints, and changes in the production of cortisol and other stress hormones.*

Chronic influences. Organizational politics can be a deeply ingrained aspect of an organization's climate, reflecting a salient and enduring aspect of the work context (Drory, 1993; Landells & Albrecht, in press; Rosen et al., 2009). Thus, it is probably more common for exposure to politics to be chronic in nature, such that employees experience the demands and uncertainty associated with workplace politics on a longer-term, daily basis. The AL model suggests that repeated activation of primary indicators may have adverse influences on allostatic systems, and, as a result, biological systems associated with secondary outcomes may adjust their set-points. This may occur in a relatively short period of time if exposure to the stressor is constant. Thus, as suggested by the AL model, employees who work in highly political contexts may experience chronically high levels of inflammation, elevated resting blood pressure, and harmful changes to their metabolic system that may be detected by high body mass index numbers, elevated cholesterol and triglycerides, and changes in insulin and glucose tolerance.

Relatively little research has considered the influence of workplace politics on secondary AL mediators, as most studies have focused on the effects of workplace politics on employee attitudes, feelings of anxiety, and work behaviors (Chang et al., 2009). The few studies that have considered relevant physiological outcomes (e.g., resting blood pressure) have provided results that are consistent with the notion that political social contexts have the potential to influence secondary AL mediators (Ganster et al., 2011). However, these studies have generally relied on cross-sectional research designs and have failed to consider the duration of exposure to politics. Nonetheless, several studies have shown that the combination of low control and high demands that are often associated with workplace politics are linked to a variety of indicators of secondary mediators, including metabolic syndrome (Chandola, Brunner, & Marmot, 2006), upper respiratory infections and immunoglobulin A (Xie, Schaubroeck, & Lam, 2008), cardiovascular functioning (i.e., off-the-job blood pressure; Perrewé et al., 2004; Schaubroeck & Merritt, 1997), as well as various broad AL composite measures that tap into the functioning of multiple regulatory systems (Li, Zhang, Sun, Ke, Dong, & Wang, 2007).

The AL model suggests that in the long run, exposure to workplace politics may have a cascading effect on well-being that leads to psychological and physiological disease end-points. However, this idea has not been substantiated in the organizational politics literature, as studies have not directly considered the influence of politics on tertiary health outcomes. Nonetheless, large-scale epidemiological studies, which tend to be population based, have provided evidence that employees who are exposed to conditions that have been linked to high levels of politics (i.e., high demands and low control) are at risk of experiencing a variety of tertiary physiological and mental health outcomes. The strongest evidence for an effect on physiology comes from research examining the influence of job strain on cardiovascular disease (CVD). For example, in their comprehensive review of studies containing indicators of CVD, Belkic, Landsbergis, Schnall, and Baker (2004) reported that high demands and low control demonstrate a strong relationship with CVD. More recently, using a cohort from the Whitehall II study of British civil servants, Kivimaki et al. (2011) reported that participants who were classified as experiencing the highest levels of chronic strain (e.g., those who were high in demands and low in both control and support) were at greater risk of developing CVD, even after controlling for factors such as age, cholesterol levels, blood pressure, diabetes mellitus, and smoking. Similarly, in a 15-year follow up on a cohort from the Whitehall II studies, Heraclides, Chandola, Witte, and Brunner (2009) found that job strain (i.e., high demands and low control) predicted the onset of diabetes.

Beyond physiological outcomes, epidemiological studies have also considered the relationship between job demands and control on depression, one of the most commonly studied tertiary mental health outcomes in the AL model. As with CVD, these studies provided evidence that individuals who are classified as experiencing high demands and low control are more likely to experience depression (Mausner-Dorsch & Eaton, 2000; Neidham-mer, Goldberg, Leclerc, Bugel, & David, 1998; Stansfeld, Fuhrer, Shipley, & Marmot, 1999). These findings have been further substantiated in large-sample, longitudinal research that has provided evidence that odds of de-pression are higher for individuals experiencing consistently high levels of strain relative to those who experience low levels of strain (Wang, Schmitz, Dewa, & Stansfeld, 2009).

Thus, based on studies examining the relationship between perceived politics and self-reported primary indicators (e.g., job anxiety and tension), there is relatively strong evidence for a short-term stress effect. Consistent with these findings, within-person studies suggest that when exposure to politics is more acute, these effects will be of limited duration. Few stud-ies have investigated the effects of politics on secondary mediators, but re-search suggests that chronic exposure to stressors in the workplace results in changing set-points (e.g., elevated resting blood pressure). No studies to date have directly linked politics to disease end-points. However, our review indicates that (a) researchers have repeatedly conceptualized politics as a stressor that is associated with an increase in demands and a perceived loss of control and (b) epidemiological studies indicate that these conditions are linked to tertiary AL outcomes. Thus, we propose that chronic exposure to a political work context is associated with dysregulation of physiological systems, changing set-points, and, ultimately, tertiary disease end-points.

Proposition 2: *Chronic exposure to organizational politics is associated with dysregulation of primary AL mediators and system-level subclinical perturba-tions, indicated by changes in secondary AL indicators. In the long-term, if exposure to politics persists and is not effectively managed, these conditions may lead to psychological and physiological disease end-points.*

Mitigating Factors

Propositions 1 and 2 suggest that organizational politics have a variety of negative effects on employee well-being. JDC and resource theories of stress, however, suggest that several factors are likely to mitigate these in-fluences, including coping strategies and individual differences that serve to enhance personal resources. In the current chapter, we focus on two of these factors, political behavior and political skill, which have been linked to the ability of employees to exert control over and gain understanding of the work environment.

Political behavior as a coping response. One way that employees may cope with workplace politics is by engaging in political behaviors, as a prima-ry motivation for employees to engage in political behavior is to reduce uncertainty by exerting control over the environment (Ferris & Hochwarter, 2011; Mayes & Ganster, 1988). Specifically, as noted by Hochwarter, Ferris, Zinko, Arnell and James (2007), the ability to secure information through political behavior is likely to "minimize much of the ambiguity generated strain experienced on the job" (p. 567). As mentioned previously, the JDC model suggests that the interaction between demands and control is important for the development of strain, and control is likely to attenuate the effects of demands on well-being. Thus, consistent with the JDC model, we argue that political behavior represents a coping mechanism that serves to alleviate the effects of workplace politics (a psychosocial demand) by allowing employees to exert control over their work environment and access information that provides them an increased understanding of the political context (Harrell-Cook, Ferris, & Dulebohn, 1999; Hochwarter, 2003).

Empirical research has provided some evidence to support this proposition, indicating that employees respond to ambiguity at work by engaging in political activity (Mayes & Ganster, 1988; Nonis, Sager, & Kumar, 1996). Moreover, there is evidence that political behaviors attenuate the negative effects of working in environments that are more stressful or ambiguous (e.g., Harrell-Cook et al., 1999; Harvey, Stoner, Hochwarter, & Kacmar, 2007), which is consistent with a coping perspective (Brown, Westbrook, & Challagalla, 2005). Thus, we posit that because political behaviors serve to increase control and understanding, they are likely to moderate the effects of workplace politics on employee well-being, such that the relationship between perceptions of politics and well-being will be weaker for employees who effectively engage in political behavior. Moreover, consistent with the AL model, we posit that when employees effectively cope with workplace politics via political behavior, the effects of perceived politics will be more acute and will demonstrate a relatively limited influence on secondary AL mediators and should, therefore, have little to no influence on tertiary outcomes.

Proposition 3: *Political behavior moderates the relationship between perceived politics and psychological and physiological health outcomes, such that the relationship between politics and health outcomes is weaker for those who engage in political behavior.*

Political skill as a personal resource. Consistent with COR theory, we propose that some employees possess resources that make them more effective at coping with the unique forms of social stress that are present in political work contexts. Specifically, a growing body of research suggests that politically skilled employees are "better equipped to participate in work environments that are perceived as political" (Brouer et al., 2006, p. 191). In particular, the combination of political astuteness and the ability to adapt one's behavior to fit the situation provides politically skilled employees with an advantage in terms of influencing others and, hence, exerting control over the work environment. Supporting this idea, several studies have indicated that political skill interacts with social stressors and acts to buffer the effects of stressors on both psychological and physiological indicators of well-being. For example, a study by Perrewé et al. (2004) demonstrated that political skill neutralized the effects of role conflict on strain, indicating that the positive relationship between perceived role stress and physiological indicators of strain (i.e., elevated heart rate and blood pressure) was weaker for those who were politically skilled. Similarly, multiple studies have shown that the negative relationship between perceived politics and various affective indicators of well-being (e.g., job satisfaction, depressive symptoms) is weaker for employees who are more politically skilled (Brouer et al., 2006; Rosen & Levy, 2013). Thus, we propose that political skill acts as an interpersonal resource that provides employees with a sense of control over political work environments and, therefore, attenuates the negative effects of perceived politics on employee well-being

> **Proposition 4:** *Political skill moderates the relationship between perceived politics and well-being, such that the relationship between politics and psychological and physiological health outcomes is weaker for those who are politically skilled.*

Implicit in all previous descriptions of political skill as a neutralizer of the effects of stressors is the notion that politically skilled employees (a) can utilize their social astuteness to recognize which behaviors are appropriate across situations and (b) are able to effectively engage in those behaviors. This suggests that there is an interaction between political skill and political behavior, such that political skill *enhances* the effectiveness of political behaviors. In other words, there is likely to be a three-way interaction between perceived politics, political behavior, and political skill, such that political behavior attenuates the effects of perceived politics on well-being, but this relationship is substantially stronger for those who are politically skilled. In particular, politically skilled employees possess an ability to subtly influence others (i.e., interpersonal influence) and present themselves as honest and sincere (i.e., apparent sincerity). Thus, when these employees engage in political activities (e.g., passing the buck, impression management, ingratiation), they are likely to be more effective and have the anticipated effect on the environment (i.e., promoting or protecting self-interest by influencing others) and, thus, go a long way towards restoring their sense of control over the political environment. Alternatively, those who are low in political skill are unlikely to be as effective in their influence attempts and will, therefore, be less likely to reap the positive benefits associated with engaging in political behavior (e.g., acquiring information or exerting control over the environment) as a means of coping with the ambiguity and uncertainty that exists in highly political work contexts.

Therefore, consistent with the JDC model, we propose that politically skilled employees who engage in political behavior will be the most effective in terms of coping with workplace politics. This suggests that there is a three-way interaction between politics, political behavior, and political skill, such that the effects of politics are more acute and less likely to demonstrate an influence on secondary AL mediators and tertiary outcomes for politically skilled employees who engage in political behavior as a means of exerting control over the political work environment. Consistent with this perspective, we posit that political behavior demonstrates only a modest buffering effect on the relationship between politics and well-being for those who are low in political skill, as the political behaviors of those who are not politically skilled will be less successful in terms of restoring one's sense of control over the political environment.

Proposition 5: *Political skill enhances the effectiveness of political behavior as a coping response, such that the relationship between perceived politics and well-being will be weaker and relatively more acute for politically skilled employees who engage in political behavior.*

DISCUSSION AND FUTURE RESEARCH

In this chapter, we integrated the workplace politics literature with the AL model in an attempt to explain the underlying processes that link workplace politics to acute and chronic forms of strain. Building on our review of the literature, we presented a model that explains how the effects of politics on psychological and physiological well-being emerge over time, with a focus on describing the cascading process suggested by the AL model. Moreover, our model serves to further integrate the politics and stress literatures and extend fundamental thinking about these relationships by explicitly focusing on the significance of the joint effect of political behavior and political skill in the process by which individuals cope with politics at work.

The proposed model has several implications for future research. In particular, the first stage of our model focuses on the *joint influence* of political skill and political behavior in moderating the effects of politics on primary AL outcomes, which reflect the types of strains that are generally considered in organizational research. However, previous studies have generally considered these effects in isolation, without considering whether political skill enhances the efficacy of political behavior as a coping response. Nonetheless, research that has identified political skill as a coping resource suggests that it enhances employee effectiveness, implying that the behaviors of politically skilled employees will be more successful at acquiring desired results or outcomes. Thus, future researchers should explicitly consider the role of political skill in enhancing the efficacy of political behavior in terms of coping with workplace stressors and, similarly, identify the specific behaviors (e.g., upward influence tactics, impression management) that are most likely to be enhanced by political skill.

A broader implication is that our model suggests that the effects of politics on well-being unfold over time in a sequential, cascading process. Specifically, our model suggests that employees who have the resources (i.e., political skill) to effectively engage in political behaviors will likely demonstrate only short-term changes in well-being as a result of exposure to politics. However, those who lack the resources to engage in effective coping behaviors will experience more chronic effects and, in the long-term, may be at risk of suffering serious health outcomes such as those that appear in the secondary and tertiary stages of the AL model.

Unfortunately, the various stages of the AL model include outcomes that are not examined very often in the organizational sciences. For example, the majority of studies that have examined the effects of politics on health outcomes have focused on self-reported measures of affective well-being (e.g., job anxiety and tension, depressive symptoms). To our knowledge, no published studies have investigated the relationship between the political climate (either objective or perceived) and physiological indicators of well-being. Thus, a first step should be for future studies to systematically evaluate the role of politics in eliciting a stress response, as indicated by physiological outcomes.

Primary AL indicators are the most likely to fluctuate in response to the presence of workplace stressors (Ganster & Rosen, in press), even for those who effectively cope with stressors in the short run. Therefore, a good starting point would be to assess relationships between politics and primary physiological outcomes, such as ambulatory blood pressure and cortisol. Once these effects have been established, it would behoove researchers to conduct large scale longitudinal studies that consider how political environments and related social stressors at work affect employee well-being over time, with a focus on (a) linking politics to the cascading sequence suggested by the AL model and (b) testing the notion that primary indicators demonstrate a weaker relationship with secondary and tertiary outcomes for politically skilled employees who engage in political behavior.

CONCLUSION

For decades, scholars have identified organizational politics as an ubiquitous aspect of work life that is a source of stress to employees. However, relatively little is known about the underlying processes that link organizational politics to short- and long-term health outcomes. In the current chapter, we draw from the AL model to present a framework for organizing and understanding how the effects of politics on well-being develop over time. In addition, we integrate the AL model with popular theories of work stress (e.g., JDC and COR theories) that explain how the joint effect of political behavior and political skill moderates the effect of organizational politics on well-being. Though this chapter is likely to generate more questions than it answers (e.g., Which political behaviors are most enhanced by political skill? Which physiological outcomes are most influenced by politics? How long does it take for this process to unfold?), we hope that it has provided a platform for systematically examining short- and long-term stress-based outcomes of organizational politics, as an examination of the process that links politics to well-being will contribute to a better understanding of both phenomena.

REFERENCES

Ahearn, K. K., Ferris, G. R., Hochwarter, W. A., Douglas, C., & Ammeter, A. P. (2004). Leader political skill and team performance. *Journal of Management, 30,* 309–327.

Belkic, K. L., Landsbergis, P. A., Schnall, P. L., & Baker, M. D. (2004). Is job strain a major source of cardiovascular disease risk? *Scandinavian Journal of Work, Environment, and Health, 30,* 85–128.

Bellingrath, S., Weigl, T., & Kudielka, B. M. (2009). Chronic work stress and exhaustion is associated with higher allostatic load in female school teachers. *Stress, 12,* 37–48.

Brouer, R. L., Ferris, G. R., Hochwarter, W. A., Laird, M. D., & Gillmore, D. C. (2006). The strain-related reactions to perceptions of organizational politics as a workplace stressor: Political skill as a neutralizer. In E. Vigoda-Gadot & A. Drory (Eds.), *Handbook of organizational politics* (pp. 187–206). Northhampton, MA: Edward Elgar Publishing, Inc.

Brown, S. P., Westbrook, R. A., & Challagalla, G. (2005). Good cope, bad cope: Adaptive and maladaptive coping strategies following a critical negative work event. *Journal of Applied Psychology, 90,* 792–798.

Chandola, T., Brunner, E., & Marmot, M. (2006). Chronic stress at work and the metabolic syndrome: Prospective study. *British Medical Journal, 332,* 521–525.

Chang, C. -H., Rosen, C. C., & Levy, P. E. (2009). The relationship between perceptions of organizational politics and employee attitudes, strain, and behavior: A meta-analytic examination. *Academy of Management Journal, 52,* 779–801.

Demerouti, E., Bakker, A. B., Nachreiner, F., & Schaufeli, W. B. (2001). The job demands-resources model of burnout. *Journal of Applied Psychology, 86,* 499–512.

Drory, A. (1993). Perceived political climate and job attitudes. *Organization Studies, 14,* 59–71.

Ferris, G. R., & Hochwarter, W. A. (2011). Organizational politics. In S. Zedeck (Ed.), *APA handbook of industrial and organizational psychology* (Vol. 3, pp. 435–459). Washington, DC: American Psychological Association.

Ferris, G. R., & Judge, T. A. (1991). Personnel/human resources management: A political influence perspective. *Journal of Management, 17,* 447–488.

Ferris, G. R., Russ, G. S., & Fandt, P. M. (1989). Politics in organizations. In R. A. Giacalone & P. Rosenfeld (Eds.), *Impression management in organizations* (pp. 143–170). Newbury Park, CA: Sage.

Ferris, G. R., Treadway, D. C., Kolodinsky, R. W., Hochwarter, W. A., Kacmar, C. C., & Frink, D. D. (2005). Development and validation of the political skill inventory. *Journal of Management, 31,* 126–153.

Folkman, S., & Lazarus, R. S. (1990). Coping and emotion. In N. L. Stein, B. Leventhal, & T. Trabasso (Eds.), *Psychological and biological approaches to emotion* (pp. 313–332). Hillsdale, NJ: Lawrence Erlbaum.

Ganster, D. C., & Perrewé, P. L. (2011). Theories of occupational stress. In J. C Quick & L. E. Tetrick (Eds.), *Handbook of occupational health psychology* (2nd ed, pp. 37–53). Washington, DC: American Psychological Association.

Ganster, D. C., & Rosen, C. C. (in press). Work stress and employee health: A multidisciplinary review. *Journal of Management.*

Ganster, D. C., Rosen, C. C., & Mayes, B. T. (2011, May). Organizational politics and blood pressure: Divergent effects of political behavior and political climate. Paper presented at the 11th annual Work, Stress, and Health, 2011 Conference, Orlando, FL.

Grandey, A. A., & Cropanzano, R. (1999). The conservation of resources model applied to work-family conflict and strain. *Journal of Vocational Behavior, 54,* 350–370.

Hall, A. T., Hochwarter, W. A., Ferris, G. R., & Bowen M. G. (2004). The dark side of politics in organizations. In R. W. Griffin & A. M. O'Leary-Kelly (Eds.), *The dark side of organizational behavior* (pp. 237–261). San Francisco, CA: Jossey-Bass.

Harrell-Cook, G., Ferris, G. R., & Dulebohn, J. H. (1999). Political behaviors as moderators of the perceptions of organizational politics-work outcomes relationships. *Journal of Organizational Behavior, 20,* 1093–1105.

Harvey, P., Stoner, J., Hochwarter, W., & Kacmar, C. (2007). Coping with abusive supervision: The neutralizing effects of ingratiation and positive affect on negative employee outcomes. *The Leadership Quarterly, 18,* 264–280.

Heraclides, A., Chandola, T., Witte, D. R., & Brunner, E. J. (2009). Psychosocial stress at work doubles the risk for type 2 diabetes in middle-aged women. *Diabetes Care, 32,* 2230–2235.

Higgins, C. A., Judge, T. A., & Ferris, G. R. (2003). Influence tactics and work outcomes: A meta-analysis. *Journal of Organizational Behavior, 24,* 89–106.

Hobfoll, S. E. (2001). The influence of culture, community, and the nested-self in the stress process: Advancing conservation of resources theory. *Applied Psychology: An International Review, 50*, 337–421.

Hochwarter, W. A. (2003). The interactive effects of pro-political behavior and politics perceptions on job satisfaction and affective commitment. *Journal of Applied Social Psychology, 33*, 1360–1378.

Hochwarter, W. A., Ferris, G. R., Zinko, R., Arnell, B., & James, M. (2007). Reputation as a moderator of political behavior-work outcomes relationships: A two-study investigation with convergent results. *Journal of Applied Psychology, 92*, 567–576.

Ilies, R., Johnson, M. D., Judge, T. A., & Keeney, J. (2011). A within-individual study of interpersonal conflict as a work stressor: Dispositional and situational moderators. *Journal of Organizational Behavior, 32*, 44–64.

Juster, R. -P., McEwen, B. S., & Lupien, S. J. (2010). Allostatic load biomarkers of chronic stress and impact on health and cognition. *Neuroscience and Biobehavioral Reviews, 35*, 2–16.

Karasek, R. (1979). Job demands, job decision latitude, and mental strain: Implications for job redesign. *Administrative Science Quarterly, 24*, 285–306.

Karasek, R., & Theorell, T. (1990). *Healthy work: Stress, productivity, and the reconstruction of working life.* New York, NY: Basic Books.

Kipnis, D., Schmidt, S. M., & Wilkinson, I. (1980). Intraorganizational influence tactics: Explorations in getting one's way. *Journal of Applied Psychology, 65*, 440–452.

Kivimaki, M., Nyberg, S. T., Batty, G. D., Shipley, M. J., Ferrie, J. E., Virtanen, M., ... Hamer, M. (2011). Does adding information on job strain improve risk prediction for coronary heart disease beyond the standard Framingham risk score? The Whitehall II study. *International Journal of Epidemiology, 40*, 1577–1584.

Landells, E., & Albrecht, S. L. (in press). Organizational political climate: Shared perceptions about the building and use of power bases. *Human Resource Management Review.*

Levy, P. E., & Williams, J. R. (2004). The social context of performance appraisal. *Journal of Management, 30*, 881–905.

Li, W., Zhang, J. Q., Sun, J., Ke, J. H., Dong, Z. Y., & Wang, S. (2007). Job stress related to glycol-lipid allostatic load, adinonectin visfatin. *Stress and Health, 23*, 257–266.

Mausner-Dorsch, H., & Eaton, W. W. (2000). Psychosocial work environment and depression: Epidemiological assessment of the demand-control model. *American Journal of Public Health, 90*, 1765–1770.

Mayes, B. T., & Ganster, D. C. (1988). Exit and voice: A test of hypotheses based on fight/flight responses to job stress. *Journal of Organizational Behavior, 9*, 199–216.

Neidhammer, I., Goldberg, M., Leclerc, A., Bugel, I., & David, S. (1998). Psychosocial factors at work and subsequent depressive symptoms in the GAZEL co-host. *Scandinavian Journal of Work, Environment, and Health, 24*, 197–205.

Nonis, S. A., Sager, J. A., & Kumar, K. (1996). Salesperson use of upward influence strategies in coping up role stress. *Academy of Marketing Science Journal, 24*, 44–56.

Perrewé, P., Rosen, C. C., & Maslach, C. (2012). Organizational politics and stress. In G. R. Ferris & D. Treadway (Eds.), *Politics in organizations: Theory and research considerations* (pp. 213–255). New York, NY: Taylor & Francis Group.

Perrewé, P. L., Zellars, K. L., Ferris, G. R., Rossi, A. M., Kacmar, C. J., & Ralston, D. A. (2004). Neutralizing job stressors: Political skill as an antidote to the dysfunctional consequences of role conflict. *Academy of Management Journal, 47,* 141–152.

Perrewé, P. L., Zellars, K. L., Rossi, A. M., Ferris, G. R., Kacmar, C. J., Liu, Y., Zinko, R., & Hochwarter, W. A. (2005). Political skill: An antidote in the role overload—strain relationship. *Journal of Occupational Health Psychology, 10,* 239–250.

Rosen, C. C., Harris, K. J., & Kacmar, K. M. (2009). The emotional implications of perceived organizational politics: A process model. *Human Relations, 62,* 27–57.

Rosen, C. C., & Levy, P. E. (2013). Stresses, swaps, and skill: An investigation of the psychological dynamics that relate work politics to employee performance. *Human Performance, 26,* 44–65.

Rosen, C. C., Levy, P. E., & Hall, R. J. (2006). Placing perceptions of politics in the context of the feedback environment, employee attitudes, and job performance. *Journal of Applied Psychology, 91,* 211–220.

Seeman, E., McEwen, B. S., Rowe, J. W., & Singer, B. H. (2001). Allostatic load as a marker of cumulative biological risk: MacArthur Studies of Successful Aging. *Proceedings of the National Academy of Sciences of the United States of America, 98,* 4770–4775.

Seeman, E., Singer, B. H., Rowe, J., Horwitz, R. I., & McEwen, B. (1997). Price of adaptation—allostatic load and its health consequences: MacArthur Studies of Successful Aging. *Archives of Internal Medicine, 157,* 2259–2268.

Schaubroeck, J., & Merritt, D. E. (1997). Divergent effects of job control on coping with work stressors: The key role of self-efficacy. *Academy of Management Journal, 40,* 738–754.

Schuler, R. S. (1980). Definition and conceptualization of stress in organizations. *Organizational Behavior and Human Performance, 25,* 184–215.

Selye, H. (1955). Stress and disease. *Science, 122,* 625–631.

Stansfeld, S., Fuhrer, R., Shipley, M. J., & Marmot, M. G. (1999). Work characteristics predict psychiatric disorder: Prospective results from the Whitehall II study. *Occupational and Environmental Medicine, 56,* 302–307.

Totterdell, P., Wood, S., & Wall, T. (2006). An intra-individual test of the demands-control model: A weekly diary study of psychological strain in portfolio workers. *Journal of Occupational and Organizational Psychology, 79,* 63–84.

Treadway, D. C., Hochwarter, W. A., Kacmar, C. J., & Ferris, G. R. (2005). Political will, political skill, and political behavior. *Journal of Organizational Behavior, 26,* 229–245.

Valle, M., & Witt, L. A. (2001). The moderating effect of teamwork perceptions on the organizational politics-job satisfaction relationship. *Journal of Social Psychology, 141,* 379–388.

Vigoda, E. (2002). Stress-related aftermaths of workplace politics: The relationship among politics, job distress, and aggressive behaviors in organizations. *Journal of Organizational Behavior, 23,* 571–591.

Wang, J., Schmitz, N., Dewa, C., & Stansfeld, S. (2009). Changes in perceived job strain and the risk of major depression: Results form a population-based longitudinal study. *American Journal of Epidemiology, 169,* 1085–1091.

Xie, J. L., Schaubroeck, J., & Lam, S. S. K. (2008). Theories of job stress and the role of traditional values: A longitudinal study in China. *Journal of Applied Psychology, 93,* 831–848.

CHAPTER 2

OCCUPATIONAL DEMANDS, ENVIRONMENTAL RESOURCES, AND PERSONAL RESOURCES EFFECTS ON PRESENTEEISM AND HEALTH

Lois E. Tetrick and Clifford R. Haimann
George Mason University

ABSTRACT

Considerable research has focused on absenteeism over the years, and absenteeism, especially sickness absenteeism, has been considered to be a major indicator of occupational stress (Ervasti et al., 2011). The focus of this chapter is on the seeming obverse of sickness absenteeism—presenteeism. Presenteeism, defined as going to work when ill, has been related to poor health for a number of purported reasons, such as lack of recovery and subsequent poorer health as well as loss of productivity and potential job loss (Johns, 2011; Poms, 2012; Prochaska et al., 2011). However, the literature on presenteeism lacks a clear conceptual definition and measure of presenteeism (Johns, 2012); this

Improving Emploee Health and Well-Being, pages 25–34

chapter will examine the implications of two of the general conceptualizations of presenteeism. In addition the literature generally has not provided a theoretical framework for understanding the motivation for presenteeism and the potential outcomes. In this chapter, the job demands-resources model of stress (Demerouti, Le Blanc, Bakker, Schaufeli, & Hox, 2009) provides such a framework. Empirical data to support this conceptualization is presented, and the implications for theory and practice are provided.

CONCEPTUALIZATIONS OF PRESENTEEISM

Johns (2010, 2012) provides an excellent overview and discussion of the various definitions of presenteeism. He suggests that the literature has come to a consensus that presenteeism involves "going to work ill…and any productivity deficit that this might occasion" (Johns, 2012, p. 206). Johns suggests, however, that including these two aspects—working while ill and productivity loss—confounds two different factors. Therefore, he suggested that one should measure them separately, with the first aspect reflecting "presenteeism" and the latter reflecting productivity loss. If one incorporates both in the definition of presenteeism, then one can't examine factors that affect individuals' decisions to go to work when ill separate from the possible effect of going to work when ill—productivity loss. It is conceivable that one might be ill but not actually experience a productivity loss as a result of being ill.

Recently, an anonymous reviewer suggested that presenteeism must be a "good thing." I can only assume that this perspective is formed, at least in part, from years of research and concern about how to get employees to come to work, which admittedly is not an insignificant cost to employers. Thus increasing attendance when employees are ill would logically only be considered if (a) by doing so employees experience no productivity loss, or, (b) from a public health perspective, by doing so employees do not transmit their illness to other employees, potentially increasing sickness absence in the organization or unit, or (c) by working when ill employees do not actually further compromise their own well-being. Indeed the empirical literature supports the fact that presenteeism is related to increased absenteeism (Aronsson, Gustafsson, & Dallner, 2000) and may prevent recovery and increase the risk of more serious illnesses (Grinyer & Singleton, 2000). Therefore, the potential effects of going to work when ill may actually have even more negative consequences for employers and employees in the long run (Demerouti et al., 2009).

What does appear to be needed to further our understanding of presenteeism and its effect on individuals and organizations is an assessment of the frequency of going to work when ill separate from potential effects such as productivity loss and decreased well-being. This has been recommended, and it has been implemented by Aronsson and colleagues (Aronsson et al., 2000; Aronsson, Svensson, & Gustafsson, 2003; Aronsson & Gustafsson, 2005), Johns (2011), and Demerouti et al. (2009). Johns (2012) articulates several limitations in trying to assess productivity loss, reviewing several attempts to do so, and concludes that there is insufficient evidence for the validity of the construct. This has not curtailed further attempts with additional measures being developed, such as Prochaska, Evers, Johnson, Castle, Prochaska, Sears, Rula and Pope's (2011) *well-being assessment for productivity*, with some initial supporting evidence that it captures performance barriers of presenteeism.

THE JOB DEMANDS-RESOURCES MODEL AS A FRAMEWORK

The job demands-resources (JD-R) model of burnout (Bakker & Demerouti, 2007) posits that job demands such as high levels of effort being required of an employee can lead to impaired health through strain or burnout, whereas resources such as support and autonomy can lead to well-being through positive motivational processes such as work engagement (Schaufeli, Bakker, & van Rhenen, 2009). According to this framework then, there are dual processes by which the work environment and personal characteristics can foster either engagement or burnout (Bakker, Demerouti, & Schaufeli, 2003). In addition, the JD-R posits that resources can buffer the effects of job demands on burnout and work engagement, and this has generally been supported empirically. For example, Xanthopoulou, Bakker, Dollard, Demerouti, Schaufeli, Taris, and Schreurs (2007) found that the effects of job demands on burnout were ameliorated by the resources of autonomy, social support, and opportunities for professional development, and these buffering effects were strongest for emotional demands. Also, Schaufeli, Bakker, and van Rhenen (2009) found that as job demands increased and resources decreased (with resources considered being social support, autonomy, opportunities to learn, and feedback) burnout increased, and increases in resources predicted work engagement.

Only a few studies have used the JD-R framework to examine the effect of demands or resources on health outcomes such as general health, presenteeism, and absence. Schaufeli et al. (2009) did find support for burnout positively predicting sickness absence and engagement negatively predicting sickness absence. Similarly, in a three-wave longitudinal study, Demerouti, Le Blanc, Bakker, Schaufeli and Hox (2009) found support for job demands leading to burnout and burnout leading to presenteeism, but they did not include resources in this study, examining only the impairment process of the JD-R.

From our review of the literature, it appears that the role of resources has been under-studied in examinations of the JD-R model of burnout and engagement. Further, although there have been some studies that have included social support from coworkers and/or supervisors as specific resources (e.g., Korunka, Kubicek, Schaufeli, & Hoonakker, 2009; Taipale, Selander, Anttila, & Natti, 2010), the role of perceived organizational support (POS) has yet to be examined. Perceived organizational support (Eisenberger, Huntington, Hutchison, & Sowa, 1986; Eisenberger & Stinglhamber, 2011) is defined as employees' beliefs that their organization values them as individuals, and it affects employees' attitudes and behaviors through social exchange theory's norm of reciprocity (Blau, 1964; Gouldner, 1960). Like other resources, such as social support, we expect that POS would be positively related to work engagement and employee well-being, consistent with the JD-R model of burnout and engagement. And, in fact, there is some support for this. For example, Panaccio and Vandenberghe (2009) found that POS was positively related to psychological well-being. Similarly, Zhao, Zhang, Wei, Lu, Bai, and Zhang (2010) found POS to be positively related to both psychological well-being and physical health. Kinnunen, Feldt, and Mäkikangas (2008) also provide support for the notion that POS is positively related to all three dimensions of work engagement (vigor, dedication, and absorption).

Therefore, based on the POS literature and the JD-R model, we propose that health outcomes are affected by the amount of effort required by the job (e.g., job demands) and POS (e.g., resources), as mediated by work engagement (see Figure 2.1). Additionally, we have incorporated another resource, adjustment latitude. Adjustment latitude (Johansson & Lundburg, 2004) is the degree to which employees can "adjust" their work conditions when feeling ill by reducing their effort by choosing among tasks or slowing their pace. This reflects a certain level of control or autonomy over the

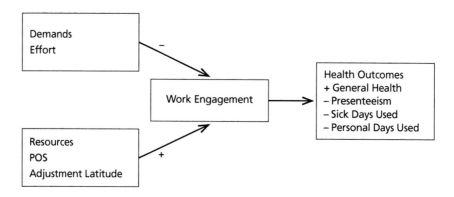

Figure 2.1 JD-R framework.

work environment, which has been previously incorporated in the JD-R as a resource (Bakker & Demerouti, 2007; Schaufeli et al., 2009; Xanthopoulou et al., 2007). Adjustment latitude seems to have some relevance to an individual's productivity, although this may be a function of the job and the duration of the sickness presenteeism episode. Adjustment latitude is a more proximal resource that POS, and therefore our model allows examination of the effect of the more global concept of POS compared to the more proximal resource of control within the JD-R framework.

Not reflected in Figure 2.1, although consistent with the literature on the buffering effects of resources in the JD-R, we also expected, consistent with Hu, Schaufeli, and Taris (2011), that both resources—POS and adjustment latitude—would lessen the effects of effort, such that the more resources employees have to meet the demands of their jobs, the less the job demands will reduce work engagement. It is also feasible that there would be an interaction between the two resources. The literature supports a positive relation between POS and work engagement; however, if adjustment latitude reflects control over the work environment and is more proximal than POS, the literature on the job demands-control model (Karasek & Theorell, 1990) and JD-R suggest that POS might have a stronger effect on work engagement when individuals also have higher levels of adjustment latitude.

AN EMPIRICAL EXAMINATION OF JD-R, ENGAGEMENT, AND HEALTH

Methodology

Recognizing differences in sick leave policies across organizations, we sought to obtain a diverse sample of working adults using Mechanical Turk, which has been demonstrated to provide high quality data from diverse samples (Buhrmester, Kwang, & Gosling, 2011; Paolacci, Chandler, & Ipeirotis, 2010). Responses were obtained from 347 individuals who reported working 44 hours, on average, the week before completing the survey. Forty-six percent of the sample were male, 42% earned $20,000–39,000 in the past year, 26% earned $40,000–59,000, 30% reported having some college studies, 36% reported having a college degree, 47% were married, and 61% reported having no dependent children.

General health was measured with a single item from the Centers for Disease Control and Prevention's Health-Related Quality of Life instrument (Centers for Disease Control and Prevention, 2000; Hennessy, Moriarty, Zack, Scherr & Brackbill, 1994), the number of days they had gone into work when ill in the last six months, or presenteeism (Aronsson, Gustafsson, & Dallner, 2000); the number of sick days allowed by their employer and the number of sick days used (sickness absence balance); and the number of personal days allowed by their employer and the number of personal days used (personal days absence balance). These latter two variables were computed such that negative balances would reflect taking more time off than granted. Participants completed the nine-item Utrecht Work Engagement Scale with a seven-point response scale (Schaufeli, Bakker, & Salanova, 2006). Effort, reflecting job demands, was measured using five items with a five-point response scale (Siegrist et al., 2004); POS was measured using eight items from Eisenberger et al. (1986) with a seven-point response scale; and adjustment latitude was measured with Johansson and Lundburg's (2004) item that asked respondents how frequently they could adjust their work to how they were feeling. All multi-item measures had acceptable levels of reliability (alpha > .72).

Results and Discussion

The data were fit to Figure 2.1 using LISREL 8.7. This model did not fit the data well (RMSEA = .14). POS was positively related to work engagement, but neither effort nor adjustment latitude were related to work engagement. Work engagement was positively related to general health but not to presenteeism or use of sick days and personal days. These results support POS as a resource affecting the motivational process of the JD-R. The lack of fit resulted from correlations among the residuals of the health outcomes as incomplete mediation effects.

Therefore, we conducted moderated regression analyses for each of the health outcomes as shown in Table 2.1, including the hypothesized interactions. Interestingly, adjustment latitude interacted with effort in predicting both general health and presenteeism (see Figures 2.2 and 2.3), but POS did not interact with effort or adjustment latitude. Therefore, while POS

TABLE 2.1   Moderated Regression Analyses

Independent variables	General health	p	Presenteeism	p
Work engagement	0.039	0.555	0.010	0.882
Effort	−0.536	0.036	0.461	0.070
POS	0.536	0.055	−0.296	0.274
Adjustment latitude	0.103	0.709	−0.020	0.943
Adjustment latitude × POS	−0.612	0.071	0.255	0.445
Effort × POS	−0.181	0.419	0.201	0.367
Effort × Adjustment latitude	0.606	0.003	−0.477	0.019
R-squared	0.099	0.000	0.111	0.000

and adjustment latitude may both be resources, the mechanisms appear to be different. POS operates through the motivational pathway of the JD-R, and adjustment latitude seems to operate more as a source of control within the framework of the JD-control framework (Karasek & Theorell, 1990).

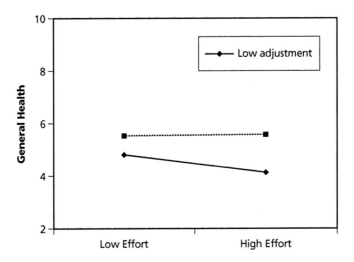

Figure 2.2 Interaction of effort and adjustment in predicting general health.

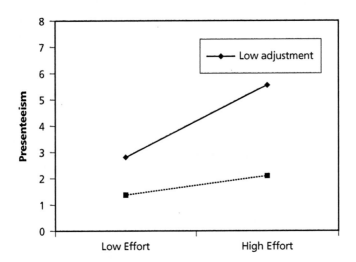

Figure 2.3 Interaction of effort and adjustment latitude in predicting presenteeism.

REFERENCES

Aronsson, G., & Gustafsson, K. (2005). Sickness presenteeism: Prevalence, attendance-pressure factors, and an outline of a model for research. *Journal of Occupational and Environmental Medicine, 47*(9), 958–966. doi:10.1097/01. jom.0000177219.75677.17

Aronsson, G., Gustafsson, K., & Dallner, M. (2000). Sick but yet at work: An empirical study of sickness presenteeism. *Journal of Epidemiology and Community Health, 54*, 502–509. doi:10.1136/jech.54.7.502

Aronsson, G., Svensson, L., & Gustafsson, K. (2003). Unwinding, recuperation, and health among compulsory school and high school teachers in Sweden. *International Journal of Stress Management, 10*(3), 217–234. doi:10.1037/1072-5245.10.3.217

Bakker, A. B., & Demerouti, E. (2007). The job demands-resources model: State of the art. *Journal of Managerial Psychology, 22*(3), 309–328. doi:10.1108/02683940710733115

Bakker, A. B., Demerouti, E., & Schaufeli, W. B. (2003). Dual processes at work in a call centre: An application of the job demands-resources model. *European Journal of Work and Organizational Psychology, 12*(4), 393–417. doi:10.1080/13594320344000165

Blau, P. M. (1964). *Exchange and power in social life.* New Brunswick, NJ: Transaction.

Buhrmester, M., Kwang, T., & Gosling, S. D. (2011). Amazon's Mechanical Turk: A new source of inexpensive, yet high-quality, data? *Perspectives on Psychological Science, 6*(1), 3–5. doi:10.1177/1745691610393980

Centers for Disease Control and Prevention. (2000). *Measuring healthy days.* Atlanta, GA: U.S. Department of Health and Human Services. Retrieved from http://www.cdc.gov/hrqol/pdfs/mhd.pdf

Demerouti, E., Le Blanc, P. M., Bakker, A. B., Schaufeli, W. B., & Hox, J. (2009). Present but sick: A three wave study on job demands, presenteeism and burnout. *Career Development International, 14*(1), 50–68. doi:10.1108/13620430910933574

Eisenberger, R., Huntington, R., Hutchison, S., & Sowa, D. (1986). Perceived organizational support. *Journal of Applied Psychology, 71*(3), 500–507. doi:10.1037/0021-9010.71.3.500

Eisenberger, R., & Stinglhamber, F. (2011). Perceived organizational support. Washington, DC: American Psychological Association. doi: 10.1037/12318-002

Ervasti, J., Kivimäki, M., Pentti, J., Suominen, S., Vahtera, J., & Virtanen, M. (2011). Sickness absence among Finnish special and general education teachers. *Occupational Medicine, 61*(7), 465–471. doi:10.1093/occmed/kqr087

Gouldner, A. W. (1960). The norm of reciprocity: A preliminary statement. *American Sociological Review, 25*, 161–178.

Grinyer, A., & Singleton, V. (2000). Sickness absence as risk-taking behavior: A study of organisational and cultural factors in the public sector. *Health, Risk & Society, 2*(1), 7–21.

Hennessy, C., Moriarty, D. G., Zack, M. M., Scherr, P., & Brackbill, R. (1994). Measuring health-related quality of life for public health surveillance. *Public Health reports, 109*, 665–672.

Hu, Q., Schaufeli, W. B., & Taris, T. (2011). The job demands-resources model: An analysis of additive and joint effects of demands and resources. *Journal of Vocational Behavior, 79*, 181–190. doi: 10.1016/j.jvb.2010.12.009

Johansson, G., & Lundberg, I. (2004). Adjustment latitude and attendance requirements as determinants of sickness absence or attendance. Empirical tests of the illness flexibility model. *Social Science & Medicine, 58*(10), 1857–1868. doi:10.1016/S0277-9536(03)00407-6

Johns, G. (2010). Presenteeism in the workplace: A review and research agenda. *Journal of Organizational Behavior, 31*(4), 519–542. doi:10.1002/job.630

Johns, G. (2011). Attendance dynamics at work: The antecedents and correlates of presenteeism, absenteeism, and productivity loss. *Journal of Occupational Health Psychology, 16*(4), 483–500. doi: 10.1037/a0025153

Johns, G. (2012). Presenteeism: A short history and a cautionary tale. In J. Houdmont, S. Leka, & R. R. Sinclair (Eds.), *Contemporary occupational health psychology* (pp. 204–220). West Sussex, UK: Wiley-Blackwell.

Karasek, R. A., & Theorell, T. (1990). *Healthy work: Stress, productivity, and the reconstruction of working life.* New York, NY: Basic Books.

Kinnunen, U., Feldt, T., & Mäkikangas, A. (2008). Testing the effort-reward imbalance model among Finnish managers: The role of perceived organizational support. *Journal of Occupational Health Psychology, 13*(2), 114–127. doi:10.1037/1076-8998.13.2.114

Korunka, C., Kubicek, B., Schaufeli, W. B., & Hoonakker, P. (2009). Work engagement and burnout: Testing the robustness of the job demands-resources model. *Journal of Positive Psychology, 4*, 243–255. doi: 10.1080/17439760902879976

Panaccio, A., & Vandenberghe, C. (2009). Perceived organizational support, organizational commitment and psychological well-being: A longitudinal study. *Journal of Vocational Behavior, 75*(2), 224–236. doi:10.1016/j.jvb.2009.06.002

Paolacci, G., Chandler, J., & Ipeirotis, P. G. (2010). Running experiments on Amazon Mechanical Turk. *Judgment and Decision Making, 5*, 411–419.

Poms, L. (2012). *Presenteeism: The dark side of employee attendance.* Unpublished doctoral dissertation, George Mason University, Fairfax, VA.

Prochaska, J. O., Evers, K. E., Johnson, J. L., Castle, P. H., Prochaska, J. M., Sears, L. E., Rula, E. Y., & Pope, J. E. (2011). The well-being assessment for productivity: A well-being approach to presenteeism. *Journal of Occupational and Environmental Medicine, 53*(7), 735–742. doi:10.1097/JOM.0b013e318222af48

Schaufeli, W. B., Bakker, A. B., & Salanova, M. (2006). The measurement of work engagement with a short questionnaire: A cross-national study. *Educational and Psychological Measurement, 66*, 701–716.

Schaufeli, W. B., Bakker, A. B., & van Rhenen, W. (2009). How changes in job demands and resources predict burnout, work engagement, and sickness absenteeism. *Journal of Organizational Behavior, 30*, 893–917.

Siegrist, J., Starke, D., Chandola, T., Godin, I., Marmot, M., Niedhammer, I., & Peter, R. (2004). The measurement of effort-reward imbalance at work: European comparisons. *Social Science & Medicine, 58*(8), 1483–1499. doi:10.1016/S0277-9536(03)00351-4

Taipale, S., Selander, K., Anttila, T., & Natti, J. (2010). Work engagement in eight European countries: The role of job demands, autonomy, and social support. *International Journal of Sociology and Social Policy. 31,* 486–504.

Xanthopoulou, D., Bakker, A. B., Dollard, M. F., Demerouti, E., Schaufeli, W. B., Taris, T. W., & Schreurs, P. J. G. (2007). When do job demands particularly predict burnout? The moderating role of job resources. *Journal of Managerial Psychology, 22*(8), 766–786. doi:10.1108/02683940710837714

Zhao, J., Zhang, X. -c., Wei, S. -y., Lu, J. -w., Bai, J., & Zhang, T. -j. (2010). Organizational justice, psychological well-being, physical health of flight attendants: Mediating role of perceived organizational support. *Chinese Journal of Clinical Psychology, 18*(4), 498–500.

CHAPTER 3

QUALITY OF WORKING LIFE

Meaning and Sense for Companies and Employees

Raphael Henrique C. Di Lascio

ABSTRACT

The objective of this study was to establish the distinction between sense and meaning of work with quality of working life, as well as to understand to whom quality of working life is most relevant—the employee or the employer. For analysis and comparison, we used the results of a study that investigated factors of quality of working life for 180 nursing professionals in the pediatric wing of two hospitals. It consisted of a questionnaire with 21 open-ended questions and used the qualitative-description and quantitative methods. An evaluation of the results revealed that in terms of factors of quality of working life, there are often imperceptible difficulties that cause stress and low self-esteem in the employee. This study aims to use this, and analyze, correlate, and compare with other data, information and theories. Quality systems seek to identify performance indicators for companies; however, these might hide dissatisfaction, which stems from not meeting the basic needs of the professionals in their working environment. The sense and meaning of quality of working life are often absent for the employee if this issue is seen simply as an obligation, and this generates problems for both the company and the employee.

Improving Emploee Health and Well-Being, pages 35–51

THE SENSE OF WORK

For the most part, people look for work so that they are able to meet their basic needs, to consume, to feel satisfied, and to be socially and professionally accomplished. In other words, they do so in order to be able to exercise their right to citizenship.

In order to better understand the issue, and the importance of doing work that carries meaning, it is necessary to revisit some facts concerning human behavior that are forgotten in the majority of environments in which the work is carried out.

The world and its economy are changing. Workplace relations are no longer as they once were. Careers and jobs are going through a period of profound transformation.

The concept of work harbors enormous ambivalence and paradox, and once it evolved from something associated with punishment, it now has the ability to create, define, and guarantee human existence (under the right conditions).

Increasingly, the outline—or concept—of the job is becoming broader, more flexible, and more dynamic, with people receiving a task and identifying the steps they judge to be most appropriate. Responsibilities are attributed in a more participative way, and subordination gives rise to mutual trust in the workplace. Self-determination and self-direction are becoming key words in the revolution of work within companies.

Etymologically speaking, the word "*sentido*" (in Portuguese, or "meaning" in English) derives from the Latin *sensus*, which pertains to perception, meaning, sentiment, or to the Latin verb *sentire*, meaning to perceive, feel, and know (Harper, 2001). It is found that this word "*sentido*" (or "sense" in English) can be used as a synonym for the word "*significado*" (or "meaning" in English) and that its origin refers principally to the occurrence of basic psychological processes. As a result, a considerable number of studies on meaning and sense are being developed by psychologists, but also by sociologists, administrators, and professionals in the field of social communication.

Initially, psychologists Hackman and Oldham (1975, and cited in Tolfo & Piccinini, 2007) related the "sense" of work to the quality of working life. According to these authors, a job that is makes sense is important, useful, and legitimate for the person doing it, and it presents the following three fundamental characteristics: (a) a variety of tasks that facilitate the use of diverse skills, so that the worker identifies with doing the work; (b) work that is not isolated, meaning that the worker can identify the whole process from beginning to end and can identify the meaning of it, contributing to the social environment, autonomy, freedom, and independence that determine the way in which the tasks will be carried out, and this will increase the worker's sense of responsibility; and (c) feedback on the performance, allowing the individual to make the necessary adjustments for improvement.

Well-being and life satisfaction are closely linked to the way in which the work is perceived, and the meaning and sense that are present for the individual and for society. As a result, the "senses" attributed to work are always unique, concrete, and historical, as they correspond to the human need to grant meaning to their surroundings, their actions, and their lives (Araújo & Sachuk, 2007). Experiencing sense in one's work is closely linked to the phenomenon of human motivation.

QUALITY OF WORKING LIFE AS SATISFACTION AND MOTIVATION AT WORK

Quality of working life is something that has concerned man from very early on, in an attempt to facilitate tasks and bring satisfaction and well-being to the workers.

It is also known that overall quality does not exist without quality of life. Factors that determine how efficient a company is are directly linked to the employees and their methods of thinking, acting, and their involvement in questions related to the company.

A company is not able to offer quality products or services if their employees do not have a good quality of life. It is fundamental, therefore, that the company concerns itself with the performance of its employees and with attitudes related to quality of their work. This is only possible once there is a good relative standard of living, as a good perspective on life results from stimuli that stem from work itself—that is to say, the capacity for and commitment to improvement, doing your best every day, and always improving through motivation and direct stimuli.

This concerns both the company and the individual—who looks for self-actualization through objectives and personal goals that are not necessarily related to the company. It is also recognized that people do not adopt particular attitudes for the same reasons, and it is within this diversified context that we can find many behaviors governed by motivation—the nontransferable force of each separate individual.

It is therefore necessary to understand humans as bio-psychosocial and emotional beings in order to understand motivation. Employees must feel pleasure and pride in the work they carry out and pride in the organization for which they work. This motivation might be the result of incentives provided by challenges or the result of sharing an environment that is favorable to effective participation and suggestions. Since successful professional and personal actualization is the source of motivational behavior, it is important that the company should carry out a personal and professional development program, which aims to recognize work that is successfully carried out.

For Chiavenato (1997), "the company constitutes an environment in which people work and lead most of their lives" (p. 9). With this in mind, people give a part of themselves and expect something in return, whether it is in the long- or short-term. The way in which this environment is modeled and structured has a huge impact on people's quality of life. More than that, it influences the behavior itself and each person's individual objectives. This, in turn, affects the functioning of the company itself.

With this in mind, companies should make it their aim to encourage the actualization of each employee with the intention of promoting an environment that is increasingly pleasant and promising. Quality of life should ensure that the activities of human beings, principally work activities, are developed with harmony, integration, and in balance with their personal life.

What are the real meanings and senses of "quality of working life"? According to Cavalheiro (2010), speaking from a socio-historical perspective in which meaning and sense are attributed to the everyday, it is necessary to differentiate between activity and action. For Leontiev (1978), human activity consists of a collection of actions. From this point of view then, for the individuals who participate in the activity, meaning is appropriate for them. In such actions, sense corresponds to its meaning. In this way, over the course of human experience, people accumulate ways of carrying out these activities, of understanding the reality in which they live, of expressing themselves and of feeling; and meaning is the reflection of this reality. This conception demonstrates how individuals construct themselves using the results of the social story in which they participate (Basso, 1998).

The following questions therefore arise:

1. What is the *sense* of quality of working life for the employee and for the company?
2. What is the *meaning* of quality of working life for the employee and for the company?

It is perhaps possible to assert that "sense" is well-being in the workplace, and the "meaning" is being happy. It would also be possible to say that the "meaning" of quality of life is well-being and the "sense" is being happy at work.

In reality, the answers to these questions seem obvious, though they have the potential to become dreams or fantasies, nightmares or suffering, or a marketing product that in the end interests the employee as much as the company. When desired by all involved, they can, if correctly implemented, generate good results in terms of productivity, satisfaction, actualization and well-being.

The company needs to be doing well, not just for its survival, but in order to be able to compete against its competitors, to obtain positive results, and to be able to work within its expenses, spending, and production needs. In addition, the factors that drive the corporate world of business also depend on the well-being of the employees.

Working is important as it makes it possible to achieve the satisfaction and professional actualization that we refer to as "well-being" or "quality of working life."

Pressures and demands are put on employees in order that they meet targets and objectives. Strategic planning involves non-favorable and favorable situations that are simulated within the organization in order to visualize possible problems. Everything must be sufficiently researched and planned for a positive result to be reached. This is the meaning of productivity and results, in other words, a human inserted into this context as a productive being.

Cavalheiro (2010), quoting Molon (1999), claims that meaning is inherent in the sign and belongs to consciousness, being felt as a product and result of meaning. Meanings are historical and social productions permeating communication and the socialization of experiences. It addition to this they refer to established content that is fixed and shared and appropriated by humans.

> Sense is much broader than meaning, as the former constitutes the articulation of psychological events that the subject produces when faced with reality. . . . Sense refers to the needs that are often not yet being realized but that mobilize the subject, which constitute his/her being and that generate ways of drawing sense from activities. The term sense highlights historically constructed singularity. (Aguiar, 2006, p. 12–13)

As a result of this, sense defines the subjectivity of the subject with greater precision, as it is the sum of all the affective, cognitive, and biological processes. In order to understand what it is that distinguishes the subject, it is important to analyze the process of forming a meaningful word, and grasping the meaning of the word requires an analytical and interpretive effort in approaching "zones" of meaning (Aguiar, 2006).

> The sense of a word varies greatly depending on the situation and the people attributing it, to the extent that it is considered almost unlimited. This means that words and senses present a high degree of independence from each other, which is something that does not happen between words and meanings. (Molon, 1999, p. 9)

What is the sense of quality of life for the employees of an organization? And how do they define quality of working life? Below are some key questions and answers on the subject that were taken from a study of 180 nurses in the pediatric wing of two hospitals in Curitiba in the Brazilian state of Paraná (Di Lascio, 2003).

- What does quality of life mean to you?

    It's physical, psychological and emotional well-being. Being able *to carry out professional and personal tasks to the desired standard. Having a healthy lifestyle and doing activities with the family.*

- What does quality of working life (QWL) mean to you?

    It's feeling good at work, having a good environment to work in and a good company atmosphere.

- How important is QWL to you?

    QWL is extremely important for being able to carry out our activities well.

- What, for you, is the meaning of quality of working life?

    Getting well-being and satisfaction from your work (the activity as well as the physical environment).

- Are you satisfied with your job?

    Yes, I like my job.

- For you, what is most important for ensuring quality of working life? Activities related to caring for the body or for psychological factors?

    Both are equally important.

- How do you understand quality of working life in terms of caring for your body?

    It's about doing exercise, eating well and having good physical conditions in the workplace.

- What do you understand by quality of working life in terms of psychological care?

    It's taking care of your mind and your emotions, doing relaxing activities and well-being exercises, showing respect in general (companies, supervisors, colleagues/employees, clients etc.) and it's *motivation.*

It is interesting to note that when we look at how people answered the question "What, for you, is the meaning of quality of working life?" people answered by saying "well-being and satisfaction from work," referring both to the activity that they are carrying out and to the climate and environment of the company. It is a broad question mainly because of the meaning that the sentence conveys to people, because it carries a lot of sense.

This is where a link arises between the sense of work and the meaning of quality of working life.

Work carries its own importance and significance in society, creating motives and senses that could be identified as realization and actualization of potential, security and autonomy, forging relationships with others and participating in groups, contributing to society, having a sense for life, and keeping occupied. Literature on the subject indicates that the terms "sense" of work and "meaning" of work are commonly used interchangeably (Meaning of Work International Research Team, 1987; Borges, 1998). Alternatively, no differentiation is made between them, as both are treated as complementary elements that correspond to the same construct.

In a study investigating human needs, Maslow (cited by Chiavenato, 1997) identified five basic common needs, which are organized into a hierarchy using a pyramid shape. At the base of the pyramid are the most basic and common needs, while those at the top are the most sophisticated and intellectual ones (see Figure 3.1).

The five human needs are: physiological needs, safety needs, social needs, esteem needs, and self-actualization needs.

Physiological needs (also known as biological needs) guide human life from birth. They are related to food (thirst and hunger), sleep and rest (fatigue), shelter (heat and cold), and sexual desire (reproduction of the species).

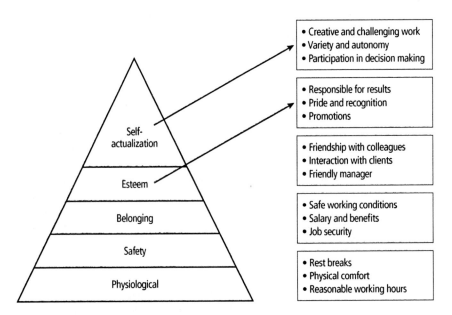

Figure 3.1   Maslow's hierarchy of human needs. *Source:* Chiavenato, 1997.

Safety needs relate to the pursuit of protection from a threat or deprivation, escaping danger, the desire for stability, and the search for an ordered and predictable world (protection of the routine).

Social needs, also known as the need for love and affection, refer to the social life of an individual—association, participation, acceptance by colleagues, and exchange of friendship, affection, and love.

Esteem and ego needs consider the way in which people perceive and evaluate themselves, that is, their self-evaluation and self-esteem. These needs concern self-appreciation, self-confidence, the need for social approval and recognition, status, prestige, and consideration.

Self-actualization needs motivate each person to realize their potential and to progress continuously throughout their lives—to search for "actualization." In discussing this, Cobra (1992) considers that:

> ... when an individual feels hungry, thirsty, tired or sleepy, few other things seem important. A person will aim to satisfy their most pressing need first... when these basic needs begin to be satisfied, the individual will look to satisfy their safety needs, which represent the second level of realization... social needs represent the individual's wish to be accepted by a social group they form part of, and factors such as love and being socially accepted become important. (p. 218)

This does not mean, however, that at any one stage in life, an individual cannot strive to fulfill more than one need at a time, meaning that safety, social, and self-esteem needs can be pursued all at the same time.

Needs vary from person to person, producing different behavior patterns. Social values also vary, as do individuals' capacity to reach their objectives.

When we want to find sense in our work, there are various objectives and needs to consider that give importance to it. Similarly, when considering the sense of quality of working life, if our needs are not fulfilled within the work environment, it carries no meaning, neither in terms of work nor in terms of quality of life.

In Maslow's hierarchy of needs (cited by Chiavenato, 1997), each factor is linked to motivation, which is linked to work and in turn to quality of life.

Herzberg too, put forward an important theory on the same subject (cited in Chiavenato, 1997) known as the *two factor theory*. It goes further in explaining the behavior and motivation of people in work situations. It involves two factors: hygiene factors and motivational factors.

1. *Hygiene factors*, also called "extrinsic factors" or "environmental factors" can be found in the surrounding environment and comprise the conditions in which work is performed. The main hygienic factors are salary, social benefits, how people are managed, the physical

conditions of the working environment, the company policies, the atmosphere within the company, internal regulations, and so on. As these factors are all determined by the company, they are outside of the individual's control.

2. *Motivational factors* are also known as "intrinsic factors." They relate to the requirements of the role and the nature of the tasks that the person carries out. As motivational factors concern what the person does or performs, these factors fall under the individual's control. They involve feelings of personal growth, professional recognition, and the needs of self-actualization. The most important characteristic of motivational factors is that when they are at their optimum, they bring work satisfaction. Conversely, inadequacy breeds dissatisfaction.

This theory is summarized in Figure 3.2, developed by students of Gouveia and Baptista (2007).

Motivation, therefore, is something that exists within individuals and that can be greatly influenced by sources external to the individual, or by their work within the company. Intrinsic and extrinsic motivation must therefore be completed by management, as both cannot be left to chance. This takes the form of satisfaction; in other words, this mixture of the two factors cited includes a good salary, good atmosphere, recognition, opportunities for growth, good management, a good team, and other conditions that are met by the employer—from the perspective of the employee—which are what influence the work environment, and it could be said that this represents the practical application of quality of life at work.

In terms of the motivational situation scheme cited by Hersey and Blanchard (1986), Maslow's work is useful for identifying the needs or motives, and Herzberg can provide suggestions as to the targets and incentives that meet these needs.

The business environment has sought competitiveness because of profound changes in terms of the global economy, social and political relations, technology, production organization, and work relations (Fleury et al., 2002).

These changes generate a dynamic social-corporate environment in which factors linked to survival often overlap with the objectives of long-term

MOTIVATIONAL FACTORS	HYGIENE FACTORS
Feeling and actualization	Relationship with manager
Recognition	Relationship with colleagues
Varied and challenging work	Technical supervision
Personal development	Work environment

Figure 3.2 Hygiene and motivational factors. *Source:* Gouveia & Baptista, 2007.

changes in society that lead to improved living conditions and the well-being of citizens (Fleury et al., 2002).

According to Albuquerque (1992), a context in which organizations pursue productivity and processes of change that look to improve their competitive position (within the market as well as the quality of working life) will gain importance as an intrinsic value in the practices of competitiveness that are concomitant to the well-being of the company.

It is clear that questions related to quality of life have been an important focus for companies over recent years. A study of quality of working life is essential for any company that intends to generate knowledge of decision-making skills; draw attention to the development of tasks, principles of compensation, and good interpersonal relations, among other factors; or promote the construction of work methodologies that are more human and that result in high satisfaction and productivity of employees. Quality of life at work is fundamentally important in being able to successfully carry out activities (Mendonça, 2010).

According to Minayo, Hartz, and Buss (2000), quality of life can be understood as a social representation built on subjective parameters such as well-being, happiness, love, pleasure, and personal actualization. Additionally, it is based on objectives whose references are the satisfaction of basic needs and of the obligations created by the degree of socio-economic development of a given society. With this concept in hand, it is possible to see that quality of working life influences the subject's personal quality of life, as it is a question of *well-being and satisfaction.*

An analysis of quality of life in a broad sense leads us to identify quality of working life, which has been widely used in administration and company activities related to caring for the health of employees. Some specialists propagate concepts of psychopathology at work, disaggregating suffering and creative suffering at work, questions of power, myths, and envy in companies (Rossi, Quick & Perrewé, 2009).

In agreement with Dolan (2006; also cited in Ogata & Simurro, 2009), quality of working life is a philosophical concept that aims to improve the life of employees within companies, increasing their involvement and satisfaction at work and reducing stress and exhaustion, as this in turn influences the success of the business.

It is necessary to implement preventive actions based on stress theories such as those focused on quality of life programs, with an emphasis on individual conditions of life management on the part of workers and not on the conditions and organization of work. Studies in this field contributed to the popularity and increased concern for mental health at work, granting greater visibility to studies, and the detection of the relationship between health and work, which is intrinsically linked to quality of life at work.

A study carried out by the International Stress Management Association (Brazil) showed that a large proportion of Brazilians (76%) feel unhappy with their professional life, clearly highlighting the lack of regard for this issue within companies.

Having said that, it can be seen that quality of working life has been used as an indicator in experiments in the workplace for measuring satisfaction levels of people performing the work. In order to reach high levels of quality and productivity, companies require employees to be motivated, to participate actively in the work they carry out, and to be adequately compensated for their work.

New paradigms of lifestyles inside and outside the company are being developed by diverse sections of society, and in terms of scientific knowledge, two of these are particularly important:

- *health*: aiming to preserve physical, psychological, and social integrity rather than simply acting to control illnesses, to ensure longer life expectancy and professional reintegration for the person who falls ill; and
- *psychology*: shows the influence of the person's internal attitudes and perspectives on life, and the importance of the intrinsic sense of individual needs in order to be committed to their work (Fleury et al., 2002).

Using representative samples from different countries, the Meaning of Work International Research Team (MOW) conducted research between 1981 and 1983 that intended to define and identify variables that explain the meanings that subjects attribute to their work. Using the main components of the heuristic model, the meaning of work was understood as a multi-dimensional, dynamic, and psychological construct formed by the interaction between personal and environmental variables, and influenced by changes within individuals, their surroundings, or their work.

Therefore, sense is essential to the experience of coherence, cohesion, balance, and fulfillment and is also associated with purpose for being and living. Given this assumption, Frankl (1963; cited in Cavalheiro, 2010) defines the sense of work using three components. The first component of senses that are attributed to work can be defined as the *meaning* of the work for people, their representation, the value they give to it, and the level of centrality that it occupies in their life. This way of conceiving the sense of work contributes to establishing parameters for defining it. Research conducted by the MOW group (1987) stated that different variables, such as family situation, socio-economic environment, and social norms, can influence the definition people give to work. The combination of these variables helps the individual arrive at a personal sense and a definition of what work is for him or her.

The second component is defined as *orientation* for work or, alternatively, the projects that guide actions. In reference to this definition, Cavalheiro (2010) cites Morin and Forest (2007) in their discussion of studies carried out by Super and Sverko (1995) and Wrzesniewski, McCauley, Rozin, and Schwartz (1997). They demonstrate that most people see their work in three ways: as employment (a way of earning a living, a need), as a career (personal investment and a way of progressing within a professional hierarchy), and as a vocation (as something that is necessary, socially desirable, and that involves pleasurable activities). Different ways of seeing work have different consequences for the daily life of workers. A further study conducted by Morin (2002), also cited by Cavalheiro (2010), considers the basis of this category identified in studies carried out by the MOW group, which is related to the function that the work has for the individual. In agreement with the results of the MOW group studies, two functions of work were identified. The first is an expressive function, which refers to an activity that provides satisfaction, social prestige, moral approval, and fulfilling relationship experiences. The second is a utilitarian function, which corresponds to the economic dimension—earning money via a scheduled and routine activity as an occupation.

The third component is the effect of *coherence* between people and their work or the degree of harmony and balance that a person feels in relation to his or her work. Cavalheiro (2010) states that Morin and Forest (2007) formulate the concept of coherence using existential psychology that is related to logic or congruence. These authors work with the notion that ideas tend to be organized into balanced systems, and instability between the activities (intellectual, emotional, or behavioral) can cause individuals to try to re-establish this balance. When a person chooses an activity (or work) with a high potential for personal expression, he or she is more likely to experience a feeling of alignment or adequacy, of being full of energy, and fulfilled as a person. This is related to an individual's engagement or commitment, which refers to the idea of transcendence. Coherence is linked to a person's engagement or responsibility as a human being, referring to that which motivates and defines their existence.

It can be stated, therefore, that for an employee within a company, quality of life amounts to physical, psychological, and emotional well-being; and quality of working life is feeling good at work, within a an environment conducive to working, and with a good company atmosphere.

There is a link between these two concepts: improved productivity means motivation, dignity, participation in planning, and performance of work within the company. It means having employees whose lives can be productive in all senses. Improved productivity does not simply refer to producing more and providing better services. It also refers to having effective and participative management that allows more efficient communication and that helps people to progress in the full sense through a supportive attitude (Fleury et al., 2002).

Promoting the health of workers refers to a combination of activities and educational programs concerning the company and the environment that are designed to motivate and support healthy lifestyles for workers and their families. This helps to reduce barriers to health and to create opportunities that facilitate healthy choices (Ogata, Fonseca, da Costa, Nahas, & Bramante, 2012).

Improvements to working conditions that fall within the scope of quality of working life programs can help a company to be competitive and to encourage people to commit to business matters within the company. Quality of working life programs should aim to develop awareness of the essential quality of a person's engagement in a company in producing better working conditions (Fleury et al., 2002).

THE REAL SENSE AND MEANING OF QUALITY OF WORKING LIFE

It is clear, therefore, that in terms of some factors related to quality of life such as decent living conditions and conditions for professional development, problems that might appear insignificant when considered superficially are, on closer examination, small cracks in the system that, if left unrepaired, will soon compromise and hinder progress.

In discussing basic needs, Chiavenato (1997) cites Maslow's reference to physiological needs as the basis for his theory, says that if these needs are not met, it is not possible to make progress and meet other needs, and individuals will experience frustration and lose motivation.

In discussing quality of working life, we must therefore consider some important points. As a point of reference it is useful to draw on the data collected by Di Lascio's study (2003) of nurses in the pediatric wing of two hospitals in Curitiba (Paraná State, Brazil).

The most common complaint was the absence of a space in which to relax during the shift. Over a 12-hour night shift employees were entitled to a one-hour rest period. This professional is entrusted with caring for the health of patients throughout the night, administering medicine and post-operative care, ensuring cleanliness and hygiene of the hospital and room, and alerting a doctor if necessary. Such a situation could make the difference between life and death, and this is therefore an issue that deserves considerable attention.

Professionals within a hospital setting who are charged with looking after the hygiene of others also require appropriate facilities for looking after their own personal hygiene when there are shift changeovers, as this may also directly influence self-esteem. It is therefore necessary for organizations to meet the basic needs of their professionals, as they will in doing so avoid dissatisfaction on the part of the workers. There are also motivational questions, as there are issues of job insecurity, and additionally they consider their salary inadequate for supporting their family.

There are therefore clear shortcomings when we discuss quality of working life. These issues might appear insignificant for companies, but they are essential in order for employees to carry out their roles successfully. As a result, it is necessary to find a balance in order to avoid future problems, as these issues can compromise or damage systems and cause harm to the professionals involved. This might take the form of occupational illnesses such as depression and stress, for example, or compromise the quality of the service and the image of the institution because of mistakes made or lack of care.

Quality of working life can be ensured through simple actions. Our study of hospitals in Curitiba (Di Lascio, 2003) shows an example that could be applied to all organizations if correctly adapted.

1. The need for a designated place where nursing professionals can:
   a. relax during the breaks they are entitled to in a more appropriate way, which would improve their working conditions; and
   b. shower and change clothes at the end of their shift if necessary, which would improve satisfaction and self-esteem.
2. The need to structure a career plan that would reduce employees' fear of losing their jobs and enable them to visualize professional development and a raise in salary, or even to know how best to benefit from their salary through training in family budgeting. This would increase their level of financial security.

It is clear that professionals need to be motivated, attentive, and willing in order to be able to carry out their roles and tasks, and factors of quality of working life are vital in achieving good levels of satisfaction.

It is the company's responsibility to give sense to work, in order to be a locus of quality of life for the employee, as the workplace is where people spend most of their time, and it is this that that makes the difference and improves people and the organization.

It appears obvious to say that quality of life is necessary at work, as quality of working life already forms part of the sense of working, as do well-being, professional actualization, and a good atmosphere at work. Companies know that improvement leads to increased productivity, but it is still possible to see that many companies need to make adjustments, changes, and adaptations in order to improve the working environment of their employees. Despite the fact that there has already been ongoing discussion of the benefits for company (and employee), many have not yet made the necessary changes to their environments and processes either because they do not believe in it, or they do not think it makes sense.

Creating a pleasant environment, with rooms for reading, music, games, or relaxing, and other benefits, such as refreshments, is completely meaningless if the workload is overwhelming, too much is expected of employees, and competition is favored over cooperation. Likewise, motivational talks and good salaries are of no use if the computers are outdated, there is insufficient lighting, it is very hot or cold, the chairs are broken, and managers are authoritarian. In the majority of cases, the most difficult problems to resolve are those that concern relationships within the team and management. A good atmosphere at work is what motivates employees to be happy, make fewer mistakes, and be more productive.

Quality of working life takes on sense when there is a concern for what people want, with what is important to us, and when there is interaction (listening to others and being listened to). The meaning is the consequence of this or, alternatively, the gains that are made that will be reflected by both the company and the employee, creating sense for both.

Therefore, everything has sense when we see the reason behind the facts and everything has a meaning when we see what this represents.

With this in mind, the well-being of employees should be a long-term goal for the company, as the benefits are numerous for both the people and the organization.

Giving sense and meaning to quality of working life is simple and easily achieved. It is necessary for employees and the company to discuss how to *be happy*. Believing in the happiness of employees will ensure the success of their business.

REFERENCES

Aguiar, W. M. J. (2006). A pesquisa junto a professores: Fundamentos teóricos e metodológicos. In W. M. J. Aguiar (Org.), *Sentidos e Significados do Professor na Perspectiva Sócio-Histórica* (pp. 12–13). Relatos de Pesquisa. São Paulo: Casa do Psicólogo.

Albuquerque, L. G. (1992). Competitividade e recursos humanos. *Revista da Administração, 27*(4), 16–29.

Araújo, R. R., & Sachuk, M. I. (2007). Os sentidos do trabalho e suas implicações na formação dos indivíduos inseridos nas organizações contemporâneas. *Revista de Gestão USP, 14*, 53–66.

Basso, I. S. (1998). Significado e sentido do trabalho docente. *Cad. Cedes* [online]. *Campinas, 19*(44), 19–32. Retrieved on Decemter 20, 2012 from http://dx.doi.org/10.1590/s0101-32621998000100003

Borges, L. O. (1998). Os pressupostos dos estudos do significado do trabalho na psicologia social: No caminho do existencialismo. *Vivência, 12*(2), 87–105.

Cavalheiro, G. (2010). *Sentidos atribuídos ao trabalho por profissionais afastados do ambiente laboral em decorrência de depressão.* UFSC: Florianópolis. Retrieved on December 20, 2012 from http://www.cfh.ufsc.br/~ppgp/Gabriela%20Cavalheiro.pdf

Chiavenato, I. (1997). *Gerenciando Pessoas.* São Paulo: Makron Books.

Cobra, M. (1992). *Administração de Marketing.* São Paulo: Atlas.

Di Lascio, R. H. C. (2003). *Modelo para Análise de qualidade de vida no trabalho dos profissionais dos serviços de enfermagem em hospital pediátrico.* UFSC: Florianópolis. Retrieved from http://repositorio.ufsc.br/bitstream/handle/123456789/86448/195054.pdf?sequence=1

Dolan, S. L. (2006). *Estresse, auto-estima, saúde e trabalho.* Rio de Janeiro: Qualitymark.

Fleury, M. T. L., Shinyashiki, G., França, A. C. L., Casado, T., Fischer, R. M., Oliveira, M. d. M., Jr.,... Fischer, A. L. (2002). *As pessoas nas organizações.* São Paulo: Editora Gente.

Frankl, V. (1963). *O sentido da vida.* São Paulo: Martins Fontes.

Gouveia, C., & Baptista, M. (2007). *Teorias Sobre a Motivação: teorias de conteúdo.* Instituto Politecnico de Coimbra, Coimbra. Retrieved on December 28, 2012 from http://prof.santana-e-silva.pt/gestao_de_empresas/trabalhos_06_07/word/Motiva%C3%A7%C3%A3o-Teorias%20de%20conte%C3%BAdo.pdf

Hackman, J. R., & Oldham, G. R. (1975). Development of the job diagnostic survey. *Journal of Applied Psychology, 60*(2), 159–170.

Hersey, P., & Blanchard, K. H. (1986). *Psicologia para Administradores.* São Paulo: EPU.

Leontiev, A. (1978). *O desenvolvimento do psiquismo.* Lisboa: Livros Horizonte.

Meaning of Work International Research Team. (1987). *The meaning of working.* London: Academic Press.

Mendonça, A. C. D. (2010). *Qualidade de vida no trabalho: Implantação de um programa com atividades de Lazer como caminho para aliviar as tensões no ambiente de trabalho.* Natal: Instituto Federal de Educação, Ciência e Tecnologia do RN

Minayo, M. C. S., Hartz, Z. M. A., & Buss, P. M. (2000). Qualidade de vida e saúde: um debate necessário. *Ciência saúde coletiva [online], 5*(1), 7–18. Retrieved on December 20, 2012 from http://www.scielo.br/pdf/csc/v5n1/7075.pdf

Molon, S. I. (1999). *Cultura: A dimensão psicológica e a mudança histórica e cultural: Subjetividade e constituição do sujeito em Vygotsky.* Unpublished doctoral dissertation, Department of Psychology at the Center for Philosophy and Human Sciences, Federal University of Santa Catarina, Brazil.

Morin, E. M. (2002). Sentidos do trabalho. In T. Wood, Jr. (Coord.), *Gestão empresarial: O fator humano* (p. 49). São Paulo: Atlas.

Morin, E., & Forest, J. (2007). Promouvoir la santé mentale au travail: Donner un sens au travail. *Gestion, 32*(2), 31–36.

Ogata, A., & Simurro, S. (2009). *Guia prático de qualidade de vida: Como planejar e gerenciar o melhor programa para a sua empresa.* Rio de Janeiro: Elsevier.

Ogata, A. (Coord.), Fonseca, C. H., da Costa, L. P., Nahas, M., & Bramante, A. C. (2012). *Profissionais saudáveis, empresas produtivas: como promover um estilo de vida saudável no ambiente de trabalho e criar oportunidades para trabalhadores e empresas.* Rio de Janeiro: Elsevier-Sesi.

Rossi, A. M., Quick, J. C., & Perrewé, P. L. (2009). *Stress e qualidade de vida no trabalho: O positivo e o negativo.* São Paulo: Atlas.

Sense [Def. 1] (n.d.). *Online Etymology Dictionary.* In Etymonline. Retrieved December 20, 2012, from http: http://www.etymonline.com/index.php?allowed_in_frame=0&search=sense&searchmode=none

Super, D. E., & Sverko, B. (Eds.). (1995). *Life roles, values, and careers.* San Francisco, CA: Jossey-Bass.

Tolfo, S. R., & Piccinini, V. (2007). Sentidos e significados do trabalho: explorando conceitos, variáveis e estudos empíricos brasileiros. *Psicol. Soc. [online], 19,* 38–46. Retrieved on December 20, 2012 from http://www.scielo.br/scielo.php?script=sci_arttext&pid=S0102-71822007000400007

Wrzesniewski, A., McCauley, C., Rozin, P., & Schwartz, B. (1997). Jobs, careers, and callings: People's relations to their work. *Journal Of Research In Personality, 31,* 21–33. Retrieved on December 20, 2012 from http://faculty.som.yale.edu/amywrzesniewski/documents/Jobscareersandcallings.pdf

CHAPTER 4

EVALUATION OF STRESS IN NURSING STUDENTS

Analysis Standardization[1]

Rodrigo Marques da Silva, Carolina Tonini Goulart, Luis Felipe Dias Lopes, Ana Lucia Siqueira Costa, and Laura de Azevedo Guido

ABSTRACT

Introduction: During the undergraduate nursing program, students join the nursing work process and thus get exposed to the stressors that affect the profession, which are added to the stressors resulting from their education. Accordingly, it is very important to identify nursing students' stress levels. *Goal:* Analyze the stress and propose a general measure for evaluating the stress level of nursing students from a standardized score. *Method:* It is a descriptive, cross-sectional and quantitative study conducted from a database built between April and May 2011. For data collection we used the Evaluation of Stress in Nursing Students (AEEE) tool, which was administered to 130 students of a public university in Rio Grande do Sul state, Brazil, to identify the stress level by student and by domain from the standardized score. Stress classification at levels was done based on tertiles. *Results:* According to the study, 67.69% of students had a medium level of stress, and a high level of stress was

Improving Emploee Health and Well-Being, pages 53–64

identified in the domains "environment" (42.31%) and "time management" (30%). *Conclusions:* The standardized score enabled the identification of the stress level by student and by AEEE domain and its comparison with other studies carried out with students.

INTRODUCTION

The Industrial Revolution, which occurred in the 18th and 19th centuries, was characterized by remarkable economic development and was marked by individuals' migration from the rural areas to factories in the cities, which led to radical changes in workers' living conditions and health (Mendes & Dias, 1991). This change process was characterized by a fast and inhuman mode of production, unhealthy conditions, and long working days. This would put at risk the survival and maintenance of the production process itself and favor the emergence of discussions focusing on individuals' health-disease process, from their relationship with the work process, which culminated in the current workers' health care model (Mendes & Dias, 1991; Ornellas & Monteiro, 2006).

In this context, we highlight the nursing worker, whose work process consists of different tasks that may or may not occur concomitantly. In this activity of caring, administering, researching, and participating politically, the nursing worker experiences stressful situations that can lead to the development of stress-induced neuroendocrine changes (Sanna, 2007).

Based on the interactionist model, which considers the interrelation between the individual and the environment as responsible for this process, stress has been defined as any stimulus that places demands on the external or internal environment and taxes or exceeds the person's sources of individual adaptation or social system (Lazarus & Folkman, 1984).

However, although linked to the work process, and thus studied in different populations (Guido, Umann, Stekel, Linch, Silva & Lopes, 2009; Guido, Silva, Goulart, Kleinübing & Umann, 2012; Linch & Guido, 2011), stress has also been studied in the nurse's professional training process (Costa & Polak, 2009). In this context, nursing students begins the teaching-learning process in different care contexts, thus being exposed to stressors characteristic of the profession, which implies a negative impact on their health condition and learning (Jones, 1988; Costa & Polak, 2009).

Moreover, the nursing teaching-learning process may have a threatening or challenging meaning for students because an error inherent in this process implies injury or damage to another individual (Costa & Polak, 2009). Accordingly, since the professional training is focused on the care of humans, students need to spend some time adapting to the conditions related to caregiving, that is, a close contact with pain, perception of others' suffering, care given to terminally-ill patients, and physical contact. In addition to these, the situations concerning the academic environment such as students' examination period, their insertion into the university environment, out-of-class tasks, group activities, and communication with professors are the most frequently cited stressors among students. As a result, one notes that nurses are exposed to stressful situations from their academic training period (Costa & Polak, 2009).

Noting the importance of analyzing the stress factors among nursing students, and noticing that there is no measurement tool available in the relevant Brazilian literature to assess the stress factors of these individuals within their own social and cultural context, the Evaluation of Stress in Nursing Students (AEEE) tool was developed in 2009 (Costa & Polak, 2009).

In the current study, we analyzed stress among nursing students based on the AEEE. Additionally, since this is the only specific tool for assessing stress in nursing students available in Brazil, a general measure was proposed to assess nursing students' stress level from a standardized score based on this tool. This will allow the association of students' stress level with different psychological constructs, such as coping, burnout syndrome, and hardiness. Propositions for interventions to decrease stress among these students will be made from the results obtained in this survey.

METHOD

It is a descriptive, cross-sectional, and quantitative approach study whose data were collected among students of the undergraduate nursing program of the Federal University of Santa Maria. Students enrolled from the first to the eighth semester and aged 18 years or older were included. Students not enrolled in professional-cycle courses and who, during the data collection period, would not complete the syllabus for exceeding the time limit determined by the educational institution (12 semesters) were excluded.

During the data collection period, there were 159 students, out of whom 10 were excluded because they were not enrolled in professional-cycle courses, four because they were under 18 years old, three for their inability to complete the program within 12 semesters, and one for taking part in the project as a researcher. Additionally, four students refused to participate in the survey, and seven did not return the tools. As a result, the study sample consisted of 130 students.

After approval by the Ethical Review Board under number 0380.0.243.000-10, the data collection was done through a form for students' sociodemographic and academic characterization and the Evaluation of Stress in Nursing Students (AEEE) tool, developed and validated by Costa and Polak (2009; see Appendix). Students were contacted in the classroom, at a time previously scheduled with students and teachers and with the consent of the program coordinator. For the data collection operationalization we presented the characteristics of the study, and their participation occurred by signing the free and informed consent form (Conselho Nacional de Saúde, 1996).

The sociodemographic and academic data form involved the following variables: date of birth, gender, marital status, number of children, who they live with, sports practice, and leisure activities.

AEEE, developed by Costa and Polak (2009), is an instrument that assesses possible stress situations experienced by nursing students during their education and training (sample used for validation of the original tool). It is a four-point, Likert-type scale consisting of 30 items with answers varying from 0 to 3, in which zero (0) is applied when the student does not experience the situation portrayed in the item; one (1) when the student does not feel stressed with the situation; two (2) when he/she feels little stressed with the situation; and three (3) when he/she feels very stressed about the situation. By using factor analysis, the 30 items were grouped into six different domains: practical activities, professional communication, time management, environment, professional training, and theoretical activity. Alpha values in the original scale have good reliability by domain, these being respectively 0.806, 0.768, 0.717, 0.866, 0.772, and 0.720.

The data collected were organized and stored in an Excel 2007 (Office XP) spreadsheet so that, subsequently, they could be analyzed electronically with the aid of the Statistical Analysis System (SAS, version 8.02.). Quantitative variables were exhibited in terms of descriptive measures: minimum and maximum values, mean values, and standard deviation. Qualitative variables were presented as absolute (n) and relative (%) frequencies. The analysis of the internal consistency of the tool was performed by using Cronbach's Alpha Coefficient.

As the total sum of the values assigned by the student in each domain is not directly comparable, since the domains consist of a different number of items, the score had to be standardized. Thus, in order to identify the stress level by student, the standardized score (Sp) calculation followed the formula below:

$$Sp = 50 \cdot \left(\frac{\sum Values \text{ answered}}{No. \text{ of Items Answered}} - 1 \right)$$

Accordingly, to obtain the stress level, the values answered in each of the 30 items were summed, and this sum was divided by the number of items answered, excluding the number of zeros, defined in AEEE as "I don't experience the situation." Then, we had to subtract one from the result and multiply the value obtained by 50.

To identify the stress level presented by the individual in each domain, the values answered in the items were summed, and this sum was divided by the number of items of the domain, excluding the number of zeros. Then, again, we had to subtract one from the result and multiply the value obtained by 50. This calculation followed the formula below:

$$Sp_i = 50 \cdot \left(\frac{\sum Values \text{ answered}}{No. \text{ of Items Answered}} - 1 \right), \quad i = 1, 2, 3, \ldots, 6$$

In this formula, i indicates the number of the domain whose standardized score (Sp_i) was calculated, which allows the replication of the formula in the six AEEE domains. So Sp_1 refers to the score of "practical activities," Sp_2—"professional communication," Sp_3—"time management," Sp_4—"environment," Sp_5—"professional training," and Sp_6—"theoretical activity."

Stress classification in levels was based on tertiles. Thus, after calculating these measures, we defined the parameter for students' classification from the standardized score, ranging from 0 to 100% according to the intervals shown in Table 4.1.

To identify items of greater and lesser stress by domain, the average of the items that comprise it was calculated. Those items presenting the highest average were considered the items of highest stress in the domain for the students.

RESULTS

In the analysis of the internal consistency of the 30 items that make up the AEEE, a total Cronbach's Alpha of 0.898 was obtained. As for the items that comprise the domains of this tool, the Cronbach's Alpha values were: 0.798—practical activities, 0.783—professional communication, 0.708—time management, 0.778—environment, 0.840—professional training, and 0.525—theoretical activity. According to Bailar and Mosteller (1992), these values are sufficient to attest to the satisfactory internal reliability of the tool.

It was found that female students (86.92%), aged between 20 and 24 years (69.23%), unmarried (86.92%), and without children (93.08%) prevailed.

TABLE 4.1 Nursing Students' Stress Level Classification Based on Tertiles: Santa Maria, 2011

Standardized Score (%)	Stress Level
0.00 to 33.33	Low
33.34 to 66.67	Medium
66.68 to 100.00	High

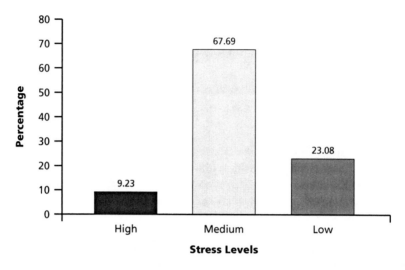

Figure 4.1 Distribution of nursing students according to their stress level: Santa Maria, 2011.

Among the students who participated in the survey, 60% live with their family, 70.77% do not practice sports, and 68.46% do some leisure activity.

One notes 67.69% of nursing students having a medium stress level (Figure 4.1).

The stress level per AEEE domain in nursing students is shown in Table 4.2.

TABLE 4.2   Distribution of Nursing Students According to Their Stress Level per AEEE Domain: Santa Maria, 2011

| Domain | Stress Level | | | | |
	Low	Medium	High	WC[a]	Total
Practical Activities	52.30%	38.50%	9.23%	0.00	100%
	($n = 68$)	($n = 50$)	($n = 12$)	($n = 0$)	($n = 130$)
Professional Communication	50.77%	36.92%	7.69%	4.62%	100%
	($n = 66$)	($n = 48$)	($n = 10$)	($n = 6$)	($n = 130$)
Time Management	18.46%	51.54%	30.00%	0.00	100%
	($n = 24$)	($n = 67$)	($n = 39$)	($n = 0$)	($n = 130$)
Environment	20.77%	32.31%	42.31%	4.62%	100%
	($n = 27$)	($n = 42$)	($n = 55$)	($n = 6$)	($n = 130$)
Professional Training	39.23%	40.77%	20.00%	0.00	100%
	($n = 51$)	($n = 53$)	($n = 26$)	($n = 0$)	($n = 130$)
Theoretical Activity	40.77%	45.38%	13.85%	0.00	100%
	($n = 53$)	($n = 59$)	($n = 18$)	($n = 0$)	($n = 130$)

[a] WC = Without Classification (When all answers were 0 for the domain)

In the "environment" and "time management" domains, the items with the highest means are: "Public transport used to get to college" ($\bar{x} = 2.23$; sd = 1.00) and "Being out of social life brings feelings of loneliness" ($\bar{x} = 2.29$; sd = 0.79).

DISCUSSION

The interactionist model, proposed by Lazarus and Folkman, assumes the occurrence of stress from the cognitive assessment, or how the individual assesses a certain situation or event. So if the individual defines a certain situation as a threat or challenge, the stress reaction occurs (Lazarus & Folkman, 1984; Guido, Silva, Goulart, Kleinübing, & Umann, 2012).

Accordingly, 67.69% of the nursing students were found to have a medium stress level. In research conducted with students of the second and third years of a nursing school in Chile, using Hamilton's Assessment Questionnaire, the prevalence of students with medium stress level, both in the second (46.2%) and third years (57.8%) of the program, was identified (Basso et al., 2008). In research among freshman students of the State University of Campinas (Unicamp) and using a specific tool designed for such research (Fioravanti, Shayani, Borges & Balieiro, 2005), it was found that 42.86% of students showed a low stress level, and 41.90% presented a medium stress level (Gama, Junqueira, Silva, Abbade & Costa, 2010). Moreover, in a survey conducted among graduate nursing students, it was found that 51.35% of them had low levels of stress (Guido, Goulart, Silva, Lopes & Ferreira, 2012).

Thus, although students are exposed to teaching-learning process situations, a medium level of stress was found in three studies, and a low level of stress was observed in two of them. This may suggest that undergraduate students, especially nursing students, are using effective strategies for coping with situations appraised as stressful. This context is positive in view of the possible outcomes of stress on students' health, such as the burnout syndrome and depression. However, research carried out among graduate students from different professions showed a statistically significant correlation between the high level of stress and the occurrence of burnout syndrome ($r = 0.68$; $p = 0.00$) among these individuals (Guido, Goulart, Silva, Lopes & Ferreira, 2012). Regarding depression, in research done with medical students, it was found that 11.5% of these students presented a diagnosis of depression requiring intervention (Kongsomboon, 2010). Moreover, those who were in the clinical phase of learning showed a higher level of stress when compared with pre-clinical period students (Kongsomboon, 2010).

Based on these findings, one notes that students' stress levels depend on the assessment they make of the situation experienced and varies according to time in which they experience it. Thus, understanding which aspects are perceived as stressors by students in a given context facilitates the development of actions aiming to reduce stress and its effects on nursing students' health.

Accordingly, it was found that 42.31% of students showed a high level of stress in the "environment" domain. In this domain, the "Public transportation used to get to college" ($\bar{x} = 2.23$; sd = 1.00) was rated by students as the item of highest stress. In research done with final-year students of the undergraduate nursing program, having to move home to the internship field and/or study site was considered an exhausting activity (Silva, Chiquito, Andrade, Brito, & Camelo, 2011). The "environment" domain refers to the degree of difficulty felt in the access to the fields of practical activities or internship and/or university and the stress situations perceived by the students with the means of transportation used (Costa, 2011). So, for students, the hours they spend traveling to these places decreases the time they have to study, which seems to be an important stressor (Silva, Chiquito, Andrade, Brito, & Camelo, 2011).

It was found that 30% of students showed a high level of stress, and 51.54% presented a medium level of stress in the "time management" domain. In this domain, "Being out of social life brings feelings of loneliness" ($\bar{x} = 2.29$; sd= 0.79) was the item with the highest stress mean for students. In research with fourth-year students of the undergraduate nursing program from the University of Franca and using the Stress Identification and Measurement Questionnaire, "balancing work and college" (63.6%) and "difficulty to balance study and leisure" (40.9%) were considered stressful activities by students (Ribeiro et al., 2011).

In this sense, one notes that students report difficulty in balancing the activities established in the syllabus and their personal, emotional, and social requirements (Ribeiro et al., 2011). This situation may be related to the changes experienced in the transition to the university world, such as a possible change of environment, separation from family and friends, meeting different professors and experiencing diverse teaching methods, and new ways of relating to the scientific and technological knowledge (Ramos & Carvalho, 2008; Gama et al., 2010). Internationally, researchers emphasize that for students, especially in the first year, this is a period of vulnerability, in which young people need to establish, test, and adapt to a new psychological identity (Verger et al., 2009). Additionally, many times, due to fact that they are very young when they enroll in college, students are not mature enough to deal with the changes of this period and the curriculum requirements, which have become more demanding due to competitiveness in the labor market (Ramos & Carvalho, 2008; Gama et al., 2010). This may explain the situations assessed as stressful by students in the time management domain, as well as the high and medium stress levels observed in it.

According to researchers, the factors that can lead students to stress are not well known, mainly those related to changes in their living conditions after they start the undergraduate course at college (Verger et al., 2009). Therefore, it is necessary to analyze the aspects concerning students' entrance to higher education institutions and the syllabus or program frameworks in order to prevent and/or reduce the effects of stress among these individuals, aiming at a good performance, quality education and training, and entering the labor market with less stress and greater satisfaction.

CONCLUSION

From the proposed standardized score, it was possible to identify a general measure of stress, in other words, the stress level per nursing student, as well as the stress level per student per AEEE domain.

With the general measure (stress level per student), it will be possible to compare stress with other studies among nursing students in different realities and institutions. However, since the AEEE tool was recently developed and is currently being deployed in different research studies, the manuscripts resulting from the deployment of this tool are still in the editorial boards of scientific journals waiting for approval to be published. For this reason, it was not possible to compare the results found in the present study with other studies that have used the same tool.

Furthermore, one notes that the environment and time management domains were the highest scored ones in the stress factor assessment. These results indicate the need for public policies to improve the means of transportation as an indicator of quality of life for the students analyzed here. Additionally, the construction of curriculum programs should include a course load and contents that allow students to exercise social and family activities, which are considered so important for the mental health of these individuals.

Thus, it is believed that through this analysis it will be possible to relate students' stress level to the occurrence of burnout and hardiness among this population, as well as to associate the coping strategies most and least used by students and their relation with the stress level.

Based on the findings, this study contributes to the establishment of future research, whose resulting hypotheses can be tested and interventions can be proposed either to change or strengthen the reality found.

ACKNOWLEDGMENTS

We thank the *Coordenação de Aperfeiçoamento de Pessoal de Nível Superior* (CAPES) for the Social Demand Grant of Rodrigo Marques da Silva.

APPENDIX
Tool for Evaluation of Stress in Nursing Students

Read each item below and mark with an "X" the number corresponding to the stress intensity that the situation causes to you, according to the following legend:

0	1	2	3
I do not experience the situation	I do not feel stressed with the situation	I feel a little stressed with the situation	I feel very stressed with the situation

1	Have concern for the professional future	0	1	2	3
2	Obligation to do extracurricular activities	0	1	2	3
3	Being out of social life brings feelings of loneliness	0	1	2	3
4	Perform the patient care procedures in general	0	1	2	3
5	The new situations that you may experience in clinical practice	0	1	2	3
6	Communication with other workers of the internship unit	0	1	2	3
7	The environment of the internship clinical unit	0	1	2	3
8	Communication with workers from other sectors in the internship unit	0	1	2	3
9	Being afraid of making mistakes during patient care	0	1	2	3
10	The way adopted for assessing the theoretical content	0	1	2	3
11	Distance between college and home	0	1	2	3
12	Perform certain patient care procedures	0	1	2	3
13	Feel insecure or afraid of taking the theoretical exams	0	1	2	3
14	The degree of difficulty to do extracurricular activities	0	1	2	3
15	The similarity between the situations that you experience in the internship and those that you may experience in the professional life	0	1	2	3
16	Realize the difficulties involving the relationship with other workers of the same field	0	1	2	3
17	Think about the situations that you may experience as a nurse	0	1	2	3
18	Reduced time to be with your family	0	1	2	3
19	Realize the professional responsibility when working in the internship field	0	1	2	3
20	Observe conflicting attitudes in other workers	0	1	2	3
21	You feel you have acquired little knowledge to take the practical exam	0	1	2	3
22	Public transport used to get to college	0	1	2	3
23	Time required by the teacher to deliver extracurricular activities	0	1	2	3
24	Distance between most internship sites and place of residence	0	1	2	3
25	Experience activities, as a nurse in training, in the internship field	0	1	2	3
26	Lacking time for leisure	0	1	2	3
27	Realize the relationship between the theoretical knowledge acquired in the course and the future professional performance	0	1	2	3
28	Assimilate the theoretical and practical content offered in the classroom	0	1	2	3
29	Public transport used to get to the internship site	0	1	2	3
30	Lacking time for moments of rest	0	1	2	3

NOTE

1. This paper is a subproject of the project *Stress, Coping, Burnout, Depressive Symptoms and Hardiness in Nursing Students and Teachers,* developed by the Work, Health, Education and Nursing research group, Stress, Coping and Burnout research line.

REFERENCES

Bailar, J., & Mosteller, F. (1992). *Medical users of statistics.* Boston: Nejm Books.

Basso, M. L., Vargas, B. A., Torres, M. B., del Canto, M. J. C., Meléndez, C. G., Balloqui, M. F. K., & Cornejo, A. S. (2008). Factors derived from the intrahospitable laboratories that cause stress in infirmary students. *Revista Latino-Americana de Enfermagem, 16*(5), 805–811. Retrieved on October 13, 2012 from http://www.scielo.br/pdf/rlae/v16n5/02.pdf

Conselho Nacional de Saúde. (1996). Resolução n.196, de 10 de outubro de 1996. Dispõe sobre diretrizes e normas regulamentadoras de pesquisas envolvendo seres humanos. *Bioética, 4*(2),15–25.

Costa, A. L. S. (2011). Stress in nursing students: Construction of determining factors. *Revista Mineira de Enfermagem, 11*(4), 414–419.

Costa, A. L. S., & Polak, C. (2009). Construction and validation of an instrument for the assessment of stress among nursing students. *Revista da Escola de Enfermagem USP, 43*, 1017–1026. Retrieved on October 13, 2012 from http://www.scielo.br/pdf/reusp/v43nspe/en_a05v43ns.pdf

Fioravanti, A. R., Shayani, D. A., Borges, R. C., & Balieiro, R. C. (2005). Estudo sobre os fatores de stress entre alunos da UNICAMP. *Revista Ciência do Ambiente On-Line, 1*(1), 41–48. Retrieved on September 13, 2009 from http://sistemas.ib.unicamp.br/be310/index.php/be310/article/viewFile/21/9

Gama, A. B., Junqueira, B. F. P., Silva, E. G., Abbade, F. L., & Costa, J. F. B. (2010). Estudo sobre o stress dos alunos calouros da UNICAMP. *Revista Ciências do Ambiente On-Line, 6*(1), 39–43. Retrieved on July 10, 2012 from http://sistemas.ib.unicamp.br/be310/index.php/be310/article/viewFile/224/170

Guido, L. A., Goulart, C. T., Silva, R. M., Lopes, L. F. D., & Ferreira, E. M. (2012). Stress and burnout among multidisciplinary residents. *Revista Latino-Americana de Enfermagem, 20*(6), 1064–1071. Retrieved on December 9, 2012 from http://www.scielo.br/pdf/rlae/v20n6/08.pdf

Guido, L. A., Silva, R. M., Goulart, C. T., Kleinübing, R. E., & Umann, J. (2012). Stress and coping among surgical unit nurses of a teaching hospital. *Revista da Rede de Enfermagem do Nordeste, 13*(2), 428–436. Retrieved on August 11, 2012 from http://www.revistarene.ufc.br/revista/index.php/revista/article/view/226/pdf

Guido, L. A., Umann, J., Stekel, L. M. C., Linch, G. F. C., Silva, R. M., & Lopes, L. F. D. (2009). Stress, coping and health conditions of nurses in a medical clinic of a university hospital. *Ciência, Cuidado e Saúde, 8*(4), 615–621. Retrieved on July 10, 2012 from www.revenf.bvs.br/pdf/ccs/v8n4a14.pdf

Jones, L. H. (1988). How to assess stress: A significant step for the nursing student. *Journal of Nursing Education, 27*(5), 227–229. Retrieved on November 9, 2012 from http://www.ncbi.nlm.nih.gov/pubmed/2839643

Kongsomboon, K. (2010). Psychological problems and overweight in medical students compared to students from faculty of humanities, Srinakharinwirot University, Thailand. *Journal of the Medical Association of Thailand, 93*(2), 106–113.

Lazarus, R. S., & Folkman, S. (1984). *Stress, appraisal, and coping.* New York, NY: Springer.

Linch, G. F. C., & Guido, L. A. (2011). Stress in nurses at a hemodynamics ward in Rio Grande do Sul, Brazil. *Revista Gaúcha de Enfermagem, 32*(1), 63–71. Retrieved on December 5, 2012 from http://www.scielo.br/pdf/rgenf/v32n1/a08v32n1.pdf

Mendes, R., & Dias, E. C. (1991). From occupational medicine to workers' health. *Revista de Saúde Pública, 25*(5), 341–349. Retrieved on October 5, 2012 from http://www.scielo.br/pdf/reben/v59n4.pdf

Ornellas, T. C. F., & Monteiro, M. I. (2006). Historical, cultural and social aspects of labor. *Revista Brasileira de Enfermagem, 59*(4), 552–555. Retrieved on December 5, 2012 from http://www.scielo.br/pdf/reben/v59n4/a15v59n4.pdf

Ramos, C. I. V., & Carvalho, A. J. R. (2008). Nível de stress e estratégias de *coping* dos estudantes do 1° ano do ensino universitário de Coimbra. *Psicologia.*. Retrieved on December 5, 2012 from http://www.psicologia.pt/artigos/textos/A0368.pdf

Ribeiro, C. B., Melo, L. A., & Ribeiro, J. C. (2011). The stress of nursing students in college. *Neurobiology, 74*(2), 59–74.

Sanna, M. C. (2007). Work processes in nursing. *Revista Brasileira de Enfermagem, 60*(2), 221–224. Retrieved on October 14, 2012 from http://www.scielo.br/pdf/reben/v60n2/a17v60n2.pdf

Silva, V. L. S., Chiquito, N. C., Andrade, R. A. P. O., Brito, M. F. P., & Camelo, S. H. H. (2011). Stress factors in the final year of undergraduate nursing: Students' perceptions. *Revista de Enfermagem da UERJ, 19*(1), 121–126. Retrieved on October 14, 2012 from http://www.facenf.uerj.br/v19n1/v19n1a20.pdf

Verger, P., Combes, J. B., Kovess-Masfety, V., Choquet, M., Guagliardo, V., Rouillon, F., & Peretti-Wattel, P. (2009). Psychological distress in first year university students: Socioeconomic and academic stressors, mastery and social support in young men and women. *Social Psychiatry and Psychiatric Epidemiology, 44*(8), 643–650. Retrieved on December 7, 2012 from http://www.ncbi.nlm.nih.gov/pubmed/19096741

CHAPTER 5

BUILDING RESILIENCE TO IMPROVE EMPLOYEE WELL-BEING

Matthew R. Leon
Jonathon R. B. Halbesleben
University of Alabama

ABSTRACT

While stress is an inevitable part of a work environment, the psychological construct of resilience buffers the negative outcomes of stress. Resilience helps an individual maintain stable functioning and performance during and following exposure to stressful situations. Common properties of resilience include positive coping strategies to deal with stress, an ability to adapt to stressful environments, and the ability to maintain stable mental and physical functioning during times of stress. By implementing environmentally- or individually-focused strategies to increase employee resilience, employers can decrease the costs and consequences associated with stress. This chapter provides an overview of resilience and discusses the positive effects of resilience to employee health and well-being. We discuss individual and environmental factors contributing to resilience development and maintenance, including hardiness, self-efficacy, supervisor and coworker support, and job crafting. In addition, we review resilience assessments in order to provide tools for practitioners to select and develop resilient employees.

Improving Emploee Health and Well-Being, pages 65–81

Consider the following scenario: two employees at the fictional company ResCorp are placed into a newly developed division in an emerging market. Work conditions are uncertain, and stress levels are high—the hours are long, the market is unpredictable, and the new roles of the employees are not clear. Over the course of a year, Employee 1 falls ill several times, and work performance suffers due to the demands of the new position. Meanwhile, Employee 2 is able to thrive in the novel environment and use the challenges to grow professionally and personally. Employee 1 eventually leaves the company, while Employee 2 maintains stable levels of performance and is able to adjust well to the demands of the new position. Both of these employees were exposed to the same stressors, but one left the company while the other was able to successfully adjust. What underlying mechanisms allowed the second employee to handle the stress and navigate through it? Is it possible to identify and select employees that are better able to handle stress? On the other hand, could the environment have been changed to alleviate stressors and promote employee well-being? In order to answer these questions, we will focus on the concept of resilience and its impact on the ability of employees to better handle workplace stressors.

Stress, which occurs when an individual appraises something as a source of harm, challenge, threat, or loss, is a pervasive force that affects many areas of an employee's work life and is a well-documented hazard to individual mental and physical health (Lazarus & Folkman, 1984; Richardson & Rothstein, 2008; Selye, 1956). For example, stress is associated with roughly 80% of injuries and 40% of turnover in American organizations (Atkinson, 2004; Richardson & Rothstein, 2008). Excessive amounts of stress can decrease physical health and mental health, while simultaneously increasing turnover, absenteeism, and worker's compensation claims in organizations (Brock & Buckley, 2011; Dextras-Gauthier, Marchand, & Haines, 2012; Park, 2007). It comes as no surprise, then, that management of employee stress remains a high priority for organizations. Since stress begins as a perceptual process (i.e., stress originates from the perception of and reaction to threats), it follows that the most direct strategy towards negating stress would focus on individual appraisal and reaction to stress (Lazarus & Folkman, 1984). The psychological construct of resilience deals directly with these aspects of the stress process and, if fostered, can improve the well-being of employees.

This chapter provides an overview of resilience among employees and discusses the positive effects of resilience to employee health and well-being. Individual and environmental factors contributing to resilience development and maintenance will be identified and discussed. In addition, resilience assessments are reviewed in order to provide tools for practitioners to select and develop resilient employees.

RESILIENCE

Although the term resilience has been a part of behavioral science literature for over thirty years, no universally accepted definition currently exists
(Windle, 2011). Many factors have contributed to the semantic confusion
attached to resilience; in particular, the term spans a wide range of dis-
ciplines, is employed in various forms (e.g., as a human capacity, ability,
strength, etc.), and accounts for many behaviors. Resilience has separate
definitions in psychology, psychiatry, developmental psychology, human
development, change management, epidemiology, nursing, social sciences,
and medicine (Isaacs, 2003). These fields emphasize many different facets
of resilience, including personality characteristics, physiology/biology of
resilience (e.g., testosterone levels, blood pressure, heart rate), and environmental factors such as group dynamics (Windle, 2011).

For our purposes, resilience is defined as a positive force (usually expressed as an ability) that helps an individual maintain stable functioning
during and following exposure to stressful situations (Windle, 2011; Bonanno, 2004). Common properties of resilience include positive coping strategies to deal with stress (e.g., actively addressing the problem, finding alternative ways to compartmentalize the stress), an ability to adapt to stressful
environments, and the ability to maintain stable mental and physical functioning during times of stress (Isaacs, 2003; Windle, 2011). Resilient behaviors, then, are those that aid a person in maintaining performance during
and after exposure to stress (e.g., active coping, altering one's perspective
of stress, maintaining health). To help organize our understanding of resilience, we build this chapter around the model outlined in Figure 5.1.

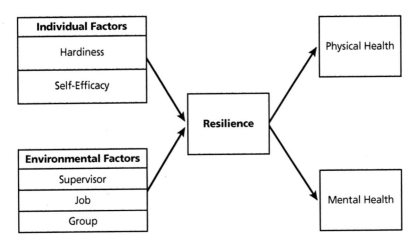

Figure 5.1 Antecedents and outcomes of resilience.

Resilient employees contribute to an organization's ability to handle dynamic conditions, uncertainty, and change in an efficient and successful manner (Lengnick-Hall, Beck, & Lengnick-Hall, 2011). A highly resilient individual can maintain stable levels of mental and physical health and performance under stress and quickly bounce back from stress; through these behaviors, resilient employees can substantially decrease the costs associated with stress in the workplace (Acquaah, Amoaka-Gyampah, & Jayaram, 2011; Howard & Dryden, 1999; Windle, Bennett, & Noyes, 2011). More specifically, resilience has been tied to behaviors such as active coping (i.e., addressing instead of avoiding problems), enhanced stress tolerance, and higher job performance (Bandura, 1994; Windle, 2011). These behaviors lead to better mental health (e.g., decreased levels of burnout) and physical health (e.g., less illness and fewer days lost due to absenteeism).

Resilient employees are more likely to manifest organizational citizenship behaviors (i.e., voluntarily helping or assisting others in the workplace), work happiness, and organizational commitment (Organ, 1988; Youssef & Luthans, 2007). Developing a resilient workforce reduces effects of stress across all levels of the organization and can create a supportive, cohesive work environment. Resilient employees contribute to a reduction in stress-related injuries and costs as well as improve individual performance and task efficiency.

These positive outcomes suggest that recruiting and developing resilient employees can improve individual and team performance and provide benefits to members of an organization and to the organization itself. However, when recruiting or training employees is not a practical solution, modifying the environment to decrease stressors and provide tools for employees to handle stress is a plausible alternative. Aligning the environment (e.g., demands of a position, available resources) to the characteristics (e.g., strengths, weaknesses, values) of employees can decrease job-related stress; this approach is known as the person-environment fit perspective (Edwards & Cooper, 1990; Parsons, 1909).

The person-environment fit perspective can be used as lens for understanding the role of resilience in the stress process, and a wealth of research exists linking each concept to resilience (e.g., Bonanno, 2004; Burton, Pakenham, & Brown, 2009; Maddi, 2002). Managers and executives possessing a broad understanding of the relationship between employees and the environment may be better able to identify coworkers and new hires that express resilient qualities and adapt the workplace to better fit their employees' strengths. We summarize some of the strategies managers could consider in Table 5.1.

TABLE 5.1   Resilience Development Strategies

Building Resilience

Environment	Supervisor support
	– Accurate and timely information
	– Transparent decision making
	– Utilization of employee input
	Group
	– Interaction/Communication
	– Group problem-solving
	Job
	– Match KSAs
	– Job crafting
Hardiness	Challenge
	Control
	Commitment
	Transformative coping
Self-efficacy	Enactive mastery
	Task familiarity
	Verbal persuasion
	Emotional arousal

ENVIRONMENTAL ANTECEDENTS OF RESILIENCE

The environment plays a major role in individual resilience and stress by providing employees with external resources and added support to cope with stressors (Kristof-Brown, Zimmerman, & Johnson, 2005). A poor work environment (e.g., hostile supervisors, unfair promotion procedures, job mismatch) can increase burnout, intentions to leave, and job dissatisfaction (Kutney-Lee, Wu, Sloane, & Aiken, in press). Altering the environment to fit existing employees may be a feasible alternative to hiring new employees or initiating training programs to increase resilience. Further, a modified environment may provide necessary tools to employees with a low internal resistance to stress.

Three major environmental factors affecting resilience include the fit between an employee and his or her supervisor, group, and job (Wheeler, Buckley, Halbesleben, Brouer, & Ferris, 2005). All of these environmental relationships, when controlled conscientiously and appropriately, can mitigate the impact of stress on work performance, job satisfaction, and engagement. In addition to the individual effects of each relationship, interactions between supervisor, group, and job exist that can further enhance employee resilience and productivity (Kristof-Brown et al., 2005). For example, employees with jobs that fit their skill sets and a supportive supervisor are more likely to express more resilient behaviors than employees with just one of these environmental supports (Kristof-Brown et al., 2005). Many similar relationships exist, with the general idea that if employee characteristics match the environment, then positive outcomes result. By understanding the different facets of the environment and their effects on the individual, employers can implement multi-level solutions to decrease stress and increase employee well-being by externally driving employee attitudes and behavior.

Supervisor Support

The relationship between an employee and his or her immediate supervisor is one of the most powerful indicators of environmental stress in the workplace (Gilbreath & Benson, 2004). Perceived supervisor support, the extent to which supervisors value their employees' contributions, plays an important role in the psychological well-being of employees by affecting employees' organizational commitment, global perceptions of the organization, and motivation (DeConinck & Johnson, 2009; Gilbreath & Benson, 2004). Because supervisors are representatives of the organization, supervisor actions are viewed as indicative of organizational support and directly affect employee attitudes towards the organization (Rhoades & Eisenberger, 2002).

Outcomes associated with low supervisor support include higher levels of burnout, increased on the job tension/anxiety, and lower engagement in coping behaviors (Halbesleben, 2006; Karasek, Triantis, & Chaudhry, 1982). Conversely, high supervisor support contributes to positive perceptions of organizational support and decreased employee turnover (Eisenberger, Stinglhamber, Vandenberghe, Sucharski, & Rhoades, 2002; Rhoades & Eisenberger, 2002). Supervisors exhibiting supportive behaviors and shared values with employees can positively impact the health of the employee-supervisor relationship and decrease mental stress associated with supervisor-employee conflicts that arise (Kristof-Brown et al., 2005).

Specific supportive behaviors include providing accurate and timely information to employees regarding work conditions and job roles, emphasizing a transparent decision making process regarding resource allocation, and encouraging input from employees when developing rules and policies. To increase employee resilience, supervisors can also formally or informally mentor struggling employees, maintain a high level of communication with employees, and provide clear and consistent feedback concerning individual performance, organization issues that may affect the employee (e.g., changes in work hours, shifting production demands, expanding/downsizing, etc.), and departmental goals. These tactics work at the individual and group level by influencing individual attitudes and coworker interactions (i.e., person–group fit; Steinhardt, Dolbier, Gottlieb, & McCalister, 2003).

Person–Group Fit

Person–group fit is the relationship match between an employee and his or her coworkers. Coworkers define the social environment of the workplace and have the power to support or undermine colleagues in social and task interactions (Fairlie, 2004; Schneider, 1987). Coworker support is a main driver of person–group fit and fosters several antecedents of resilience, such as social support and commitment (Kristof-Brown et al., 2005). Additionally, coworker support is a predictor of individual withdrawal (e.g., detachment, turnover intentions), individual effectiveness (e.g., endorsement of organizational citizenship behaviors, task efficiency), work attitudes (e.g., perceived organizational support, feelings of anxiety), and role perceptions (e.g., role conflict, role ambiguity, role overload; Chiaburu & Harrison, 2008).

High person–group fit is characterized by strong relationships among coworkers (e.g., high levels of trust and mutual respect) and high engagement (i.e., interest in achieving group objectives, maintaining individual role, helping other employees). The literature emphasizes the positive effects of coworker support behaviors, including increased performance, higher job satisfaction, and improved mental health (Karasek, Triantris, Chaudry, 1982; Kristof-Brown et al., 2005). Interventions (e.g., training, team composition) can be effectively implemented by management to increase person–group fit.

When possible, a supervisor or manager should take efforts to create teams of coworkers with 1) an already established relationship and 2) previous history of working together to increase the probability of person–group fit among employees. To increase person–group fit, it is important to encourage high levels of interactions between team members in formal and informal settings (e.g., team training or retreats involving all of the team members). Training should focus on communication and group problem-solving strategies (e.g., providing constructive feedback, integrating individual contributions into group goals, defining roles, and prioritizing tasks).

Job Matching and Crafting

Finally, person-job fit is the match between an individual's personal and professional characteristics and the knowledge, skills, and abilities (KSAs) associated with the job (Carless, 2005). This type of fit is emphasized in the selection process and job design. The most straightforward actions associated with person-job fit are to either 1) place employees in a position that most complements their skill set or 2) modify the position so that it fits the employee's skills. The primary goal of these action is to place employees in a job that matches their skills in order to minimize stress associated with job performance and task management. However, many qualified employees still burn out despite an adequate job match. In these cases, managers can turn to strategies designed to add value to the position in order to decrease stress and increase employee motivation and job satisfaction.

The job characteristics model emphasizes a humanistic management approach focusing on the development and reinforcement of the affective state of an employee to add intrinsic worth and value to the job (Hackman & Oldham, 1974, 1975). The model puts forth three psychological states—perceiving work to be meaningful, experiencing responsibility for outcomes of work, and possessing knowledge of work results—that, if achieved, inject positive reinforcement, personal reward, and meaningfulness into daily job tasks (Boonzaier, 2001; Hackman & Oldham, 1975). In turn, these outcomes improve employee motivation, job satisfaction, growth satisfaction (i.e., how satisfied the employee is with professional and personal growth opportunities within the position), and work effectiveness (Boonzaier, 2001). Job crafting provides several pathways towards enhancing each psychological state.

Job crafting is a technique used to increase person-job fit and promotes task emphasis, job expansion, and role reframing as methods of adding meaning and value to the position (Berg, Dutton, & Wrzesniewski, 2008; Berg, Grant, & Johnson, 2010). The purpose of job crafting is to configure job tasks and perceptions of the job in such a way that the job answers an occupational calling (i.e., the job is meaningful to the individual; Berg et al., 2010; Wrzesniewski & Dutton, 2001). Task emphasis involves highlighting tasks that are already a formal part of the job and relating them to personally meaningful actions (e.g., interfacing with clients is a function of helping others). Task emphasis occurs when an employee incorporates meaning into tasks or chooses to spend more time and energy on assigned responsibilities congruent with personal values. Job expansion adds tasks to pursue a calling that is not being answered. These can be short- or long-term actions designed to add meaning to work (e.g., volunteering for community service on behalf of the organization, becoming the "go-to" person for a certain knowledge or skill). Finally, role reframing consists of altering perceptions of a role to create fulfillment. Unlike task emphasis and job expansion, role reframing is a purely mental exercise used to broaden and re-evaluate the meaning of a job (Berg et al., 2010).

Matching employee KSAs to a job and encouraging employees to add personal value to job tasks can mitigate environmental stressors associated with task performance and increase job satisfaction and resilience by instilling intrinsic values to the job that negate or remove the mentally stressful properties associated with job tasks. Finding meaning in work should be encouraged as a tool for weathering stressors and promoting positive work attitudes.

Supervisor, group, and job fit can all be used to decrease stress or increase resilience. Together, these types of fit can have a cumulative effect on the resilience and well-being of employees. By remaining cognizant of factors such as supervisory behaviors, group cohesiveness, employee skills, and job design, employers can employ multiple strategies when creating environmental interventions to support employees.

INDIVIDUAL ANTECEDENTS OF RESILIENCE

It is not always feasible to restructure the work environment to meet the needs of a small number of employees. In these cases, an effective alternative is to focus on individual characteristics affecting resilience. Two factors, hardiness and self-efficacy, are commonly cited in stress and resilience literature as antecedents to resilience and higher levels of physical and mental health.

Hardiness

Hardiness is related to how a person views and manages stressors (Kobasa, 1979; Maddi, 2005). Hardiness entered the psychological research landscape in 1979, with a publication examining the workplace behaviors of managers at the Illinois Bell Telephone Company (Kobasa, 1979; Maddi, 2002). In a group of highly stressed managers, Kobasa (1979) found that those who did not fall ill exhibited certain attitudes that buffered the effects of stress, including a stronger commitment to self, an internal locus of control, and engagement with the environment. Kobasa's work spurred an interest in hardiness, and since that time, research has expanded and elaborated on the construct.

From this research, three properties—challenge, commitment, and control—were identified as the underlying components of hardiness (Maddi, 2002; Kobasa, Maddi, & Kahn, 1982). Challenge is a person's tendency to interpret stressful situations as challenges as opposed to threats (Eschleman, Bowling, & Alarcon, 2010). Commitment is the measure of how involved a person is in different areas of life such as family, friends, work, and personal hobbies (Maddi, 1990). Finally, control is a person's belief that he or she controls the events in his or her life (Eschleman et al., 2010).

Generally, commitment has been shown to be the most powerful indicator of employee well-being and performance in the hardiness literature (Eschleman et al., 2010). It is thought that an individual committed to many different areas possesses a strong and diverse social support network that can be called upon when the individual is under stress. However, challenge and control remain important contributors to employee well-being and still provide significant predictive power when measuring the effects of stress on physical and mental health. Each of the three components is important to the conceptualization of hardiness and uniquely contributes to a person's overall level of hardiness (Eschleman et al., 2010).

Hardiness has been tied to positive performance outcomes across many different populations, including adult workers, college students, and clinical patients and has been described as a pathway to resilience (Bonanno, 2004; Eschelmann et al., 2010; Maddi, 2005). Hardiness can be developed through specialized training that focuses on engaging cognition (e.g., providing mental models of how to accurately assess stressors), emotion (e.g., mood stabilization), and action (e.g., addressing problems) at an individual level to promote effective coping strategies (Maddi, Kahn, & Maddi 1998).

The two goals of hardiness training are to teach trainees the skills associated with transformational coping and for trainees to use these skills to emphasize their challenge, control, and commitment views. Transformational coping teaches individuals to successfully navigate stressful situations through action (addressing the problem), planning (creating and committing to a strategy to resolve the stressor), positive re-interpretation of events (viewing the stressor as a development opportunity as opposed to an insurmountable obstacle), and seeking help from others (building and maintaining a strong support network; Maddi & Hightower, 1999). The purpose of transformational coping is to decrease the stressfulness of an event through cognitive and emotional appraisals that broaden an individual's perspective of the event and lead to problem-solving action plans (Maddi et al., 1998). The second aim is to use the information gathered from the transformational coping strategies to deepen self-perceptions of challenge, control, and commitment. Transformational coping training should leave employees with a diverse coping skill set and the motivation to use it (Maddi et al., 1998).

Self-Efficacy

Self-efficacy has been studied in an organizational context for about 35 years and is defined as a person's belief in his or her ability to complete a task or behavior successfully (Bandura, 1977; Barling & Beattie, 1983; Gist, 1987; Taylor, Locke, Lee, & Gist, 1984). These beliefs are part of the process that determines what, if any, behavior will be initiated towards performing a task, how much effort will be put forward to complete the task, how focused the individual will remain, and how long the person will continue to engage in the task despite challenges (Bandura, 1997). That is, how well a person believes he or she can complete a task will dictate how much effort is put into the task. Similar to hardiness, self-efficacy is tied to resilience and functions as a pathway towards enhanced stress tolerance.

Self-efficacy is typically viewed as a positive trait that enhances self-belief and self-confidence (an exception to the positive effects of self-efficacy may be that too much self-efficacy can lead to overconfidence; Bandura, 2012). Self-efficacy has been shown to play a role in lower levels of burnout, higher achievement, and higher goal-setting in various populations (Bandura, 1994; Gündüz, 2012; Peetsma, Hascher, & van der Veen Ewoud Roede, 2005). We propose these relationships are strong due to self-efficacy acting as a pathway to resilience (e.g., levels of burnout are low because a person's self-efficacy is related to resilience and the ability to adapt to stress). In the context of resilience, self-efficacy could be manifested as individual belief in one's ability to manage stressors in the work environment and perform well despite challenging situations and demonstrated through behaviors such as motivation, perseverance, and engagement.

Self-efficacy can be developed at any time in an individual's life. Bandura (1982) listed four precursors to self-efficacy that can be used in an employee's development—enactive mastery, task familiarity, verbal persuasion, and emotional arousal. The most influential experience in the development of self-efficacy is enactive mastery (Bandura, 1982). Enactive mastery is the repeated performance of accomplishments and is achieved through gradual, successful trials that build the necessary knowledge, skills, and abilities needed for task completion (Bandura, 1982; Gist, 1987). In other words, enactive mastery is the process of building on past successes to achieve expertise. Task familiarity, or how comfortable and knowledgeable an employee is about a task, is generally built through the enactive mastery process as well. Increased task familiarity and mastery can lower performance related stress and chance of injury. When enactive mastery is not a safe or viable option, organizations can use modeling to increase an employee's self-efficacy. Modeling, also referred to as vicarious experience, is the second most effective strategy for developing self-efficacy (Bandura, 1982; Gist, 1987). In this case, the idea is to show an employee different examples of successful behaviors that can be emulated. The examples should display clear behaviors as well as multiple pathways to success to increase effectiveness. Modeling can teach task-specific behaviors as well as increase familiarity for employees.

The last two methods of developing self-efficacy are verbal persuasion and emotional arousal (Gist, 1987). Although less effective than enactive mastery and modeling, these are two fairly straightforward and easy to implement means of increasing self-efficacy. Verbal persuasion is the action of talking to an employee in an attempt to convince him or her that success is possible. Emotional arousal is an individual's attempt to harness any nervous energy and channel it into a productive force (Gist, 1987). Often, this requires a supervisor or coworker talking through problems and negative emotions with the target employee. Showing support while proactively and cooperatively working to overcome challenges can increase levels of self-efficacy, and ultimately resilience, in all parties.

Self-efficacy is concerned with one's belief in his or her own abilities to succeed at a task. It can be developed through several methods and leads to increased resilience from employees. If an individual's self-efficacy related to a task is low, the individual will expend less effort and energy in persisting after encountering difficulties and give up, believing that he or she is unable to complete the task at hand (Bandura, 1977). Conversely, if an individual's self-efficacy is high, he or she will persist longer because of the belief that the effort is not wasted and the obstacles can be overcome (Bandura, 1977). Following these findings, it comes as no surprise that self-efficacy leads to perseverance in the face of difficulty—a characteristic of resilience (Hamill, 2003).

HOW TO ASSESS RESILIENCE

While we have discussed several methods to increase resilience, clearly evaluation of any intervention intended to improve resilience will require measurement of resilience. Tracking resilience provides clues to how an employee is handling stress over time and can help predict how well an employee will perform under pressure or in a new environment. After discussing several strategies for increasing resilience among employees, it is important to recognize the tools needed to track these changes. Resilience is an abstract construct and can be difficult to measure through observation. For example, viewing two employees perform in a stressful environment does not necessarily allow a supervisor to quantify levels of resilience for each employee because employees may alter behavior while under observation, or the observer may be unable to keep track of multiple employees. Also, resilience encompasses personal beliefs and habits, which are sometimes impossible to observe. Due to these limitations, survey methods are generally used to assess resilience.

To date, self-report surveys are the most reliable way to measure individual resilience. Self-report surveys are frequently used to measure levels of resilience, and close to twenty resilience measures exist for different groups (e.g., adolescents, children, adults, minorities; Windle, Bennett, & Noyes,

2011). Two of the main reasons for the large number of resilience scales are the variations in resilient beliefs and behaviors of unique groups of people and the different facets of resilience that each scale emphasizes. Two highly rated scales targeted towards working adults are the Resilience Scale for Adults and the Brief Resilience Scale.

The Resilience Scale for Adults (Wagnild & Young, 1993) identifies the degree of individual resilience a person possesses, with a focus on positive personality characteristics that enhance individual adaptation. This scale can inform employers of the tools and skills an employee possesses that facilitate resilience. On the other hand, the Brief Resilience Scale (Smith, Dalen, Wiggins, Tooley, Christopher, & Bernard, 2008) emphasizes one's ability to bounce back from stress. This scale can be used as an outcome measure in the context of stress (Windle et al., 2011). In other words, this scale measures how well an individual will recover when exposed to stressors. Both of these surveys offer employers a quantifiable measure of individual resilience that can be used to predict individual behaviors in the face of stress.

The Resilience Scale and the Brief Resilience Scale vary in length, with twenty-five and six questions, respectively. The scales can be administered and completed with paper and pencil and scored afterwards. Scoring instructions are available with the surveys. When initiating individual or environmental change with the purpose of increasing resilience, take a baseline measure before implementation. This allows classification of employees into high and low resilient individuals who may need more (or less) focus during the intervention. After the change, require employees to retake the survey and track any changes that have occurred.

CONCLUSION

Stress is an inevitable part of every employee's work life, but its deleterious effects can be mitigated by an individual's resilience. Resilient employees enable a firm to capitalize on otherwise harmful events through effective coping strategies, an ability to bounce back from stressful events, and maintaining performance despite challenges. A resilient individual is able to adapt to dynamic environments and changing roles, use challenge as an opportunity for growth, and maintain high levels of production despite excessive demands or adversity.

Highly resilient employees are generally more productive, less likely to fall ill, and exhibit higher job satisfaction than other employees. By fostering resilience through a supportive work environment, training, and the development of hardiness and self-efficacy, an employer can increase the output of employees while decreasing costs associated with sick leave and attrition. Resilience can be developed through the manipulation of external, environmental factors as well as through training targeted at increasing hardiness and self-efficacy.

By providing the right resources to employees, negative outcomes associated with exposure to risks and adversity can be deterred. Resilience can be developed in employees to support physical and mental health, increase levels of performance, and equip employees with coping tools to navigate and recover from stress. Stress management through resilience development provides employers with multiple avenues to increasing employee performance, preserving mental and physical health, and creating a stable and adaptive workforce.

REFERENCES

Acquaah M., Amoako-Gyampah, K., & Jayaram J. (2011). Resilience in family and nonfamily firms: An examination of the relationships between manufacturing strategy, competitive strategy and firm performance. *International Journal of Production Research, 49*(18), 5527–5544.

Atkinson, W. (2004). Stress: Risk management's most serious challenge? *Risk Management, 51*(6), 20–24.

Bandura, A. (1977). Self-efficacy: Toward a unifying theory of behavioral change. *Psychology Review, 84,* 191–215.

Bandura, A. (1982). Self-efficacy mechanism in human agency. *American Psychologist, 37,* 122–147.

Bandura, A. (1994). Self-efficacy. In V. S. Ramachaudran (Ed.), *Encyclopedia of human behavior* (Vol. 4, pp. 71–81). New York, NY: Academic Press.

Bandura, A. (1997). *Self-efficacy: The exercise of control.* New York, NY: W. H. Freeman.

Bandura, A. (2012). On the functional properties of perceived self-efficacy revisited. *Journal of Management, 38*(1), 9–44.

Barling, J., & Beattie, R. (1983). Self-efficacy beliefs and sales performance. *Journal of Organizational Behavior Management, 5,* 41–51.

Berg, J. M., Grant, A. M., & Johnson, V. (2010). When callings are calling: Crafting work and leisure in pursuit of unanswered occupational callings. *Organization Science, 21*(5), 973–994.

Berg, J. M., Dutton, J. E., & Wrzesniewski, A. (2008). *What is job crafting and why does it matter? Theory-to-practice briefing.* Ann Arbor, MI: Ross School of Business, University of Michigan. Retrieved from http://www.bus.umich.edu/positive/pos-teaching-and-learning/job_crafting-theory_to_practice-aug_08.pdf

Bonanno, G. A. (2004). Loss, trauma, and human resilience: Have we underestimated the human capacity to thrive after extremely aversive events? *American Psychologist, 59*(1), 20–28.

Boonzaier, B. (2001). A review of research on the job characteristics model and the attendant job diagnostic survey. *South African Journal of Business Management, 32*(1), 11–34.

Brock, M., & Buckley, M. R. (2011). The role of stress in workers' compensation: Past, present and future. *Public Personnel Management, 41*(1), 1–14.

Burton, N. W., Pakenham, K. I., & Brown, W. J. (2009). Evaluating the effectiveness of psychological resilience training for hearth health, and the added value of promoting physical activity: A cluster randomized trial of the READY program. *BMC Public Health, 9*, 427–436.

Carless, S. A. (2005). Person-job fit versus person-organization fit as predictors of organizational attraction and job acceptance intentions: A longitudinal study. *Journal of Occupational and Organizational Psychology, 78*, 411–429.

Chiaburu, D. S., & Harrison, D. A. (2008). Do peers make the place? Conceptual synthesis and meta-analysis of coworker effects on perceptions, attitudes, OCBs, and performance. *Journal of Applied Psychology, 93*(5), 1082–1103.

DeConinck, J. B., & Johnson, J. T. (2009). The effects of perceived supervisor support, perceived organizational support, and organizational justice on turnover among salespeople. *Journal of Personal Selling & Sales Management, 29*(4), 333–350.

Dextras-Gauthier, J., Marchand, A., & Haines, V. (2012). Organizational culture, work organization conditions, and mental health: A proposed integration. *International Journal of Stress Management, 19*(2), 81–104.

Edwards, J. R., & Cooper, C. L. (1990). The person-environment fit approach to stress: Recurring problems and some suggested solutions. *Journal of Organizational Behavior, 11*, 293–307.

Eisenberger, R., Stinglhamber, F., Vandenberghe, C., Sucharski, I. L., & Rhoades, L. (2002). Perceived supervisor support: Contributions to perceived organizational support and employee retention. *Journal of Applied Psychology, 87*(3), 565–573.

Eschleman, K. J., Bowling, N. A., & Alarcon, G. M. (2010). A meta-analytic examination of hardiness. *International Journal Of Stress Management, 17*(4), 277–307.

Fairlie, R. W. (2004). Self-employed business ownership rates in the United States: 1979–2003. *Small Business Administration.* Research Summary 243.

Gilbreath, B., & Benson, P. G. (2004). The contribution of supervisor behaviour to employee psychological well-being. *Work and Stress, 18*(3), 255–266.

Gist, M. E. (1987). Self-Efficacy: Implications for Organizational Behavior and Human Resource Management. *Academy Of Management Review, 12*(3), 472-485.

Gündüz, B. (2012). Self-efficacy and burnout in professional school counselors. *Educational Sciences: Theory & Practice, 12*(3), 1761–1767.

Hackman, J. R., & Oldham, G. R. (1974). *The job diagnostic survey: An instrument for diagnosing the motivational potential of jobs. Technical Report no. 4.* Department of Administrative Sciences, Yale University, New Haven, CT.

Hackman, J. R., & Oldham, G. R. (1975). Development of the job diagnostic survey. *Journal of Applied Psychology, 60*(2), 159–170.

Halbesleben, J. R. (2006). Sources of social support and burnout: A meta-analytic test of the conservation of resources model. *Journal of Applied Psychology, 91*(5), 1134–1135.

Hamill, S. (2003). Resilience and self-efficacy: The importance of efficacy beliefs and coping mechanisms in resilient adolescents. *Colgate University Journal of the Sciences, 35*, 115–146. Retrieved from http://groups.colgate.edu/cjs/student_papers/2003/Hamill.pdf

Howard, S., & Dryden, J. (1999). Childhood resilience. Review and critique of literature. *Oxford Review of Education, 25*(3), 307–324.

Isaacs, A. J. (2003). *An investigation of attributes of school principals in relation to resilience and leadership practices.* Unpublished doctoral dissertation, Florida State University, Tallahassee, FL.

Karasek, R. A., Triantis, K. P., & Chaudhry, S. S. (1982). Coworker and supervisor support as moderators of associations between task characteristics and mental strain. *Journal Of Occupational Behaviour, 3*(2), 181–200.

Kobasa, S. C. (1979). Stressful life events, personality, and health: An inquiry into hardiness. *Journal of Personality and Social Psychology, 37*(1), 1–11.

Kobasa, S. C., Maddi, S. R., & Kahn, S. (1982). Hardiness and health: A prospective study. *Journal of Personality and Social Psychology, 42*(1), 168–177.

Kristof-Brown, A. L., Zimmerman, R. D., & Johnson, E. C. (2005). Consequences of individuals' fit at work: A meta-analysis of person-job, person-organization, person–group, and person–supervisor fit. *Personnel Psychology, 58*, 281–342.

Kutney-Lee, A., Wu, E. S., Sloane, D. M., & Aiken, L. H. (in press). Changes in hospital nurse work environments and nurse job outcomes: An analysis of panel data. *International Journal of Nursing Studies.* doi:10.1016/j.ijnurstu.2012.07.014

Lazarus, R. S., & Folkman, S. (1984). *Stress, appraisal, and coping.* New York, NY: Springer Publishing Company.

Lengnick-Hall, C. A., Beck, T. E., & Lengnick-Hall, M. L. (2011). Developing a capacity for organizational resilience through strategic human resource management. *Human Resource Management Review, 21*(3), 243–255.

Maddi, S. R. (1990). Issues and interventions in stress mastery. In H. S. Friedman (Ed.), *Personality and disease* (pp. 121–154). New York, NY: Wiley.

Maddi, S. R., Kahn, S., & Maddi, K. L. (1998). The effectiveness of hardiness training. *Consulting Psychology Journal: Practice And Research, 50*(2), 78–86.

Maddi, S. R. (2002). The story of hardiness: Twenty years of theorizing, research, and practice. *Consulting Psychology Journal: Practice And Research, 54*(3), 173–185.

Maddi, S. R. (2005). On hardiness and other pathways to resilience. *American Psychologist, 60*(3), 261–262. doi:10.1037/0003-066X.60.3.261

Maddi S. R., & Hightower, M. (1999). Hardiness and optimism as expressed in coping patterns. *Consulting Psychology Journal: Practice and Research, 51*, 95–105.

Organ, D. W. (1988). *Organizational citizenship behavior: The good soldier syndrome.* New York, NY: Lexington Books/DC Heath and Com.

Park, K. -O. (2007). Social support for stress prevention in hospital settings. *Journal of the Royal Society for the Promotion of Health, 127*, 260–264.

Parsons, F. (1909). *Choosing a vocation.* Boston, MA: Houghton Mifflin.

Peetsma, T., Hascher, T., & van der Veen Ewoud Roede, I., (2005). Relations between adolescents' self-evaluations, time perspectives, motivation for school and their achievement in different countries and at different ages. *European Journal of Psychology of Education, 20*(3), 209–225.

Rhoades, L., & Eisenberger, R. (2002). Perceived organizational support: A review of the literature. *Journal of Applied Psychology, 87*(4), 698.

Richardson, K. M., & Rothstein, H. R. (2008). Effects of occupational stress management intervention programs: A meta-analysis. *Journal of Occupational Health Psychology, 13*(1), 69–93.

Schneider, B. (1987). The people make the place. *Personnel Psychology, 40,* 437–453.

Selye, H. (1956). *The stress of life.* New York, NY: McGraw-Hill.

Smith, B. W., Dalen, J., Wiggins, K., Tooley, E., Christopher, P., & Bernard, J. (2008). The brief resilience scale: Assessing the ability to bounce back. *International Journal of Behavioural Medicine, 15,* 194–200.

Steinhardt, M. A., Dolbier, C. L., Gottlieb, N. H., & McCalister, K. T. (2003). The relationship between hardiness, supervisor support, group cohesion, and job stress as predictors of job satisfaction. *American Journal of Health Promotion, 17*(6), 382–389

Taylor, M. S., Locke, E. A., Lee, C., & Gist, M. E. (1984). Type A behavior and faculty research productivity: What are the mechanisms? *Organizational Behavior and Human Performance, 34,* 402–418.

Wagnild, G. M., & Young, H. M. (1993). Development and psychometric evaluation of the resilience scale. *Journal of Nursing Measurement, 1*(2), 165–178.

Wheeler, A. R., Buckley, M. R., Halbesleben, J. R., Brouer, R. L., & Ferris, G. R. (2005). "The elusive criterion of fit" revisited: toward an integrative theory of multidimensional fit. In J. Martocchio (Ed.), *Research in Personnel and Human Resource Management* (vol. 24, pp. 265–304. Greenwich, CT: Elsevier/JAI Press.

Windle, G. (2011). What is resilience? A review and concept analysis. *Reviews in Clinical Gerontology, 21*(2), 152–169.

Windle, G., Bennett, K. M., & Noyes, J. (2011). A methodological review of resilience measurement scales. *Health and Quality of Life Outcomes, 9*(8), 8–25.

Wrzesniewski, A., & Dutton, J. E. (2001). Crafting a job: Revisioning employees as active crafters of their work. *Academy of Management Review, 26*(2), 179–201.

Youssef, C. M., & Luthans, F. (2007). Positive organizational behavior in the workplace: The impact of hope, optimism, and resilience. *Journal of Management, 33*(5), 774–800.

CHAPTER 6

THE "RIGHT" TOOLS

Stress Response Lessons from the Opposite Sex

Faye K. Cocchiara
Arkansas State University

David J. Gavin and Joanne H. Gavin
Marist College

James Campbell Quick
University of Texas at Arlington

ABSTRACT

Stress is an inevitable part of the workplace experience. Managed properly, stress can be a positive contributor to peak performance. Managed poorly, stress can lead to burnout and failure. The purpose of this chapter is to help readers understand the basics of stress and increase their awareness of advances made in stress prevention and coping, particularly between men and women. The authors discuss advances in stress knowledge and experiential exercises they have used in educational and professional settings to increase awareness of potentially harmful stressors and identify differences between

Improving Emploee Health and Well-Being, pages 83–99

the stress responses of men and women. Success in preventive stress management hinges on men and women being able to not only identify sex-specific
coping strategies but to learn from them.

Since Walter Cannon (1929/1915) framed the architecture of the stress
response circa 1915, which he originally labeled the emergency response,
there has been an explosion of knowledge about the role that stress plays
in human disease and illness as well as in workplace performance and
well-being (Quick, Wright, Adkins, Nelson, & Quick, 2013), particularly
as it applies to men and women. Workplace demands, concerns about the
economy, family-related problems, financial challenges, and illness—all of
these factors can play a role in creating stress in the workplace. In fact,
stress is directly or indirectly implicated in seven of the 10 leading causes
of death, with heart disease being at the top for both men and women.
However, genetic and culture differences between men and women combine to reduce men's average life expectancy (Murray-Law, 2011). While
the actual difference in life expectancy between men and women is five
years, only one year is attributable to genetic differences; the remaining
four years may be attributable to culture differences. From this paradigm,
understanding and valuing these differences between the sexes takes on
new importance. As educators, we spend a great deal of time with our students, helping them navigate a variety of demands (stressors) to prevent
them from becoming acute and thus leading to unhealthy consequences.
While the demands with which college students are faced do not entirely
align with those faced by the majority of American workers, we believe
there is similarity in terms of the potential consequences. We also believe
the lessons we learn from the coping strategies of college-aged men and
women can inform the broader workplace.

Recent studies on stress suggest that the health risks for working men
and women are not evenly distributed between the sexes (Abdel-Khalek &
Maltby, 2009). A survey conducted by the American Psychological Association (APA) found that 81% of middle-aged men cited work as a significant
source of stress, yet only 68% of women in the same age group viewed work
in the same way (APA Practice Central, 2009). What is clear from a pre-
ponderance of evidence is that there are differences in the coping strategies that men and women use. Shelley Taylor's groundbreaking research on
females' stress responses demonstrated that women are, by design, better
equipped for the physical and emotional challenges of life (Taylor, Klein,
Lewis, Gruenewald, Gurung, & Updegraff, 2000). As a result, American
women outlive their male counterparts by over half a decade. The female
tend-and-befriend capacity provides significant protective armor against
the physical and psychological threats that lead to emotional suffering, one
key manifestation of distress.

The purpose of this chapter is multi-faceted. We look first at the basics of stress and then at the relationship between health and wealth. From there, we describe the differences that men and women have in their responses to stress and examine the prevention and coping strategies that both groups use to overcome such stress effects. While we focus our attention on the research of Taylor et al. (2000), which highlights the differences in coping mechanisms between men and women, we emphasize the importance of learning from each other. We conclude the chapter with a focus on stress mastery skills for twenty-first century working adults. Stress is not beyond their control. Rather, stress is well within their control . . . with the right tools!

STRESS: THE BASICS

The stress concept has its origins in medicine and physiology. Walter B. Cannon hypothesized the existence of the stress response circa 1915 based upon his physiological research. He first called it the emergency response (Benison, Barger, & Wolfe, 1987) and then the stress response, distinguishing stress from strain (Cannon, 1935). Cannon's primary interest was in the sympathetic nervous system components of the stress response as well as the central role of emotions, especially the "fighting emotions," as he called them, in triggering the stress response (Cannon, 1929/1915). Selye (1976) was the physician scientist most closely associated with the stress concept based upon his extensive endocrine (hormone) system research and his explication of stress's role in the diseases of maladaption and adverse health effects. The combined research of these two physician scientists, both rooted in the earlier research of Claude Bernard, framed our basic understanding of the psychophysiology of stress (Rosch, 2001).

The Stress Response

Cannon outlined the four basic mind-body changes that constitute the stress response. First, there is a shunting of blood to the large muscle groups and brain for functional fight-or-flight, and away from the extremities and vegetative organs where it is not needed in time of emergency. Second, there is an increase in sensory alertness (hearing, seeing, sensing) that psychologically focuses the individual on immediate reality. Third, there is a release of glucose and fatty acids into the blood stream as a key energy source for this heightened activity period. Finally, there is a shutting down of the immune system because the mind and body are going onto a war-footing, shifting from defense to offense. These four basic changes are highly functional for short emergency periods and to achieve peak performances in a wide range of athletic and other performance events.

Selye (1976) took Cannon's basic architecture to the next level and sketched out the General Adaptation Syndrome with its three stages. The stage one alarm response is the essence of Cannon's discovery. What Selye realized is that in stage two, the individual is engaged in a period of resistance. This stage of resistance is where the heightened risk of physical and psychological disorders becomes manifest. In the final third stage, the individual reaches exhaustion, with its accompanying elevated risk of serious psychological disorders and diseases of maladaptation. Selye's three stages of stress—alarm, resistance, and exhaustion—lead us to believe that the stressors working men and women experience are not exclusively physical; they also involve emotions (Dusselier, Dunn, Wang, Shelley, & Whalen, 2005).

HEALTH AND WEALTH

Working men and women often focus on the financial and economic aspects of their chosen professions. Few may realize that there is a positive connection between health and wealth. This important, positive relationship emerges in medical and executive health research (Adler, Boyce, Chesney, Folkman, & Syme, 1993; Quick, Gavin, Cooper & Quick, 2000; Quick, Cooper, Gavin, & Quick, 2008). The executive suite is not always a bed of roses. However, attention to the health issues of top executives and managers is important because of their role in wealth creation and the development of healthy organizations (Quick, Cooper, Gavin, & Quick, 2002).

In addition to focusing on the health and well-being of the upper echelons of the organizations, this research expanded the concept of health from just the physical and psychological to the spiritual and ethical (Quick et al., 2000). Organizations do not only suffer from the absence of the executive for physical or psychological challenges, they are equally if not more affected by issues of spiritual or ethical health (Quick et al., 2002). Executive health is important because of executives' contributions to economic activity, the success of the organization, and the creation of wealth (Quick et al., 2008). Research has supported the positive effects a CEO can have on the success of his or her company compared to its industrial peers as well as the important role the top management team plays in the strategic success of the company (Hambrick, 1987). For example, Jack Welch created $52 billion market value added during his tenure as CEO of GE, and Roberto Goizueta created $59 billion during his tenure as CEO of Coca-Cola. While both of these men were well rewarded for their efforts, so were many others. Shareholders, employees, and their families all benefited from this growth (Quick et al., 2002).

There is also strong evidence to support the importance of executive health concerns by looking at the other side of the coin. When executives are not healthy, organizations suffer. Let's examine the financial health of the Disney Company under the leadership of Walt Disney and Michael Eisner. When Walt Disney died in 1966, the stock price of the company fell dramatically, and fifteen years later the *Wall Street Journal* was still questioning if the company had ever recovered (Quick et al., 2002). Almost twenty years later, when Disney announced that Michael Eisner would have quadruple-bypass surgery, the company stock dropped again. However, within two days of his return to work, the price per share rose $5 and continued to rise (Huey, 1995).

STRESS AND SEX DIFFERENCES

Among the widely accepted responses to stress is the fight or flight response, which describes the physiological changes under stress (Cannon, 1935). As we discussed earlier, the General Adaptation Syndrome is another commonly-held stress response concept that describes what occurs beyond the initial flight or fight response (Selye, 1976). What is generally not commonly discussed is that prior to 1995, the samples used in compiling the research were comprised of only 17% females (Taylor et al., 2000). As a result, much of what we know about responding to stress is based on evidence using male samples (Taylor et al., 2000).

Even so, the ways in which women manage stress has been a topic of concern. For instance, Davidson and Cooper (1984) investigated the relationship between occupational stressors and manifestations of stress for 696 women managers representing four management levels in a variety of industries. More recently, Gyllensten and Palmer (2005) conducted a systematic review of cross-cultural studies investigating the role of gender in the workplace. Two reasons account for this increased attention. First, women have entered the labor force in record numbers over the last decade, particularly in the United States. Women comprised 59.4% of the U.S. labor force in 2006, and the rate of those with dependent children (under the age of 18 years) rose substantially from 1975 through 2006, from 47% to 71% (U.S. Bureau of Labor Statistics, 2007). The influx of women into the labor force has made them susceptible to the same occupational stressors (prolonged exposure to stressful working conditions) as men. Yet, working women, in particular, are exposed to unique stressors: multiple conflicting roles and stymied careers brought about by glass ceilings, sex discrimination, and stereotyping (Cocchiara & Bell, 2010). We believe there is value in men and women learning about these unique stressors for working women, and we discuss them in the following section.

Women's Unique Stressors

First, we look at role conflict. Nelson and Quick (2011) define inter-role conflict as "conflicting expectations related to two separate roles" (p. 225). Therefore, a sick child presents the mother who works outside the home with a conflict between her role as a mother and that of an employee. It is clear that the more roles one takes on, the higher the potential for stress (Langan-Fox, 1998). And while men's work consists primarily of paid employment, women's work tends to be diffused between paid work, childcare, and housework (e.g., Krantz, Berntsson, & Lundberg, 2005). This diffusion has had a detrimental effect on women's health in the form of increased exhaustion, heart disease, depression, anxiety, and increased and sustained stress (Cocchiara & Bell, 2010).

Multiple roles for women are not entirely harmful, however. Ruderman, Ohlott, Panzer, and King (2002) found positive outcomes for working women when multiple roles accumulated in such a way that their personal roles benefited their professional ones. For example, the planning skills women managers used to juggle familial responsibilities at home served as good practice for managing multiple responsibilities in the workplace. Ruderman et al. (2002) agree that while fewer roles are better than many, multiple roles can contribute to rather than interfere with good performance of women managers.

The lack of progress towards achieving their career goals presents another source of stress and strain for many working women (Gyllensten, & Palmer, 2005; Nelson, Quick, Hitt, & Moesel, 1990). Despite having similar credentials, women managers fail to move up corporate hierarchies as quickly as men managers (Stroh, Brett, & Reilly, 1992). How does failing to achieve one's career goals translate into negative stress? The process begins with one's appraisal of a demand. When a worker is presented with a particular demand (career mobility, in this instance), and she perceives that giving in to the demand outweighs the rewards, stress is often the result (cf., Nelson & Quick, 1985). For many working women, doing what they believe are all the "right" behaviors to achieve higher organizational levels yet failing to achieve a level representative of their efforts can result in frustration and distress. It is true that men also experience frustration and become distressed when they fail to achieve desired organizational levels. However, women tend to face a more challenging organizational climate, as we discuss in the following sections.

The "glass ceiling" describes the largely invisible barriers that limit career advancement for women, particularly in large organizations and in male-dominated professions such as engineering and medicine (Morrison, White, Van Velsor, & the Center for Creative Leadership, 1992). This issue goes beyond the notion that fewer women are represented at all levels of management; the term "glass ceiling" suggests that women face increasingly more difficulty gaining access to organizational positions that represent "real" power (Wright & Baxter, 2000). Though invisible, glass ceilings are very apparent to women who experience them and have bona fide effects on their career mobility and, consequently, their mental state.

Closely related to the lack of career progress for working women is the issue of discrimination and gender stereotyping. Perceived discrimination has been linked to a variety of outcomes, including psychological distress (e.g., Fischer & Holz, 2007). Being the object of discrimination (perceived or actual) is harmful in many ways. When women perceive they are the object of sex discrimination, they tend to have more negative views of themselves as individuals and as members of the group (Fischer & Holtz, 2007). Such negative views can lead to increased psychological distress and feelings of worthlessness, which can lead to reduced performance (e.g., Gaumer, Shah, & Ashley-Cotleur, 2005).

A final workplace stressor that affects primarily women is gender stereotyping. Women in leadership positions often find themselves in a bit of a quandary in terms of how they should behave in the workplace (Cocchiara & Bell, 2010). Ann Hopkins, a highly successful business manager with Price Waterhouse, is a prime example. Hopkins amassed more billable hours than any other prospective partner, bringing in $25 million in new business, and yet was denied partnership on the basis that she wasn't feminine enough (cf., Ryan & Haslam, 2007). However, a woman who is caring, cries, or otherwise shows her "feminine" side is deemed as not possessing the traits associated with being an effective leader (Cocchiara & Bell, 2010). This difference equates to a perceived deficiency in leadership, with the result being discrimination, although sometimes at the subconscious level.

Experiencing discrimination and being the object of gender stereotypes are common stressors for many working women. However, it should be pointed out that unhealthy job stress is not an inevitable outcome of workplace pressures for women. Women who work generally experience fewer health-related illnesses such as cardiovascular disease and enjoy increased emotional well-being through challenging jobs, emotional support, and encouragement than do unemployed women (Nelson & Burke, 2000). And as we discussed earlier, when women are successful at negotiating personal roles, it may lead to positive cross-over benefits in the ways that they handle their professional roles and vice versa (Ruderman et al., 2002).

Prevention and Coping Strategies

Whereas males tend to respond to stress and pressures by fighting or fleeing, the female response to stress is much less aggressive and is geared to nurture and protect. As we mentioned earlier, Taylor et al. (2000) confirm that the female physiology differs from that of males. That physiological difference manifests itself behaviorally as well. In the face of constant stress, females will release high levels of oxytocin, an estrogen-enhanced hormone associated with relaxation and sedation. When men have a particularly stressful day at work, they may withdraw (or "flee") from their families. While the fight or flight stress response quickly mobilizes bodily organs to react to stress, it can cause significant damage when the stress is chronic (Parker-Pope, 2007). The response for women is markedly different. Women appear to be at their most nurturing and caring (especially with their family members) on their most stressful days. This "reaching out" behavior by women (tend-and-befriend) under stress extends to relationships outside the immediate family. According to Taylor et al. (2000), women are more likely than men to maintain same-sex relationships and seek out support from those relationships, particularly in times of distress. Women derive numerous social benefits by simply living and caring for others. These benefits do not disappear when women are faced with stress. Rather, they become more essential.

Coping dispositions, like personality traits, have been found to be stable over the course of one's life (Williamson & Dooley, 2001). Therefore, without the aid of effective coping skills, men are likely to continue utilizing destructive coping behaviors into their adult years. Women use more emotion-focused coping strategies (e.g., expressing feelings, seeking emotional support, and positive reframing) compared to men (e.g., Davies et al., 2000). Gender differences in risk taking have been clearly documented in the research literature. While there are numerous individual studies to support this, the Byrnes, Miller, and Schafer (1999) meta-analysis of 150 studies overwhelmingly indicated that men were more likely to engage in risky behaviors than women. According to Davies et al. (2000), college-age men, for example, are more likely than women to engage in risk-taking behaviors like using drugs and alcohol, driving dangerously, having multiple sexual partners, and participating in violent acts.

Why do young men engage in such behaviors? Some researchers suggest that it is a combination of gender-role stereotyping and socialization. For instance, the "traditional" male is strong, aggressive, and stoic in the face of adversity. From an early age, boys are socialized to conceal their vulnerabilities and discouraged to seek help from peers, parents, and other adults in order to "be a man" (Courtenay, 1998). This typically male socialization process, often characterized by intense daring, bravado, and even violence, tends to follow a similar pattern with men's coping skills (Mejia, 2005). Moreover, males typically push each other into risky behaviors by daring taunts (Pleck, 1981).

Risk-taking behavior, particularly abusing drugs and alcohol, can have dire consequences as discussed later. Such pressure to conform to societal expectations can lead to increased risks, delayed medical diagnoses and treatment, and even death. In fact, suicide was the third leading cause of death for U.S. young people aged 15 to 24 (National Institute of Mental Health, 2003). The ratio of college-age men to women 20 to 24 years old who died by suicide in 2000 was seven to one (National Institute of Mental Health, 2003). This could be an indication of men's ability to successfully hide their pain and, perhaps, their perceived invulnerabilities to risk and illness. Psychologists advance several hypotheses to explain the link between suicidal behaviors and stress (see Spirito & Esposito-Smythers, 2006 for a review). Among them is that excessive substance abuse will heighten distress to the point where an individual might view alcohol as giving him the courage he needs to make the suicide attempt. Courtenay (1998) cites one mother's disbelief that her college junior would ever shoot himself. Apparently, no one, including his own mother, was aware of his true feelings or his inability to cope.

Learning to cope is critical to success in college and beyond. Students who enter college must learn to adapt and adjust to college life. Bonica and Daniel (2003) found that the ability to successfully cope upon entering college was critical to student success. Other research found that stress led to high levels of burnout and that this burnout may build from semester to semester (Law, 2010). Helping students learn to cope and prevent burnout will do much more than help them stay in school. Learning coping strategies early will help them reverse the "male" coping dispositions we discussed earlier and better equip them for the rigors of a professional work life.

HOW WOMEN AND MEN CAN LEARN FROM EACH OTHER

We have a unique opportunity as educators to move beyond sharing information to informing students on how to use that information to improve their personal and professional lives. One such opportunity was in the early 1980s when we developed an interactive learning framework called Sex-Role Stereotype Dialogue, in which male and female students worked in same-sexed groups to list their top five sources of stress attributable to their sex. We transitioned the framework into an experiential exercise aimed at raising awareness of the sex differences in stress and strain.

We used a variation of the gender role stressors classroom experiential exercise between 1981 and 1985 in a series of stress and marriage workshops designed for Hospital Corporation of America. This experiential exercise initially saw some dramatically different understanding between male and female groups, with men being less attuned to women's stressors but not vice versa. In the 1980s, male groups often listed rather inflammatory stressors about women, such as "looking perfect." Male groups were very uneven in their ability to predict women's stressors well. Female groups were much better predictors of male competitiveness, performance pressures, Type A behavior, and macho image. Since the mid-1990s, this has changed, and men are learning more about women while displaying greater, appropriate appreciation. We have come to realize that women now own their strength and power and have become more assertive, while not modeling men. These gender role and cultural shifts are ones that seem both appropriate and positive. The awareness gained through this exercise led to thoughtful prevention planning and action with the potential to channel energy along constructive lines as opposed to conflicted lines. However, there is still tension, conflict, and debate between opposite sexed groups in the exercise from which learning distills.

We should be clear that the learning that occurs between the sexes is not only from women to men; it goes both ways. The stress mastery tools we outline below are equally effective for helping both women and men cope with stress and strain.

Stress Mastery for the Workplace

Stress mastery is the process of developing the knowledge, skills, and abilities to prevent distress and cope with the inevitable stress that college, work, and life offer. No one ever achieves "stress mastery," yet all can develop competence by paying attention to both head and heart (e.g., Quick, Gavin, Cooper, & Quick, 2004). To really learn about stress is experiential and goes beyond the academic. The heart of stress mastery is mastery of one's body, feelings, and emotions. Cannon (1929/1915) was correct in centering his attention on the effects of the emotions and emotional excitement on human physiology. Therefore, stress mastery requires skilled practice in muscles and emotions. Stress mastery is about personal and interpersonal intelligence and about emotional competence. Hardiness, self-reliance, and positive stress are tools that working individuals can use to master stress.

Hardiness

A personality characteristic that can benefit both men and women is hardiness. Maddi (2006) describes hardy individuals as those who have learned to face conflict using a combination of three attitudes—commitment, control, and challenge. Despite the number and difficulty of upcoming workplace demands, the hardy professional remains engaged instead of withdrawing. Hardy individuals are neither powerless nor passive to events taking place around them. Finally, hardy workers view stress as a normal occurrence, as a challenge to be met rather than a hindrance, and an opportunity to grow and learn.

Self-Reliance

Researchers have described self-reliance in several ways. All of these show self-reliance as a source of strength. Levinson (1996), for example, in a follow-up to his classic article "When Executives Burn Out," noted that his basic assumption that leaders take action to prevent stress seemed outdated. Because of increasing stress from increased competition among organizations and the related reengineering and downsizings, employees no longer looked to employers for support. Instead, Levinson (1996) suggested that they look to themselves in what he termed "a new age of self-reliance." Looking inside the self is the fallback position should the job fail the individual. That is true self-reliance, which is different from macho-independence. Individuals thus express self-reliance by understanding their most characteristic behaviors and by enacting these behaviors in the workplace. This, in turn, leads to less stress and more security.

Research on self-reliance focuses attention on the interpersonal and interdependent aspects of self-reliance, stemming from the pioneering work of Ainsworth and Bowlby (1991). They proposed that the attachment process is a biological imperative and that it leads to survival of the human species. Ainsworth and Bowlby (1991) saw three distinct patterns of attachment: secure (subsequently renamed self-reliant), avoidant, and anxious-ambivalent. Self-reliant patterns represent health and secure attachments, whereas avoidant and anxious-ambivalent patterns were insecure and unhealthy. Early childhood patterns of attachment become internal working models of relationships for working adults. Good friends, colleagues, and mentors offer great shields against the slings and arrows of stress, both in and outside the workplace.

Positive Stress

The lion's share of existing stress research has focused on the prevention and resolution of negative stress; that is, its focus has been on the prevention and management of distress. The emphasis has been on the negative in terms of identifying causes of distress, ways of coping with stressors, and healing the wounds of distress. Eustress (from the Greek *eu*, meaning good) is positive, while distress (from the Latin *dis* or bad) is not. Many researchers, including Quick and Quick (1984), have acknowledged the presence of a positive form of stress, associating it with good health and high performance. Edwards and Cooper (1990) emphasized that eustress is not simply the absence of distress and that one way to study eustress is to assess positive psychological states.

This positive stress has been described in various ways and recognized in athletes and performing artists (e.g., opera singers) as being in the "zone" or in the "flow" during which time is suspended, and there is pure joy and pleasure from immersion in productive activity. Yet in the research literature on work stress and health, eustress appears very infrequently. There is a regrettable lack of attention to defining eustress, identifying causes of eustress, identifying a process (similar to coping) of managing eustress, and finding ways of generating eustress at work.

Simmons (2000) defined eustress as the positive psychological response to a stressor that is indicated by the presence of positive psychological states. Eustress reflects the extent to which individuals appraise a situation or event as beneficial or as a potential enhancement of their well-being. Work situations elicit a mixture of both positive and negative responses in individuals. When assessing eustress as we have defined it here, the indicators of eustress should be positive psychological states, such as attitudes or emotions. Positive affect (PA), meaningfulness, manageability, and hope may be good indicators of eustress (Simmons, 2000; Simmons & Nelson, 2001; Simmons, Nelson, & Neal, 2001). These indicators all represent an aspect of active engagement, which may be an important component of the eustress response at work.

Eustressed workers are actively engaged, meaning that they are immersed in and pleasurably occupied by the demands of the work at hand. Workers can be engaged and perceive positive benefits even when confronted with extremely demanding stressors. Nelson and Simmons (2011) refer to this process as savoring and offer it as a complement to what is called coping in response to distress. They further suggest that individuals who likely engage in savoring are those who are optimistic, hardy, and self-reliant and who possess an internal locus of control and a sense of coherence. As a complement to distress prevention, we need to study eustress generation, including ways that managers can help employees engender and savor the eustress response.

CONCLUSION: LESSONS TO BE LEARNED

Today's workplace has become a breeding ground of job demands that, if not properly addressed, can lead to negative job stress. The National Institute for Occupational Safety and Health (NIOSH) indicates that, especially in recent years, high levels of job stress have become the rule rather than the exception. One quarter of employees consider their jobs to be the number one source of stress in their lives, with work problems having a stronger association with health complaints than any other life stressor (NIOSH, 1999).

We believe that men and women have valuable lessons to teach one another about identifying and coping with harmful stressors, even in light of the bio-behavioral differences in the sexes (e.g., Taylor et al., 2000). While women are more likely than men to adopt coping strategies that emphasize caring and networks, these methods for coping with stress are not exclusively female. These strategies can be beneficial for males. It is important to recognize that the "female" stress response is somewhat limited, to the degree that a particular stressor is chronic or predictable. According to Taylor et al. (2000), "Under certain stressful circumstances, we might find the tend-and-befriend pattern to be quite descriptive of female responses to stress and, in other cases, not descriptive" (p. 422).

Men can benefit by seeking emotional support through networks and other interpersonal relationships. Another lesson that men can learn from women is to take better care of themselves. Men are less likely than women to go to the doctor when they have health problems, with one in four men waiting "as long as possible" before seeking help for medical problems (cf., Parker-Pope, 2007). On the other side, when women go to a gynecologist, for example, they are checked not only for gynecological problems but for diabetes, blood pressure, and depression—a well woman checkup (Parker-Pope, 2007).

Taylor et al. (2000) have expanded our knowledge of stress by bringing attention to the female's predisposition to tend-and-befriend under stress. Cannon's (1929/1915) classic fight-or-flight response is physiologically valid and one that both males and females may exhibit when conditions warrant. However, the tend-and-befriend capacity is more prevalent among women and may be one important component in their greater life expectancy. Men, especially starting early, can learn positive lessons from women that may help extend their lives (Murray-Law, 2011). This is not to say that men are devoid of healthy prevention and coping strategies, such as regular exercise, a lesson from men that many women may learn. In fact, Read and Gorman (2010) report that men engage more in, and benefit more from, physical exercise than do women. We encourage men and women to learn from each other both formally and informally. Such cooperative and collaborative behavior, rooted in the tend-and-befriend response, can set a positive pattern that they can use successfully in today's workplace.

Men and women are different. We all know that. Valuing their differences and more appreciatively understanding them allows both men and women to capitalize on the strengths of the opposite sex. In addition, appreciating the differences may allow each to defend the other against inherent limitations, or weaknesses. Us-versus-them and divisive human behaviors are inherently stressful and, in the long run, risky and unwise. By learning from each other, men and women can advance their collective physical health and psychological well-being. Mastering stress prevention and coping skills is in the collective best interest of both men and women in today's workplace.

REFERENCES

Abdel-Khalek, A. M., & Maltby, J. (2009). Differences in anxiety scores of college students from Germany, Spain, the United Kingdom, and the USA. *Psychological Reports, 104*, 624–626.

Adler, N. E., Boyce, W. T., Chesney, M. A., Folkman, S., & Syme, S. L. (1993). Socioeconomic inequalities in health: No easy solution. *Journal of the American Medical Association, 269*, 3140–3145.

Ainsworth, M. D. S., & Bowlby, J. (1991). An ethological approach to personality. *American Psychologist, 46*, 333–341.

APA Practice Central. (2009). APA poll find economic stress taking a toll on men. Retrieved on October 22, 2012 from http://www.apapracticecentral.org/news/2009/stress-men.aspx

Benison, S., Barger, A. C., & Wolfe, E. L. (1987). *Walter B. Cannon: The life and times of a young scientist.* Cambridge, MA: Belknap Press.

Bonica, C., & Daniel, J. H. (2003). Helping adolescents cope with stress during stressful times. *Current Opinions in Pediatrics, 15*, 385–390.

Byrnes, J., Miller, D., & Schafer, W. (1999). Gender differences in risk taking: A meta-analysis. *Psychological Bulletin, 75*, 367–383.

Cannon, W. B. (1929). *Bodily changes in pain, hunger, fear, and rage.* New York, NY: Appleton. (Original work published 1915).

Cannon, W. B. (1935). Stresses and strains of homeostasis. *The American Journal of the Medical Sciences, 189*, 1–14.

Cocchiara, F. K., & Bell, M. P. (2010). Gender and work stress: Unique stressors, unique responses. In C. L. Cooper, J. C. Quick, & M. J. Schabracq (Eds.), *Work and health psychology: The handbook* (3rd ed., pp. 123–145). Indianapolis, IN: Wiley Blackwell.

Courtenay, W. H. (1998). College men's health: An overview and a call to action. *Journal of American College Health, 46*(6), 279–290.

Davidson, M. J., & Cooper, C. L. (1984). Occupational stress in female managers: A comparative study. *Journal of Management Studies, 21*, 185–205.

Davies, J., McCrae, B. P., Frank, J., Dochnahl, A., Pickering, T., Harrison, B., Zakrzewski, M., & Wilson, K. (2000). Identifying male college students' perceived health needs, barriers to seeking help, and recommendations to help men adopt healthier lifestyles. *Journal of American College Health, 48*(6), 259–267.

Dusselier, L., Dunn, B., Wang, Y., Shelley, M.C., & Whalen, D. F. (2005). Personal, health, academic, and environmental predictors of stress for residence hall students. *Journal of American College Health, 54*(1), 15–24.

Edwards, J. R., & Cooper, C. L. (1990). The person-environment fit approach to stress: Recurring problems and some suggested solutions. *Academy of Management Journal, 39*(2), 292–339.

Fischer, A. R., & Holz, K. B. (2007). Perceived discrimination and women's psychological distress: The roles of collective and personal self-esteem. *Journal of Counseling Psychology, 54*, 154–164.

Gaumer, C. J., Shah, A. J., & Ashley-Cotleur, C. (2005). Enhancing organizational competitiveness: Causes and effects of stress on women. *Journal of Workplace Behavioral Health, 21*, 31–43.

Gyllensten, K., & Palmer, S. (2005). The role of gender in workplace stress: A critical literature review. *Health Education Journal, 64*(3), 271–288.

Hambrick, D. C. (1987). The top management team: Key to strategic success. *California Management Review, 340,* 88–108.

Huey, J. (1995, April 17). Eisner explains everything. *FORTUNE Magazine.* Retrieved from http://money.cnn.com/magazines/fortune/fortune_archive/1995/04/17/202090/

Krantz, G., Berntsson, L., & Lundberg, U. (2005). Total workload, work stress and perceived symptoms in Swedish male and female white-collar employees. *European Journal of Public Health, 15*(2), 209–214.

Langan-Fox, J. (1998). Women's careers and occupational stress. *International Review of Industrial and Organizational Psychology, 13,* 273–302.

Law, D. W. (2010). A measure of burnout for business students. *Journal of Education for Business, 85,* 195–202.

Levinson, H. (1996, July). A new age of self-reliance. *Harvard Business Review,* pp. 162–173.

Maddi, S. R. (2006). Hardiness: The courage to grow from stresses. *The Journal of Positive Psychology, 1*(3), 160–168.

Mejía, X. (2005). Gender matters: Working with adult male survivors of trauma. *Journal of Counseling and Development, 83*(1), 29–40.

Morrison, A. M., White, R. P., Van Velsor, E., & the Center for Creative Leadership. (1992). *Breaking the glass ceiling: Can women reach the top of America's largest corporations?* Reading, MA: Addison-Wesley.

Murray-Law, B. (2011). Why do men die earlier? *Monitor on Psychology, 42*(6), 59–62.

National Institute for Occupational Safety and Health (NIOSH). (1999). Stress... at Work. DHHS (NIOSH) Publication No. 99-101. Retrieved on November 2, 2012 from http://www.cdc.gov/niosh/docs/99-101/

National Institute of Mental Health. (2003, April 11). Suicide in the United States. *Almanac of Policy Issues.* Retrieved on June 9, 2011 from http://www.policyalmanac.org/health/archive/suicide.shtml

Nelson, D. L., & Burke, R. J. (2000). Women executives: Health, stress, and success. *Academy of Management Executive, 14,* 107–121.

Nelson, D. L., & Quick, J. C. (1985). Professional women: Are distress and disease inevitable? *Academy of Management Review, 10,* 206–218.

Nelson, D. L., & Quick, J. C. (2011). *Organizational behavior: Science, the real world, and you, Seventh Edition.* Mason, OH: Cengage/South-Western.

Nelson, D. L., Quick, J. C., Hitt, M. A., & Moesel, D. (1990). Politics, lack of career progress, and work/home conflict: Stress and strain for working women. *Sex Roles, 23,* 169–183.

Nelson, D. L., & Simmons, B. (2011). Savoring eustress while coping with distress: A holistic model of stress. In J. C. Quick & L. E. Tetrick (Eds.), *Handbook of Occupational Health Psychology* (2nd ed., pp. 55–74). Washington, DC: American Psychological Association.

Parker-Pope, T. (2007, April 24). The man problem. *The Wall Street Journal,* p. D1.

Pleck, J. (1981). *The myth of masculinity.* Cambridge, MA: MIT Press.

Quick, J. D., Cooper, C. L. Gavin, J. H., & Quick, J. D. (2002). Executive health: Building self-reliance for challenging times. In C. L. Cooper & I. T. Robertson

(Eds.), *International review of industrial and organizational psychology* (pp. 187–216). West Sussex, England: John Wiley & Sons, Inc.

Quick, J. C., Cooper, C. L., Gavin, J. H., & Quick, J. D. (2008). *Managing executive health: Personal and corporate strategies for sustained success.* Cambridge, England: Cambridge University Press.

Quick, J. C., Gavin, J. H., Cooper, C. L., & Quick, J. D. (2000). Executive health: Building strength, managing risks. *Academy of Management Executive, 14,* 34–46.

Quick, J. C., Gavin, J. H., Cooper, C. L., & Quick, J. D. (2004). Working together: Balancing head and heart. In R. H. Rozensky, N. G. Johnson, C. D. Goodheart, & W. R. Hammond (Eds.), *Psychology builds a healthy world* (pp. 219–232). Washington, DC: American Psychological Association.

Quick, J. C., & Quick, J. D. (1984). *Organizational stress and preventive management.* New York, NY: McGraw-Hill.

Quick, J. C., Wright, T. A., Adkins, J. A., Nelson, D. L., & Quick, J. D. (2013). *Preventive stress management in organizations* (2nd ed.). Washington, DC: American Psychological Association.

Read, J. G., & Gorman, B. K. (2010). Gender and health inequality. *Annual Review of Sociology, 36,* 371–386.

Rosch, P. J. (2001). On the origins and the evolution of stress. *Health and Stress, 9,* 1–7.

Ruderman, M. N., Ohlott, P. J., Panzer, K., & King, S. N. (2002). Benefits of multiple roles for managerial women. *Academy of Management Journal, 45*(2), 369–386.

Ryan, M. R., & Haslam, S. A. (2007). The glass cliff: Exploring the dynamics surrounding the appointment of women to precarious leadership positions. *Academy of Management Review, 32,* 549–572.

Selye, H. (1976). *Stress in health and disease.* Boston, MA: Butterworth.

Simmons, B. L. (2000). *Eustress at work: Accentuating the positive.* Unpublished doctoral dissertation, Oklahoma State University, Stillwater, OK.

Simmons, B. L., & Nelson, D. L. (2001). Eustress at work: the relationship between hope and health in hospital nurses. *Health Care Management Review, 26*(4), 7–18.

Simmons, B. L., Nelson, D. L., & Neal, L. J. (2001). A comparison of the positive and negative work attitudes of home healthcare and hospital nurses. *Health Care Management Review, 26*(3), 63–74.

Spirito, A., & Esposito-Smythers, C. (2006). Attempted and completed suicide in adolescence. *Annual Review of Clinical Psychology, 2,* 237–266.

Stroh, L. K., Brett, J. J., & Reilly, A. H. (1992). All the right stuff: A comparison of female and male manager's career progression. *Journal of Applied Psychology, 77,* 251–260.

Taylor, S. E., Klein, L. C., Lewis, B. P., Gruenewald, T. L., Gurung, R. A. R., & Updegraff, J. A. (2000). Biobehavioral responses to stress in females: Tend-and-befriend, not fight-or-flight. *Psychological Review, 107,* 411–429.

U.S. Bureau of Labor Statistics. (2007). Women in the labor force: A databook, Report 1002. Retrieved on May 22, 2008 from http://www.bls.gov/cps.wlf-databook-2007.pdf

Williamson, G., & Dooley, W. (2001). Aging and coping: The activity solution. In C. R. Snyder (Ed.), *Coping with stress: Effective people and processes* (pp. 240–258). New York, NY: Oxford University Press.

Wright, E. O., & Baxter, J. (2000). The glass ceiling hypothesis: A reply to critics. *Gender & Society, 14,* 814–821.

SECTION II

EXAMINING THE SOCIAL ASPECTS
OF OCCUPATIONAL STRESS

CHAPTER 7

WHEN DEALING WITH QUALITY OF WORKING LIFE, IT IS IMPOSSIBLE TO FORGET

Regrettably, Taylor Is Still Alive and Kicking!

José Vieira Leite

ABSTRACT

It is not work in itself that oppresses people who work, as we often think, but rather the way it is structured. Human beings do not manage not to think (and thus not create), even when they are submitted to extreme circumstances of denial of this condition, and the Taylorist model of production organization occupies an outstanding position in this regard.

The Taylorist model of work management—which, as we shall seek to demonstrate, currently prevails in almost all organizations in all corners of the Earth—on taking the separation between the spheres of conception and execution to its utmost, paroxysmal expression produces oppression at work for almost all workers, who are driven, day after day, throughout all the days of their lives, to repress the unwavering human condition of co-creation of the

Improving Emploee Health and Well-Being, pages 103–118
Copyright © 2014 by Information Age Publishing

world, of life. This, in our opinion, is the most essential cause that produces unease, suffering, and absence of a quality of working life in the universe of the world of contemporary production. Much beyond many tasks, low wages, authoritarian supervisors, and so on, what most affects humanity of the workers in itself—profoundly, extensively, viscerally—is oppression at work.

INTRODUCTION

This chapter discusses two axes of reflection-proposition, here called I—rationalization and II—oppression at work.

Axis I—Rationalization

Regarding axis I—rationalization, we will seek to affirm, first of all and above all, the fact that Frederick Taylor's propositions are still current. Taylor, as he is known, is the theoretical-practical genius (for the interests of capital, of course) of the worldwide explosion of capitalism, the main name of the so-called School of Scientific Management. His book *Princípios de Administração Científica* is often considered the bible of a human-centered management proposal. Even though it has a dense and totalitarian proposition about work, it still has an expressive meaning regarding rationalization and oppression of work. From those days (late 19th–early 20th century) to the present, as is also well-known, much has changed in the world of labor—in the world in general. As a result of such changes, the idea has been widely disseminated that more traditional labor management models, as we may call them (including Taylor's), are being replaced every so often by new models more appropriate to the new (always new, increasingly and more rapidly new) times. The number of "novelties" offered, already for some time, on the market of "solutions" for problems of labor management is immeasurable: CQC, re-engineering, downsizing, management by competencies, coaching, management of intellectual capital, and so on. It is appropriate here to say that these "solutions" come and go, mostly without any news for those who are their subject—people who work—regarding the reasons, both for their coming and their going, which, among other evils, leads to a great dis-enchantment by the workers regarding the initiatives of company top management, which merely adopts, sequentially and mimetically, the fashionable solution or the solution that is the current fad.

The idea that Taylor's proposal has been surpassed does not, in our opinion, correspond to reality—and this is very unfortunate for workers. What has certainly changed—concomitantly with the characteristics of production that are much more negative for the working human being, as, for instance, the brutal intensification of work in current times—are secondary aspects of the Taylorist proposition, such as time and movement control using a clipboard and a chronometer, for instance. This control became unnecessary, since it was internalized in the Fordian and post-Fordian machines themselves.

However, Taylor's central proposal, that is, the most radical possible separation between the domains of conception and implementation of production, is still the essence of work management in almost the entire contemporary productive universe. This means that, nowadays, in the world of production very few people conceive while almost all only carry out what was conceived deliberately and outside them. This reality becomes clear when one looks at the organization chart of businesses today. The organization chart is the graphic representation of the prevailing power structure in a given organization. Almost every company has one of them that, in almost all cases, reflects a strongly hierarchical, vertical, top-down model of power distribution). With the precision of a Swiss watch, the presence of instance(s) of formulation is identified, separate from instances of merely applying of what has been previously created in the first instance(s) referred to here.

Depending on the size of the organization, the instance of conception can be an advisor, an advisory department, a coordinator, a department, a board of directors, a vice-president, and so on. However, there is no doubt that it will almost always be present. And what does this mean? It unequivocally means that, regrettably, Taylor is still alive and kicking!

Axis II—Oppression at Work

Regarding axis II—oppression at work, we believe that almost all production units of the historical space and time that has come to be called modernity (and even more dominantly, in contemporary times), using the theoretical-practical armamentarium of rationalization (or other models of production organization that come in its wake), lead to practicing the most extreme oppression at work—an oppression that, materialized in the machines and the work management processes used in production, reveals itself even more harmful for those who work than the exploitation of labor itself, denounced by Karl Marx.

Thus, we consider that the greatest tragedy of contemporary workers is the fact that, while in their spirit the flame of freedom remains alive, because of oppression at work they are expropriated from thinking in their everyday doing. Thus, entrapped between the fate of freedom universally bestowed on them, and the impossibility of freedom, daily inflicted on them, contemporary workers have their privileged location, their vocation of a relationship with the world in existential anguish. No matter how good the work conditions experienced, almost always something—or everything—is lacking: freedom. Contemporary workers, thus, almost never take pleasure in what they do because, between doing and taking pleasure in it, the pleasure of doing is always absent.

A lot has certainly been said (but perhaps still too little) about rationalization, oppression at work. Karl Marx inaugurates a dense line of research on such topics, in which Hanna Arendt definitely has an outstanding position. Simone Weil, however, in our opinion, produced the most modern practical analysis-proposal on the subject. It is entirely valid and, very especially, in the historical times of today.

Thus, the present chapter finds its theoretical-practical foundation, essentially, in the life and work of Simone Weil—Frenchwoman, Jew, philosopher, militant, mystic—who was born, lived, and died in the historical space-time of the rise and implantation of the national socialism (Nazism) in Europe, during a short 34 years. However, she left an extraordinary legacy of propositions that are in fact essential to seek the edification of a world in humanist, human, and humanizing truth.[1]

RATIONALIZATION

On February 23, 1937, Simone Weil gave, to an audience of workers, a lecture in which one of the harshest criticisms ever presented against the process of rationalization of material production was made public.[2] Now we will discuss the ideas expressed there that are most relevant to us.

> In the beginning, science was only the study of the laws of nature. Afterwards it intervened in production by inventing and improving machines and with the discoveries of processes that allowed using the forces of nature. Finally, in our time, at the end of last century, one thought to apply science no longer simply to using the forces of nature but to using the human workforce... (Weil, 1951, p. 289)

The Industrial Revolution, for many, is the name of the radical change that occurred in industry when science began to be applied to production, with the beginning of the large-scale industry. Simone Weil, however, refers to two industrial revolutions: the first defining itself by the scientific use of inert matter and the forces of nature, and the second characterized by the scientific use of living matter, man. Rationalization of production is a term that acquires meaning because of the occurrence of the second industrial revolution, thus concerning the scientific use of living matter, of human labor. As to this use, Weil proposes the existence of two issues to be distinguished:

...exploitation of the working class that is defined by capitalist profit, and oppression of the working class at the workplace, which is expressed in long suffering, 48 hours or 40 hours a week, depending on the case, but which can also go beyond the factory, taking up the 24 hours of the day. (Weil, 1951, p. 293)

Distinguishing between exploitation and oppression of the workers thus is decisive in analyzing Weil insofar as it enables understanding of the reasons that allow oppression of workers to continue under socialism, even if the typically capitalist exploitation of those who work has ceased. About this she says:

...a factory is made essentially to produce. Men are there to help the machines make, every day, the greatest possible number of well-made, cheap products. But, on the other hand, these men are men; they have needs, aspirations to be fulfilled, which do not necessarily coincide with the requirements of production; and even, in fact, mostly definitely do not coincide with them. This is a contradiction that the change of regime would not eliminate. But we cannot accept that the life of men be sacrificed in the name of manufacturing products. (Weil, 1951, p. 293–294)

The change in the dominant legal-political regime does not in itself solve the fundamental contradiction that exists between the interests, *stricto sensu*, of production and the interests of those who produce the production, the workers. Ideally,

...a factory must be organized in such a way that the raw material it uses becomes products that are neither very rare, nor very expensive, nor defective, and that, at the same time, the men who enter the factory in the morning do not leave there physically or morally diminished in the evening, at the end of a day, a year, twenty years. (Weil, 1951, p. 295)

Here, according to Weil, lies the real problem, the most serious problem faced by workers: finding a method to organize the work that will be acceptable for production, work, and consumption.

Since not even the possible transition from capitalism to socialism—by definition the most acceptable social regime to defend the workers' interests—in itself ensures overcoming the contradiction among the three fields of interest of production, work, and consumption, it is the workers, under whatever social regime of production they are, who have to permanently seek a solution to this issue because, due to oppression by work to which they are permanently subjected, they are the only social force really interested in reconciling the interests among production, work, and consumption, a reconciliation that is found to be the only concrete situation that is truly favorable to the interests of people who work.

This problem, however, has not even begun to be solved, since it has not yet been adequately formulated; the socialist movement theoreticians, from Proudhon to Marx, and the workers' movement in general, including workers' unions, have not managed to think the issue through. To do so, Weil considers it essential to previously study the existing system and begin with the current regime to conceive a better one. That is why she looks at the critique of the rationalization of production, of scientific organization of work, a system formally structured by Taylor and widely disseminated in the universe of production at the time Weil gave her lecture, and we consider it to be still widely used nowadays. It was Taylor who found the essential, who gave the impulse and marked the orientation of this work method, according to Weil. The great concern was to avoid any waste of time at work. Taylor was not exactly a discoverer, an inventor. Taylor always "... sought more scientific processes to use the already existing machines to the utmost; and not only the machines, but also the men ..." (Weil, 1951, p. 301). Taylor's great discovery was, we are convinced, the articulation of thinking, word and action to overcome the limits that had until then been established for the exploitation of machines and men.

Herein lies the essence of the rational organization of work. Herein lies the permanence of Taylor in modern times,[3] a time in which everything that is solid melts in the air, as Marx famously said. Taylor, who is modern, is solid—more solid than Marx (than real socialism, at least)—and does not melt in the air; not all that is solid melts in the air could, thus, be an alternative formula to that proposed by Marx. Taylor, despite and mainly because of his essential solidity as to the interests of capitalism (and it would also be possible to refer to his solidity as to the interests of socialism, at least as to the interests of socialism inspired by Lenin), did not melt in the air throughout the already long time of domination of the rational organization of work; much the opposite, he solidified in the air, and like air itself, occupied all spaces of the material production of modernity and, in our opinion, also those of contemporary time.[4]

> His aim was to take away from the workers the possibility of determining for themselves the processes and pace of their work, and putting into the hands of management the choice of the movements to be carried out during production ... his main concern was to find the means to oblige workers to give the factory their utmost working capacity ... (Weil, 1951, p. 301)

Taylor was, greatly preceding everything, a modern Machiavelli, with a genius-like capacity to understand, formulate, and implement the policies that were most favorable to the interests of company owners, of the dominant class of his time. Taylor probably was the most effective—a sum of efficacious and efficient—political being of modern-contemporary time. His fundamental contribution does not lie in the sphere of economy, of business administration, as one generally supposes. His decisive, essential finding was in the terrain of political science, of politics, of the art of managing the destiny of the "polis," of influencing—radically, extensively, profoundly—the life of men itself, in all its dimensions.

Displacement of workers to company management, the possibility of determining the processes, work pace, and the moves to be performed during production now re-inaugurates the regime of the large-scale industry, in a way that fully carries the vocation for complete domination. This is the fullest form of organization of production in modern time/space. Marx denuded the existence of surplus value. Taylor, covering it in velvets and brocades, brought it to the highest point of its extraction. "...Egyptian foremen had whips to make workers produce. Taylor replaced the whip by offices and laboratories under the cover of science" (Weil, 1951, p. 302). After all, that is what it is all about: the oppression of workers by work.

The whips of yesterday found their expression in the offices and scientific laboratories of today; the form was changed, but the perverse content of work relations, of the exploitation of man by man, was maintained. Rationalization is more a method to make people work harder than a method to make them work better, according to Weil. In this sense, Ford takes a step forward in rationalization in inventing the assembly line.

> The assembly system in a production line allowed replacing specialized workers by workers specialized in line work; in this work, instead of performing qualified work, the worker only has to carry out a certain number of mechanical gestures that are constantly repeated. It is an improvement on the Taylor system that manages to take away from a worker their choice of method and the intelligence of their work, transferring these to the section of planning and studies. This assembly system also makes the manual skill needed by specialized workers disappear. (Weil, 1951, p. 304)

On enabling the brutal intensification of the pace of production, rationalization created a major alternative to the simple lengthening of the work day as a way to expand the extraction of surplus value. Together with the extraction of absolute surplus value, it then became feasible to have a significant expansion of the extraction of relative surplus value, by intensifying the work pace. Without changing the manufacturing methods,

> ...Taylor proudly tells that he managed to double and even triple production in certain factories simply by using the bonus system, by surveilling the workers and by inexorably dismissing those who did not want to or could not keep up with the pace. (Weil, 1951, p. 307)

Taylorization produced the disqualification of workers. Weil presents the information that, at Ford, only 1% of the workers needed more than one day to learn.[5] Rationalization led to the isolation of workers. An essential formula by Taylor is that it is necessary to address the worker individually, consider the individual in him, which is intended to destroy the workers' solidarity by means of bonuses and competition.

> ...Ford naïvely says that it is excellent to have workers who get along well, but that they should not get along too well, because this diminishes the spirit of competition and of emulation indispensable for production. (Weil, 1951, p. 310)

The worker's class division, therefore, is at the foundation of Taylorization.

> This system produced monotony at work... If it really happens that with this system, monotony is bearable for the workers, this is possibly the worst that one can say of such a system; because it is certain that monotonous work always begins as suffering. If it reaches the point of becoming a habit, this occurs at the expense of moral diminishment. (Weil, 1951, pp. 310–311)

Discipline, subjection, is another characteristic of the system, its essential character, its purpose. The decisive element of this discipline is to break down the workers' resistance. The imposition of times and movements in production takes away all power of resistance from the workers. Taylor said that his system allowed the end of the power of workers' unions in the companies.

> During an enquiry held in America concerning the Taylor system, a worker interviewed by Henri de Man told him: "Supervisors do not understand that we did not want to let them time us; however, what would our supervisors say if we asked them to show us their accounting books and said to them: 'On this much profit you have made, we think that this part should be yours, and that other part should return to us in the form of wages'? Knowledge of work times is, to us, precisely the equivalent of what industrial and trade secrets mean to them..." (Weil, 1951, pp. 311–312)

Besides ownership of the factory, machines, monopoly of the manufacturing processes, and financial and commercial knowledge of his factory, a supervisor also intending to monopolize the work and work times found in the production organization system engendered by Taylor the way to extend his dominance to a point never before achieved by those who own the means of production. Using a combination of subjection and bonuses, supervisors, under the guidance of Taylor, try to tame the workers, the touchstone of the scientific organization of work.

> It is impossible to call such a system scientific, unless one considers the principle that men are not men, that one gives science the degrading role of an

instrument of pressure. But the true role of science in organization of work is to find better techniques... (Weil, 1951, p. 313)

OPPRESSION AT WORK

The issue is to know whether one can conceive an organization of production that, although impotent to eliminate the natural needs and the resulting social pressure, at least allows it to be carried out without crushing spirits and bodies with oppression. (Weil, 1991, p. 47)

This is the main challenge to all men who work: the end of oppression at work on bodies and spirits.

But it is not work itself that produces oppression. Broeckhoven reports:

Factory N.—Complaints because we ate slices of bread at 4 o'clock. I am going to talk to X:

"Can't we eat a slice of bread?"

"Regulation!"

"And do you think that normal?"

"It is fair!"

"Is it fair? You are a worker like us..."

"It is the regulation, it is fair!"

"Do you think this really fair??"

"We can take it, but we must not let ourselves be caught..."

"It is humiliating. And is it fair that there is neither heating nor water to wash oneself...??"

"N. works at a loss. It would be better if he closed his factory."

"And do you think that he can do that? He is the only one who can say something, do we all need to dance to his tune??"

"He only works because of his own prestige; if he closes the factory he becomes a simple citizen, like anyone else." (Broeckhoven, 1982, p. 144)

Oppression derives, not from work, but from given ways of organizing production. These ways do indeed generate oppression, mostly related to work itself. Dejours defines the following:

We use the term *organization of work* to designate the division of labor, the content of the task (insofar as it derives from it), the hierarchical system, the modalities of command, power relations, issues of responsibility, etc. (Dejours, 1987, p. 25)

Dejours also proposes:

> ... *organization of work* exerts a specific action on man, whose impact is on the *psychological.* Under certain conditions, suffering emerges that can be attributed to a clash between an *individual history,* that carries projects, hopes and desires, and an organization of work that ignores them. This mental suffering begins when man at work no longer can make any changes in his task, to make it more according to his physiological *needs* and his physiological *desires*—i.e., when the man-work relationship is blocked. (Dejours, 1987, p. 133)

Weil states that Marx, substituting the idea established until then, of the power of oppressors and pure and simple usurpation, thought that it was not possible to suppress oppression if the causes that made it inevitable were maintained. These causes lie in the material conditions of the social organization. Oppression is no longer considered usurping a privilege and is now taken as an organ of a social function, a function that consists in developing the productive forces, insofar as this development requires hard effort and strict deprivations. Oppression is only established when the progress of production causes a division of work that is far enough advanced that change, military command, and government are distinct functions. And oppression, once it has been established, provokes the later development of production forces and changes its form, as required by this development, until the day when, having become an obstacle to it and not a help, it purely and simply disappears.

Considering that the Marxist scheme is progress compared to the previous interpretations, Weil understands why he does not explain the mechanism of oppression.

> He describes its birth only in part, since, why would the division of work necessarily become oppression? It does not allow in any way achieving the end reasonably; because if Marx thought to show how the capitalist regime ultimately creates an obstacle to production, he did not even try to prove that, in our times, any other regime would create the same kind of obstacle; and, further, it is not known why oppression could not manage to maintain itself, even having become a factor of economic regression. Above all, Marx does not explain why oppression is invincible during the time in which it is useful, why the angry oppressed never managed to found a non-oppressive society, be it based on the productive forces of their time, be it even at the price of an economic regression that could hardly increase their poverty; and finally, he leaves completely unexplained the general principles of the mechanism through which a given form of oppression is replaced by another. (Weil, 1991, p. 48)

How then, based on criticism of Marx, does Weil suppose that it is possible to know oppression? Just as for living beings, conditions for the existence of societies are determined, firstly by the natural environment, and then by the existence, activity, and, particularly, the competition of the other social groups. There is still a third factor involved: the disposition of the natural environment, the tool, the weapon, the procedures for working and fighting. This is the only factor that members of a society could perhaps control to a certain extent.

> This view is too abstract to guide us, but if, based on this summary view, we could achieve concrete analyses, it would finally be possible to define the social problem. The informed good will of men, all acting as individuals, is the only possible beginning of social progress... (Weil, 1991, p. 50)

Forms of social organization without any oppression are very rare and little known. All of them present an extremely low level of production, with a division of work that is practically unknown—except between sexes—and each family producing only what it needs for its own consumption.

> Force and oppression are two things...it is not the way in which one uses some force, but its own nature that determines whether it is or not oppressive...Oppression comes exclusively from objective conditions. The first of them is the existence of privileges; and it is not the laws or decrees of men that determine the privileges nor the deed of ownership of a property; it is the very nature of things... (Weil, 1991, p. 53)

The laws, the decrees, the deeds to a property, far from producing privilege, are the expression of a privilege generated previously—and in a different social region. Certain circumstances of human development produce forces that are placed between effort and the result of effort, which produces a monopoly by some, who then decide on the fate of those on whom they depend, and that is where equality perishes. Religious rites are the space to inaugurate the privilege of some priests regarding knowledge of the powers of nature. Priests have now been replaced by scientists and the technicians. The privilege of controlling weapons enables warriors to dominate workers. The presence of money in relationships of exchange among men gives specialists in organizing exchanges the privilege of earning their living, from the fruits of other people's work, and depriving the producers of what is indispensable. When the efforts of man need to be added and coordinated among them to be effective, coordination becomes the monopoly of some leaders, generating privileges. The second objective condition that leads to oppression is the struggle for power.

> Power contains a kind of inevitability that weighs as mercilessly on those who command as on those who obey; further, it is to the extent that they subject the former, that through them they crush the latter... (Weil, 1991, pp. 54–55)

This subjection of the powerful to power very often crushes them even more, in some sense, than they themselves crush those who are devoid of power.

> Preserving power is a vital need for the powerful, since it is their power that feeds them; now they have to preserve it at the same time against their rivals and against their inferiors, who certainly will try to get rid of dangerous masters, because in a vicious circle, the master is terrible to the slave, because he fears him and vice-versa; the same happens between rival powers. (Weil, 1991, p. 55)

All these conflicts around power lead society to a situation of growing oppression.

Expanded preservation of power is almost always the main reason for the action of the powerful, who, placing their lives at the service of gaining, preserving, and expanding their power, subordinate themselves to it, reducing their existence to a meaningless circular movement. Like the dog that chases its own tail and, on finding it, starts chasing it again, the powerful do not find rest until they conquer some power, and even after this, they do not find shelter, since they are occupied in maintaining and expanding their power. Power, thus, does not confer greater freedom on the powerful than on the powerless, who, in turn, mostly seek to conquer power, a search that, if successful, will place them inside the whirlpool in which the powerful are located and that, even if unsuccessful, in itself is enough to take away their freedom, which does not exist from the time in which, seduced by the siren song of the dispute for power, they think themselves powerful.

For Simone Weil, the essential evil of humankind consists in replacing the ends by the means. Except for in primitive societies, the law of all activities that dominate social existence is that each one sacrifices human life, in itself and in others, for things that are no more than means to live. Power is a means. But seeking power, because it is essentially impotent to grasp its object, excludes every consideration of an end, and, through an inevitable inversion, takes the place of all ends.

Human history, then, is simply the history of enslavement that makes men both oppressors and oppressed, simple playthings of the instruments of domination that they themselves have manufactured, thus reducing living humankind to the level of a thing of inert things. Thus, it is not men, but things that impose limits and laws on this vertiginous race.

Every so often, the oppressed manage to expel a team of oppressors and replace it with another, and sometimes they even manage to change the form of oppression; but as to suppressing oppression itself, for this it would be necessary to suppress its sources, abolish all monopolies, the magic secrets or techniques that give power over nature, weapons, money, coordination of the works.

According to Weil, the essential problem in the analysis of oppression is to know that what makes up the link that so far appears to unite social oppression and progress in the relations between man and nature. About this, she says:

> How is primitive man a slave? It is because he hardly has his own activity; he is a plaything of need, which dictates almost all of his gestures, and stirred up by its merciless sting; and his actions are ruled, not by thought itself, but by the equally incomprehensible customs and whimsy of a nature which he can only adore with blind submission. If we only consider the collectivity, apparently men have raised themselves in our days to a condition which is among the antipodes of this servile state. Almost none of their works constitute a simple response to the imperious impulse of need; work is accomplished in a way that takes possession of nature and orders it in such a way that needs are met. Humankind no longer believes itself to be in the presence of capricious deities whose favor must be conciliated; it knows that it simply has to handle inert matter, and carries out this task, regulating themselves methodically according to clearly conceived laws. Finally, it appears that we have come to that time predicted by Descartes, in which men would use "the force and actions of fire, water, air, the stars and all other bodies" just like the work of craftsmen and would thus become the masters of nature. But, by a strange turnaround, this collective domination is transformed into subjection, as soon as one comes down to the scale of the individual, and in a subjection very close to that of primitive life. Modern workers' efforts are imposed on them by a brutal, merciless coercion, which oppresses them inside as much as hunger does a primitive hunter; from this primitive hunter to the workers of our large factories, passing by the Egyptian workers who were dealt with by whipping, the ancient slaves, the serfs of the Middle Ages, constantly threatened by the sword of their lords, men have never stopped being pushed to work by an external force and under almost immediate death sentence. As to the sequence of work movements, it is also often imposed from outside on our workers, as well as on primitive men, and it is equally mysterious to both; further, in this domain, pressure is in certain cases incomparably more brutal today than ever; no matter how used primitive man was to the routine and to blind groping, at least he could try to reflect, combine, innovate with its risks and dangers, a freedom from which an assembly line worker is completely deprived. Finally, if humankind appears to have at their disposal these forces of nature, which according to Spinoza "are infinitely greater than those of man," and this almost as sovereignly as a man has his horse, this victory does not belong to men one by one; only the greater collectivities are able to manage "the force and actions of fire, water, air... and all other bodies that surround us"; as to the members of these collectivities, oppressors and oppressed are

likewise submitted to the implacable demands of the struggle for power. (Weil 1991, p. 67–68)

Despite progress, men still live under the servile condition in which they have existed since the beginning of time; they simply have transferred the power that sustains them from nature to society.

At factory N.: heaters were installed for the machines (not for us!).

G.: "It is slavery, as in the Middle Ages; the only difference is that they do not beat us and that we can return home." (Broeckhoven, 1982, p. 142)

Is slavery then an immovable component of the human condition? Weil believes that it is not so. Never, happen what may, can man accept servitude, because he thinks. He has never ceased to dream of a limitless freedom. But perfect freedom cannot be conceived as the disappearance of need, since, as long as man lives, the pressure of need will never relax, not a single moment. True freedom is not defined as a relationship between desire and satisfaction, but as a relationship between thought and action; is a man completely free, all of whose actions were to come from a prior judgment regarding the end he proposes and the sequence of specific means that lead to this end?

Man is a limited being who cannot be like the God of theologians, the direct author of his own existence; but man could have the human equivalent of this divine power, if the material conditions that allow him to exist were exclusively the work of his thinking, directing the effort of his muscles. This would be true freedom. This freedom is only an ideal, but it would be useful to think about whether we can at the same time perceive what separates us from it and what circumstances can distance us from or bring us to it.

CONCLUSION

As we see, it is not work, in itself, that oppresses those who work, as we often think, but rather the way it is structured. We, human beings, do not manage to think (and thus, don't create), even under extreme circumstances of denial of this immovable human condition, the Taylorist model of organization of production occupying an outstanding position in this regard.

Can we believe that this human condition—that we are thinking, creative beings—derives from something different and greater than ourselves (God, for instance), or believe that this condition derives from the evolution of the species. Today there is no third alternative to this matter. In other words, we all, each and every one of us, are currently dominated by the belief, the faith in something, determined in this world or outside it, and thus the dichotomy produced between faith and reason is mistaken, since all is faith, with a greater or lesser presence of reason.

The Taylorist model of work management that, as we tried to demonstrate, is in force in almost all private and public organizations in all corners of the earth, currently, on taking the separation between spheres of conception and implementation to its maximum, paroxysmal expression, produces oppression at work in almost all workers who are daily forced to repress, throughout all the days of their life, the immovable human condition of being co-creators of the world, of life.

This, in our opinion, is the most essential cause of the production of unease, suffering, absence of quality of working life in the universe of the world of contemporary production.

Much beyond any tasks, low wages, authoritarian supervisors, and so on, what most affects the humanity itself of the workers—profoundly, extensively, viscerally—is oppression at work. The main enemy of the workers is, thus, the Taylorist model of work organization, the main instrument of oppression at work. The main objective of someone who works, thus, must be the end of oppression at work, an absolute prerequisite to the possibility of the true existence of quality of working life.

Hence, and about what has been discussed in the chapter that now ends, let us see what Max Weber tells us:

> Nobody knows yet who will have to live in this prison in the future, or whether at the end of this tremendous development, entirely new prophets will arise, or a vigorous rebirth of old thoughts and ideas, or even whether none of these two—the possibility of a mechanized petrification characterized by this convulsive kind of self-justification. In this case the "last men" of this cultural development could be designated as "specialists without spirit, sensualists without heart, nobodies who imagine that they have reached a level of civilization never before attained." (Weber in Bartholo, 1986, p. 15)

NOTES

1. Information about the life and work of Weil can be obtained, for instance, in Leite (2004). We suggest consulting it, among so many others that exist, because it records the radical association, in the existence of Weil, of personal loneliness and social solidarity, emblematic dimensions of a short existence that mysteriously occurred in the fullest balance between life and work, which brings us to the level of myths, heroes, saints. Her work is in a rare symmetry with her life, and is animically marked by the being-in-the-world of who conferred life on her. Be it against capitalism—and there in a very particular and warlike way, against its most evil, most diabolic aspect—Nazi-fascism—be it also against the real socialism that was just beginning. Simone Weil fights the

good fight that antagonizes the oppressed to the oppressor, the libertarian to the repressor, the saint to the sinner. Loneliness and solidarity alone on the personal level and commitment to the social struggle are characteristic traits of a life turned toward attention to the non-I, to the service of Thou, to love of the other.

2. Only a part of the text of this conference is available. It was collected by a listener.

3. About Taylor and current times, see Valle and Peixoto (1994).

4. About Taylor's solidity regarding the interests of socialism: "the exploitation does not come from the presence of private capitalists, but more generally, from the division—in factories—among those who make all the decisions and those who only obey" (Claude Lefort in Leite, 1994, p. 71). And also: " ... the comprehension that the suppression of private property is not enough to do away with inequality and oppression (since they depend much more on the conditions of use of labor than from their purchasing conditions on the market) led to a set of criticisms about the use of the principles of capitalist organization in the work process in the socialist countries through the dissemination of Taylorism ... " (Leite, 1994, pp. 73–74).

5. See about this, the issue of professional training and workers' union movement in Brazil (Horta & Carvalho, 1994).

REFERENCES

Bartholo, R. S., Jr. (1986). *Os labirintos do silêncio—Cosmovisão e tecnologia na modernidade*. São Paulo: Editora Marco.

Broeckhoven, E. V. (1982). *Diário da amizade*. São Paulo: Editora Loyola.

Dejours, C. (1987). *A loucura do trabalho—Estudo de psicopatologia do trabalho*. São Paulo: Editora Corty-Oboré.

Horta, C. R., & de Carvalho, R. A. (1994). *Formação profissional e movimento sindical no Brasil*. XVIII Encontro Nacional da ANPOCS. São Paulo: Mimeo.

Leite, J. (2004). Contemplativo na Ação. *Notas sobre a questão do sentido no trabalho contemporâneo*. RJ, PUC.

Leite, M. P. (1994). *O futuro do trabalho—Novas tecnologias e subjetividade operária*. Rio de Janeiro: Editora PUC.

Taylor, F. W. (1971). *Princípios de Administração Científica*. São Paulo: Editora Atlas S.A.

Valle, R., & Peixoto, J. A. (1994). *Certificação da qualidade e opções organizacionais: Histórico e estudo de caso no Brasil*. XVIII Encontro Nacional da ANPOCS. São Paulo: Mimeo.

Weil, S. (1951). *La condition ouvrière*. São Paulo: Editora Papirus.

Weil, S. (1991). *Aulas de filosofia*. Paris: Éditions Gallimard.

CHAPTER 8

SOCIO-ENVIRONMENTAL RESPONSIBILITY IN PUBLIC ADMINISTRATION

Marcos Weiss Bliacheris

ABSTRACT

The present chapter discusses socio-environmental responsibility in public administration, giving a view of the international and national legal framework that organizes this matter. It shows the action model of the federal government, A3P—Environmental Agenda in Public Administration, which is based on volunteer work and on five thematic axes: the rational use of resources, sustainable public procurement, management of solid waste, quality of life at work, and environmental education. After a diagnosis of the current status was made, this model underwent a reformulation in 2012, and the Interministerial Committee of Sustainability in Public Administration was established, as well as Plans for Sustainable Logistics Management. This created a bureaucratic structure, and the mode of organization was adopted, using planning tools, designating actions, goals, objectives, and people responsible for them.

Improving Emploee Health and Well-Being, pages 119–133
Copyright © 2014 by Information Age Publishing

INTRODUCTION

If the state cannot be seen or touched, except for its symbols such as anthems and flags, when the citizen addresses himself to it he will encounter the public administration. This will be the face of the state and the entity that will implement its policies, the so-called public policies; in brief, it will provide the public services that are available to society.

Public administration will be of different sizes according to the needs and aspirations of society. Functions that are now carried out by private agents, in the past have already been public concessions, or performed by public agents.

The values of society, which are decided in the political field and expressed in its laws, will define the size of the public administration, the way in which this administration will operate, the rights of its agents, how they will be hired and fired, among so many fundamental decisions that will characterize their bureaucracy.

In the Brazilian legal system, the 1988 Constitution, which was the result of the redemocratization of Brazil, established that the administration would be ruled by four principles: legality, impersonality, morality, and publicity.

The principle of legality is explained classically as the faculty of a private person doing everything the law does not forbid, while public administration is only permitted to do what the law authorizes (Meirelles, 1997). However, it should be noted that this view is being extended by our jurists, in that "the principle of legality needs to be...understood and applied in the broader context of obedience that Public Administration owes to Law" (Freitas, 2004, p. 45).

It should be noted that this extension of a concept is important for our work, since we go from an extremely formal interpretation of this principle to a broader, more integrating, and less restrictive concept.

These principles were extended by Constitutional Amendment n° 19, in 1998, which included efficiency in the list of principles that rule public administration. Thus, we show that even in the fundamental text, the Constitution, public administrative activity is being altered according to the current values of society.

Considering that the environment has become one of the main issues at the end of the 20th century and beginning of the 21st century, it is clear that public administration is being called upon to also give its contribution to this debate. Just as there is a search for a more environmentally sustainable world, people and businesses are being required to take attitudes that are not only environmentally but also socially more just, which is also being demanded of public administration.

The way in which these actions are developed in public administration, both the legal framework and the initiatives that are being taken, is the subject of these pages. The present chapter discusses the topic of social responsibility in public administration.

In discussing this issue, we will deal with the already existing model, the A3P—Environmental Agenda in Public Administration, as well as with the model that will be implemented as a result of the normative change of 2012 that seeks to fit the environmental agenda into the bureaucratic operational model of public administration.

LEGAL FRAMEWORK

Our law, which will shape the action of public administration, will be founded on national standards inspired by international commitments signed by Brazil. Thus, to deal with the matter, it is necessary also to look at texts of international law originating at international conferences of the United Nations regarding environmental matters.

It should be highlighted that these norms rule on the behavior of public administration in two ways: in the behavior of the public administration itself, or as a producer of public policies that will influence third parties.

INTERNATIONAL TEXTS

The first United Nations conference on the human environment took place in 1972 in Stockholm, Sweden. In the Declaration generated at that meeting, it was established that "economic and social development is essential for ensuring a favorable living and working environment for man, and for creating conditions on earth that are necessary for the improvement of the quality of life" (n.p.).

This discussion was taken up again at the Earth Summit-92, as the United Nations Conference on Environment and Development (UNCED) became popularly known. It was held in Rio de Janeiro in June 1992, marking the twentieth anniversary of the Stockholm conference.

If the environmental discussion was taking place around the dichotomy of "development vs. conservation," the Earth Summit confirmed a new concept that seeks to go beyond this position and integrate these antagonisms: sustainable development. This concept is dealt with in a historical document, Agenda 21 (United Nations Conference, 1992), whose preamble uniquely defines the point of departure for what will be discussed in the next few pages:

> Humanity stands at a defining moment in history. We are confronted with the perpetuation of disparities between and within nations, a worsening of

poverty, hunger, ill-health and illiteracy, and the continuing deterioration of the ecosystems on which we depend for our well-being. However integration of environment and development concerns and greater attention to them will lead to the fulfillment of basic needs, improved living standards for all, better protected and managed ecosystems, and a safer and more prosperous future. No nation can achieve this on its own; but together we can—in a global partnership for sustainable development.

Agenda 21 was launched as a program for these changes. Regarding the matter that is being examined, it creates a new requirement: the integration of environmental concerns into the governmental decision-making process. And, in its Chapter 4, it went into details about sustainable public procurement: the change of consumption patterns.

In this chapter, when the development of national policies and strategies to encourage changes in unsustainable consumption patterns is examined, governments are expected to take on a leading role through their procurement.

This Agenda 21 (United Nations Conference, 1992) document said the following about this matter:

> Governments themselves also play a role in consumption, particularly in countries where the public sector plays a large role in the economy and can have a considerable influence on both corporate decisions and public perceptions. They should therefore review the purchasing policies of their agencies and departments so that they may improve, whenever possible, the environmental content of government procurement policies, without prejudice to international trade principles.

Since the government is a large scale purchaser, the impact of government purchases on the economy is always relevant (Costin, 2010). This impact, this influence is what Agenda 21 seeks, bringing to light the concept of "sustainable consumption," or "responsible consumption," and it proposes sustainable public procurement as a public policy aiming at influencing the business community and society as a whole.

The ten year anniversary of the Earth Summit-1992 was marked by the World Summit on Sustainable Development held in Johannesburg. The Declaration of Johannesburg discusses in its implementation plan the patterns of production and consumption, including the role of public procurement in Chapter III, called "Change in the Unsustainable Patterns of Consumption and Production," aiming at "promoting the policies of public procurement that will encourage the development and dissemination of goods and services rationally from the environmental standpoint."

If the above standards establish guidelines, the Kyoto Protocol, by its nature as an international treaty, was internalized into our Law by Decree n°

5.445/2005, which established responsibility regarding the formulation "of national programs that will contain measures to mitigate climate change, as well as measures to facilitate an appropriate adaptation to climate change," according to Article 10 of the aforementioned standards.

NATIONAL LEGAL FRAMEWORK

Although this is not the focus of the present work, considering the way public administration operates, we believe it necessary to mention, however briefly, the norms that deal with the topic of the article in public administration.

As such, we highlight:

- Law n° 12,187, of December 29, 2009, which established the National Policy on Climate Change.
- Law n° 12,305, of August 2, 2010, establishing the National Policy on Solid Waste.
- Law n° 12,349, of December 15, 2010, which changed Article 3 of the Law on Public Tenders, including the promotion of sustainable national involvement among its objectives.
- Decree n° 99,685, of October 30, 1990, which regulates, within the scope of federal public administration, the reuse, handling, alienation, and other forms of disposal of materials.
- Decree n° 2,783, of September 17, 1998, which rules on the prohibition of acquiring products or equipment that contain or use substances that destroy the ozone layer, by agencies and entities of the direct, autarchic, and foundational federal public administration.
- Decree n° 5.940, of October 25, 2006, which establishes the sorting of recyclable waste discarded by the agencies and entities of the direct and indirect federal public administration at the generating source and their disposal to the association and cooperatives of pickers of recyclable materials.
- Decree n° 7,746, of June 5, 2012, which regulates Article 3 of Law n° 8,666, of June 21, 1993, to establish criteria, practices, and guidelines for the promotion of sustainable national development in procurements by the federal public administration and establishes the Interministerial Committee of Sustainability in public administration.
- Normative Instruction n° 01, of January 19, 2010, of the Department of Logistics and Information Technology of the Ministry of Planning, Budget, and Management (SLTI/MPOG), which rules on environmental sustainability criteria in the purchase of goods,

services, or construction work by the direct, autarchic, and foundational federal public administration.

- Normative Instruction n° 10, of November 12, 2012, of SLTI/MPOG, which establishes rules to elaborate the Plans for Sustainable Logistics Management, discussed in Article 16 of Decree n° 7,746, of June 5, 2012.

A3P

The A3P—the Environmental Agenda in Public Administration is the program that structures actions of social responsibility and socio-environmental management in the Brazilian public administration. This program, which is the responsibility of the Ministry of the Environment, was established in 1999, and its characteristic is that it is voluntary both as to the agencies that join it and as to the members that participate in it, who are organized in committees.

The Environmental Agenda in Public Administration (A3P) appeared in 1999 as a volunteer initiative of the Ministry of the Environment (MMA—*Ministério do Meio Ambiente*) employees who tried to change the MMA routine, providing an example of sustainability for the entire public administration (Abreu, Feitosa, & Motta, 2012).

The way in which people joined the program changed progressively to establish a greater commitment of the department to the agenda. Initially, a letter of intent was adopted. Currently it is necessary to sign a Terms of Acceptance, with a work plan that includes delivering an annual report evaluating the actions taken.

It should be pointed out that the following can join A3P: entities of the federal, state, and local administration; of the executive, legislative and judiciary powers; of the direct and indirect public administration.

The A3P is structured around five thematic axes, which we will now examine, namely: the rational use of resources, sustainable public procurement, management of solid waste, quality of life at work, and environmental education.

In general, the rational use of resources is considered a way of making the public administration fulfill its functions with less environmental impact, be it by the reduction of natural resources used or by the reduction in greenhouse gases emissions, not forgetting the management and reduction of solid waste generated by their activities. The axis of rational use of resources deals with the use of resources within the public administration, mainly observing those that are most used by government agencies, such as electricity, water, and paper, and educating users to avoid wasting them.

Sustainable public procurement, also known as Eco procurement or green public procurement, play an essential role in the socio-environmental position of the government by introducing environmental sustainability criteria in public contracts. As already mentioned in this chapter, considering the weight of the state in the economy, its option for products with an environmentally more responsible origin is expected to play an inducing role in the economy.

Solid waste management is one of the important issues of the socio-environmental agenda insofar as the state acts as a regulator of the issue when legislating and ordering sanitation and the management of solid wastes, not forgetting that the issue also affects the great works sponsored by the state.

However, in the everyday work of public administration, the greatest impact will be caused by the Solidary Waste Sorting, in which the state acknowledges that it is a polluter. As Teresa Villac Pinheiro Barki said, "the reusable and recyclable solid waste is recognized as an economic good with social value that generates work and income and promotes citizenship" (Barki, 2012, p. 68).

Thus, government action has an environmental character when it promotes the sorting of waste and garbage, and social character when it gives this waste to the waste pickers, who are part of the so-called sustainability tripod: environmental, social, and economic.

The thematic axis of quality of life is described as follows by the A3P site:

> Public administration must permanently seek a better Quality of Working Life (QoWL) promoting actions for personal and professional development of government employees. For this purpose, public organizations must develop and implement specific programs that will involve the level of satisfaction of a person with their work environment, improved overall environmental conditions, promotion of health and safety, social integration, development of human capacities, among other factors. (Brazil, n.d.-a, n.p.)

On dealing with this issue, the Administrative Decree that establishes the Plans for Sustainable Logistics Management considers the following as good practices of sustainability in quality of life: taking measures to promote a physical environment with safe, healthy work; adopting measures for the evaluation and control of the air quality in air-conditioned environments; performing the maintenance or replacement of equipment that causes noise in the workplace; carrying out campaigns, workshops, lectures, and exhibitions to make employees sensitive to sustainable practices with dissemination via the intranet, posters, labels, and newsletters; and producing newsletters concerning socio-environmental topics, successful experiences, and progress achieved by the organization.

Finally, one of the highlights of A3P is environmental education, a thematic axis that has also been called "employees' awareness raising and training." Environmental education is an integrating function insofar as there is need for sensitization, awareness raising, and collaboration from the employees for these initiatives to succeed. Furthermore, new needs require training for the employees to adapt their administrative routines to them (Brazil, n.d.-b).

According to Maria Augusta Soares de Oliveira Ferreira, relating environmental education to the organizational mission of A3P itself:

> Environmental education, as one of the basic pillars of A3P, supports all other thematic axes to achieve its ends. Education will generate a change in habits and organizational culture and enable promoting the program as a whole.

> Therefore, the A3P program has a special multiplying and transforming effect, since it is based on environmental education, on the change in culture and habits by public employees and managers, and these changes will also be extended to the rest of society, to their homes, neighborhoods and cities. Furthermore, this environmental awareness will change the way in which these public employees work, providing a better performance in government service, especially in the field of environmental governance. (Ferreira, 2012, p. 33)

This model was gradually implemented during the first decade of this century, and it is undergoing a review. It is to be adapted to a new reality resulting from Decree n° 7,746/2012.

It should be mentioned that the previous model of socio-environmental responsibility of the federal public administration was exhausted, as found by Decision 1752/2011, of the Plenary of the Federal Audit Court (TCU), which evaluated the actions adopted by the federal public administration regarding the rational and sustainable use of natural resources. This led to a number of recommendations to public agencies, especially to the Ministries of Planning, Budget, and Management and the Environment.

The study performed by the TCU found that:

> the sustainability and efficiency measures have not yet been widely disseminated in Public Administration, and they do not yet constitute a broad, coordinated and continuous State policy, which will favor the saving of natural and financial resources by means of the rational use of natural resources. A great heterogeneity is found within Public Administration, in the inclusion of the concepts of sustainability and rational use of resources in its activities. (n.p.)

In other words, there were agencies that had taken very advanced initiatives, while at the same time other public agencies had not taken any initiative whatsoever in this sense, showing a low degree of institutionalization of these public policies. As the aforementioned decision warns "this is reflected in the personification of management, founded on the personal evaluation of the managers, who establish priorities to put the rationalization measures into effect or not, according to their convenience and opportunity."

Specifically concerning the A3P Program described above, and despite all the undeniable merits it has (which are not few), only 34% of the public agencies surveyed by the TCU had joined this program. There are indeed initiatives. Besides the A3P we also have the Program of Efficiency in Public Spending (PEG); the National Program for the Conservation of Electric Energy (Procel), discussed in the aforementioned decision; the Solidary Waste Sorting; Sustainable Federal Administration Project (PES); and Sustainable Public Procurement.

However, as the aforementioned decision says, there is a low level of knowledge and compliance with these initiatives.

In the diagnosis performed, it is pointed out that:

> An important reason for the heterogeneous behavior of public institutions is the lack of a clear direction by the Central Government, that the topic should be treated as a priority. The action or lack of action by the agencies does not generate repercussions from the Central Government, be they positive or negative. Furthermore, the actions and results are not followed, and therefore, for instance, it is not demanded from the institutions that make less of an effort in this subject that they improve their performance, and there are also no performance indicators to guide public agencies and organizations. (n.p.)

This situation, with a low level of information and institutionalization, is what one wishes to change.

BUREAUCRATIC STRUCTURE

Decree n° 7,746/2012, among other aspects, innovated by establishing the CISAP—Interministerial Committee of Sustainability in Public Administration—an advisory agency to SLTI/MPOG, and establishing the requirement for Plans of Sustainable Logistics Management.

Thus, we went from a model focused solely on the non-mandatory nature of participation to its institutionalization, formatting it within a bureaucratic structure and subjecting it to planning together with the other operational and financial actions of the administration.

Socio-environmental management is no longer centered on the Ministry of the Environment, and now it goes into the sphere of the Ministry of Planning, Budget and Management. To understand this new allocation in the organization chart of the federal government it is necessary to understand the role of this ministry and the aforementioned SLTI.

The Ministry of Planning is the agency responsible for the policies and guidelines to modernize the federal public administration, and it is the central agency of federal bureaucracy. It coordinates and manages the different systems that structure the federal public administration, such as budget, staff, general services, and actions for the administrative organization and modernization of the federal government.

In this context, it will be the agency responsible for regulating purchases and procurements by the Federal Government, an attribution that will be internally assigned to the aforementioned Department of Logistics and Information Technology of the Ministry of Planning, Budget and Management (SLTI/MPOG), the central department of the System of General Services—SISG, to which the logistics sectors also responsible for the public purchases and procurement are attached (Brazil, 2012a).

This department, for purposes of implementing the public policy of sustainable public procurement, following the principle of sustainable national development as set forth in the Law of Tenders, will have in CISAP a permanent advisory agency, for the purpose of proposing sustainability criteria aimed at the goods purchased by the federal public administration, sustainability practices to be required from companies that provide services to the federal public administration, and sustainable actions within the scope of the federal public administration.

CISAP is formed by representatives and various ministries, including the Ministry of Planning, Budget, and Management. There is a representative of the Department of Logistics and the Ministry of the Environment.

Likewise, CISAP is the advisory body responsible for proposing to the agency in charge, in other words, to SLTI/PPOG, the norms of the Plans for Sustainable Logistics Management, which will be discussed next.

The Plans for Sustainable Logistics Management (PLS) are set forth in Article 16 of Decree n° 7,746/2012 and regulated by Normative Instruction SLTI/MPOG n° 10, of November 12, 2012, of SLTI/MPOG.

This instruction begins with the pertinent definitions, first of all on sustainable logistics, the concept that rules it, which is defined as: "the process of coordinating the flow of materials, services and information, from supply to disposal, which considers environmental protection, social justice, and balanced economic development" (Brazil, 2012b).

It should be pointed out that the concept concerns not only goods and services purchased and procured by the administration, but also the flow of information on the issue. It is also noted that the norm expressly adopts the already mentioned tripod of sustainability, besides going all the way from the supply to disposal of the products purchased or used by the administration.

In other words, and this is very important, each purchase or procurement must be considered as a process that does not begin nor becomes fully exhausted at the time of the purchase. As such, it is necessary to present the criticism, namely, that administration must take into account not only the specific moment when things are supplied, but also the manufacturing and packaging processes of the products it consumes, observing the chain of production itself, where it will be included by the action of that purchase or the use of a given product.

The norm deals with the inclusion of sustainability criteria, defined as parameters used to evaluate and compare goods, materials, or services based on their environmental, social, and economic impact, through sustainability practices, actions that aim at constructing a new model of institutional culture by including the aforementioned sustainability criteria into the activities of public administration.

At the same time, it deals with the practices of rationalization, actions that aim at improving the quality of public expenditures and the management of processes, showing both economic and environmental concern.

The norm also points to the bureaucratic instruments for this purpose, such as performing a financial physical inventory and, for instance, distinguishing consumables from permanent materials—the former being that which loses its physical identity and/or whose use is limited to two years.

The norm mentioned encourages shared purchases performed by a group of agencies, through a price registration procedure. Shared purchases are those in which several agencies get together to perform a single price registration procedure that will be managed by one of these agencies, on the one hand saving in procedures, and on the other achieving gains in scale (Silva & Barki, 2012).

The definition of the PLS itself indicates the incorporation of the socio-environmental agenda to the bureaucratic *modus operandi.* The plans are defined as a planning tool, which is the fundamental principle of administrative activity, in the form of the regulation itself, which organizes administrative activity, namely, Decree-Law nº 200, of February 25, 1967. Thus, the issue of sustainability is incorporated to planning under the responsibility of the public administrator.

The PLS require that defined objectives and responsibilities be established through actions and goals. In the prescribed content are also execution schedules and monitoring and evaluation mechanisms that allow the agency or entity to establish practices for sustainability and rationalization of expenditures and processes in public administration.

To begin with, it is clear that the PLS is a management tool. The "thinking about efficient, effective and democratic public management" itself "includes policies for the development of a high degree of professionalism of its agents, who are expected to be conscious of the objectives, goals and results to be achieved, and committed to them" (Pereira Júnior & Dotti, 2008, p. 15).

In other words, the current model of public management works with actions that lead to achieving goals and results, clearly delegated to responsible government employees. These goals or results will be followed half-yearly and discussed in an annual report that will show the results reached and the actions to be developed the next year.

Socio-environmental management then begins to use this new model, replacing the previous one, marked by voluntary work. However, there is no way to achieve these goals by simply setting goals and objectives to be met— here the commitment, the involvement promoted by A3P and emulated by the norm involved are essential since a minimum of sustainability and rationalization practices are required to cover the consumables (paper, disposable cups, and printing cartridges; electricity); water and sewage; waste sorting; quality of life in the work environment; sustainable public procurement, including purchases, procurements and works, and staff travel.

Staff travel is focused both on the reduction of expenditure and on that of emissions of polluting substances. We should know that the Brazilian government chose to use ethanol fuel in its fleet of cars.

Annex II of this norm lists the sustainability practices and indicators that are considered a reference for public administration to elaborate their own plans. Next we will list briefly the good practices mentioned, because, in fact, they show the results expected in the early stages of the implementation of this model.

There is a section for consumables, as mentioned above. As to paper, digitalization is encouraged, using electronic messages (e-mail) in communications, avoiding the use of paper, and replacing the use of printed documents with digital documents. Expenditures on printing paper are another concern, and one should print only if strictly necessary; documents should be proofread before printing in order to avoid unnecessary printing and control the consumption of printing paper and copies. The documents should be printed on both sides of the paper, and paper printed on only one side of the page should be reused to make drafting blocks. The use of recycled or non-chlorinated white paper is also encouraged. Additionally, maintenance or replacement of printers should be programmed for reasons of efficiency, and one should preferably print using a text font that will save ink or toner (Eco fonts). As to disposable cups, it is recommended to use those produced with materials that will favor reuse or recycling.

A number of steps are also recommended concerning power, beginning by checking the status of the electrical wiring and proposing the changes needed to reduce power consumption. Among the other practices are the following: power consumption monitoring, simple measures such as switching off lights and computer monitors when one leaves the room, closing doors and windows when one switches on the air-conditioning, and making use of the natural conditions of the work environment—ventilation, natural light. Slightly more sophisticated are the use of sensors that detect movement and diminishing the number of lamps, establishing a standard per square meter. It is also recommended to switch off some elevators in the hours when there is no rush, and when replacing air-conditioners, prefer more modern and efficient ones, aiming to reduce power consumption. A measure that has lately been successful in various agencies is to review the power supply contracts, trying to rationalize them according to the actual demand for power by the government agency.

As to water and sewage, the first step is also to perform a diagnosis and monitor consumption. There is a preference for individualized systems to measure water consumption and water reuse, and to treat wastewater. The use of rainwater, more efficient flushes and taps, and ecological washing are encouraged.

As regards quality of life in the work environment, the goal is to have a physical work environment that is safe and healthy. As such, attention should be given to the quality of air in air-conditioned environments and also to machines that produce noise in the working environment.

Sustainable practices in purchases and procurement are a vital point of the socio-environmental agenda of the administration, and they should be taken into account. As such, several guidelines are presented to complement the already existing ones.

Thus, one should rather use printers that print both sides of the page and purchase recycled paper, without any elemental chlorine or bleached with oxygen, hydrogen peroxide and ozone, and the option of printing both sides of the papers should be included in the printing service contracts.

One should rather buy recycled or recyclable goods, and in the contracts for catering and cleaning services procedures to promote the rational use of resources and utilization of recycled, reusable, and biodegradable products should also be included.

Likewise, it is recommended that proof of origin of wood be demanded when goods are purchased and works and services are procured, as well as prioritizing employment of local labor, materials, technologies, and raw materials.

It is recommended that electronic means be used for communication, besides adopting a telephone communications network between the units of a same agency or organization.

Contracts should be reviewed several times to rationalize and size the object according to actual needs: cleaning contracts, surveillance contracts, and telephones (landlines and mobile).

In the case of surveillance and security, one should seek to replace the armed guards by unarmed ones and the physical presence of a guard by electronics, whenever possible.

Finally, group shared purchasing should be encouraged. This has already been mentioned in the present chapter.

These measures can only be enabled by environmental education. As such, awareness-raising is essential to influence and change behaviors. The planned goals can only be achieved with the involvement of government employees.

In this sense, that norm includes the implementation of several educational measures, such as awareness-raising campaigns to reduce the consumption of paper and to make employees aware of the need to reduce the consumption of disposable cups. Awareness-raising campaigns should be directed to the reduction in power consumption and irrational use of water.

Additionally, the norm includes campaigns, workshops, lectures, and awareness-raising exhibitions of sustainable practices to be held for government employees, disseminated by intranet, posters, labels, and newsletters, newsletters about socio-environmental topics, successful experiences, and progress made by the institution, and the promotion of integration and quality of life activities at the workplace.

CONCLUSION

This chapter attempted to discuss the socio-environmental responsibility in public administration, providing a view of the international and national legal framework that organizes this matter, focusing on the internal aspects of administration itself. We observed the transition from the federal government action model, A3P—the Environmental Agenda in Public Administration, centered on voluntary work to the bureaucratic model, established with the reformulation by the Interministerial Committee of Sustainability in Public Administration and the Plans of Sustainable Logistic Management.

The implementation of this new model, without discarding the advances already achieved, is the challenge facing the federal public administration, and that will determine management according to the aspirations of society.

REFERENCES

Abreu, G. V., Feitosa, A. R., & Motta, L. (2012). Título. In M. W. Bliacheris & M. A. S. O. Ferreira (Coords.), *Sustentabilidade na administração pública: Valores e práticas de gestão socioambiental* (pp. 155–171). Belo Horizonte: Fórum.

Barki, T. V. P. (2012). O compromisso socioambiental do estado na gestão adequada de resíduos. In M. W. Bliacheris & M. A. S. de O. Ferreira (Org.), *Sustentabilidade na administração pública: Valores e práticas de gestão socioambiental* (pp. 65–81). Belo Horizonte: Fórum.

Brazil. (n.d.-a). Quality of Life in the Working Environment. Retrieved on January 4, 2013 from http://www.mma.gov.br/responsabilidade-socioambiental/a3p/eixos-tematicos/item/527

Brazil. (n.d.-b). Awareness-raising and Training of Civil Servants. Retrieved on January 4, 2013 from http://www.mma.gov.br/responsabilidade-socioambiental/a3p/eixos-tematicos/item/528

Brazil. (2012a). Decreto n° 7.675, de 20 de janeiro de 2012. Aprova a Estrutura Regimental e o Quadro Demonstrativo dos Cargos em Comissão e das Funções Gratificadas do Ministério do Planejamento, Orçamento e Gestão. Retrieved on January 9, 2013 from http://www.planalto.gov.br/ccivil_03/_Ato2011-2014/2012/Decreto/D7675.htm

Brazil. (2012b). Ministério do Planejamento, Orçamento e Gestão. Secretaria de Logística e Tecnologia da Informação. Instrução Normativa n° 10, de 12 de novembro de 2012. Estabelece regras para elaboração dos Planos de Gestão de Logística Sustentável de que trata o art. 16, do Decreto n° 7.746, de 5 de junho de 2012, e dá outras providências. Retrieved on January 9, 2013 from http://www.planejamento.gov.br/secretarias/upload/Legislacao/Instrucao_Normativa/121114_IN10.pdf

Costin, C. (2010). *Administração Pública.* Rio de Janeiro: Elsevier.

Ferreira, M. A.S.O. (2012). Apontamentos sobre a gestão socioambiental na administração pública brasileira. In M. W. Bliacheris & M. A. S. O. Ferreira (Coords.), *Sustentabilidade na administração pública: valores e práticas de gestão socioambiental* (pp. 21–43). Belo Horizonte: Fórum.

Freitas, J. (2004). *O controle dos atos administrativos e os princípios fundamentais.* São Paulo: Malheiros.

Meirelles, H. L. (1997). *Direito administrativo Brasileiro.* São Paulo: Malheiros Editores.

Organização das Nações Unidas. (1972). Declaração da Conferência das Nações Unidas sobre o Meio Ambiente Humano—1972. Retrieved on January 9, 2013 from www.onu.org.br/rio20/img/2012/01/estocolmo1972.pdf

Pereira Júnior, J. T., & Dotti, M. R. (2008). *Políticas públicas nas licitações e contratações administrativas* (2nd ed.). Belo Horizonte: Fórum.

Silva, R. C., & Barki, T. V. P. (2012). Compras públicas compartilhadas: A prática das licitações sustentáveis. *Revista do Serviço Público, 63*(2), 157–176.

United Nations Conference. (1992). Agenda 21. Retrieved from http://sustainabledevelopment.un.org/content/documents/Agenda21.pdf

SECTION III

THE ROLE OF PREVENTION AND INTERVENTION
IN THE QUALITY OF WORKING LIFE

CHAPTER 9

SAV-T FIRST

A Risk Management Approach
to Workplace Violence

E. Kevin Kelloway and Kate Calnan
Saint Mary's University

Jane Mullen
Mount Allison University

Mike Teed
Bishop's University

ABSTRACT

In this chapter we present a risk management approach to workplace violence. We begin by distinguishing between workplace aggression and workplace violence and, drawing on extant research, make the point that most incidents of workplace violence are perpetrated by members of the public rather than by organizational insiders. Based on this observation we review the situational risks for workplace violence and suggest that some commonly recommended strategies (e.g., the formulation of anti-violence policies) are unlikely to be effective. Rather, situational risks are more appropriately addressed through

Improving Emploee Health and Well-Being, pages 137–151
Copyright © 2014 by Information Age Publishing

robbery reduction strategies (e.g., target hardening, reducing reward, staff training). Finally, we introduce the notion of imminent risk based on the notion of the assault cycle. The SAV-T (Swearing, Agitation, Volume—Threat) model is presented as a means of diagnosing escalating situations and identifying appropriate responses to reduce the likelihood of violence.

Sparked by high profile events such as the United States Post Office shootings, research on workplace violence has burgeoned in recent years (Kelloway, Barling, & Hurrell, 2006). It is now common to specifically address workplace violence in occupational health and safety policies, and a growing number of jurisdictions have enacted legislation requiring employers to take specific steps to manage the risks associated with workplace violence. Unfortunately, organizational policies and regulations are frequently based on the many myths that surround workplace violence (Barling, Dupre, & Kelloway, 2009) and, as a result, do not address the real risks in the workplace.

In this chapter we begin to address this situation. We begin by defining workplace violence and aggression and examining data that speak to the prevalence of these phenomena. We then introduce the notion of situational risk by identifying the specific tasks associated with a greater risk of workplace violence (e.g., LeBlanc & Kelloway, 2002) and the strategies that can be used to mitigate these risks (Kelloway & Teed, 2011). We then move to a consideration of imminent risk (Calnan, Kelloway & Dupre, 2012) and describe the use of the SAV-T first model as a behavioral decision making guide.

Definitions and Prevalence

Aggression and violence are two commonly used, but conceptually and empirically distinct (LeBlanc & Kelloway, 2002), terms. Schat and Kelloway (2005) defined workplace aggression as "*behavior by an individual or individuals within or outside an organization that is intended to physically or psychologically harm a worker or workers and occurs in a work-related context*" (p. 191). This definition (a) is consistent with broader definitions of aggression (e.g., Baron & Richardson, 1994; Berkowitz, 1993; Geen, 2001), (b) includes behaviors enacted by a variety of sources both internal (e.g., coworkers, supervisors, subordinates) and external (e.g., clients) to the organization, and (c) includes a wide range of physical and non-physical behaviors. Thus aggressive acts in organizations include a wide range of behaviors, ranging from relatively minor, non-physical behaviors (e.g., being glared at) to more serious non-physical aggression (e.g., swearing, name calling, threats) and, at the most extreme, physical assault with or without the use of a weapon.

In contrast to this general and wide-ranging definition, Schat and Kelloway (2005) suggested that workplace violence is best understood as a distinct form of workplace aggression that comprises behaviors that are intended to cause physical harm (e.g., physical assaults and/or the threat of assault). Thus, while not all aggressive behavior constitutes violence, all violent behaviors are by definition a form of aggression. (For similar distinctions see, Anderson & Bushman, 2002; Greenberg & Barling, 1999; Neuman & Baron, 1998.)

Deriving accurate estimates of the prevalence of workplace violence and aggression is not as straightforward as one might think. Accurate surveillance of the forms and frequency of workplace violence requires meeting a set of criteria that are rarely adhered to. Thus, Peek-Asa, Schaffer, Kraus, and Howard (1998) suggested that accurate prevalence estimates could only be derived from studies that employed representative sampling procedures and standardized definitions, measures, and reporting mechanisms.

Perhaps the best estimates of prevalence come from Schat, Frone, and Kelloway's (2005) analysis of data from a representative sample of U.S. workers. They found that 41% of their national probability sample reported experiencing acts of workplace aggression in the preceding year. Only 6% of the sample reported experiencing acts of physical violence in the same time periods. Although the incidence of physical violence is obviously lower than that of aggression, it is important to note that this figure represents approximately seven million American workers being exposed to acts of workplace violence in a 12 month period. Assault with an object was reported by 4.2% of respondents. Being pushed, grabbed, or slapped in anger was reported by 3.9% of respondents; being kicked, hit, or bitten was reported by 3%; and being attacked with a knife, gun, or other weapon was reported by 0.7%.

Although we are aware of no comparable data (i.e., based on rigorous sampling and measurement procedures) from other jurisdictions, there is some indication that there may be national differences even across very similar economies. Leseleuc (2004) reanalyzed data (n = 24,000) from the Canadian 2004 General Social Survey (GSS) to derive estimates of criminal victimization in Canadian workplaces. Leseleuc (2004) reports that 17% of all violent victimizations reported by respondents occurred in the workplace. This represents approximately 356, 000 workplace violence incidents in a 12 month period in Canada. Of these, 71% were physical (i.e., nonsexual) assaults. Anomalies in the way the estimates are derived systematically excluded some (high risk) occupations (e.g., cab drivers, transit operators), suggesting that the data systematically underestimate the extent of workplace violence in Canada.

Sources of Workplace Violence

One of the most enduring myths about workplace violence is that of the disgruntled co-worker—the suggestion that violence and the risk of violence stems primarily from the people with which we work (Barling et al., 2009). In fact, the available data resoundingly suggest that most incidents of workplace violence are perpetrated by individuals who are not employees of the organization.

The most widely cited classification of workplace violence identifies four categories of violence defined in terms of the relationship between the perpetrator and the victim (California Occupational Safety and Health Administration, 1995). Thus, Type I workplace violence encompasses criminal acts committed by an individual(s) with no prior relationship to the organization. In this context the particular organization is the target of a crime such as a robbery (Braverman, 1999). Type II workplace violence involves a physical and/or psychological attack from a client or customer (Braverman, 1999). In this context the perpetrator has a relationship with the organization. Together, Type I and Type II (i.e., violence committed by organizational outsiders) are the most common types of workplace violence (Barling et al., 2009; LeBlanc & Kelloway, 2002). For example, Schat et al. (2005) found that employees are four times more likely to experience violence from an outsider than from an organizational insider.

Type III violence involves former or current employees (Braverman, 1999) committing violent acts toward supervisors, coworkers, subordinates, and other staff. Perceived injustice, abusive supervision, or role stressors (Barling, 1996; Dupré & Barling, 2006; Greenberg & Barling, 1999) are often identified as the triggers of such behaviors. However, it should also be noted that Type III violence is extraordinarily rare. Indeed, it is often the case that researchers in a given study find no respondents reporting any experience of Type III violence (e.g., LeBlanc & Kelloway, 2002).

Intimate partner violence constitutes the final (Type IV) form of violence identified in the Cal/OSHA framework. Overall, Type IV violence is thought to account for 1% to 3% of all incidents of workplace violence (Duhart, 2001). Intimate partner violence typically involves work disruptions (Pollack, Austin, & Grisso, 2010), stalking, or on-the-job harassment (Swanberg, Logan, & Marke, 2006) and can have several damaging effects for organizations, such as tardiness and absenteeism, property damage, and production setbacks (Barling et al., 2009).

Situational Risk Management

Overall then, most incidents of workplace violence are perpetrated by organizational outsiders rather than by coworkers. This observation has direct implications for the experience, and management, of workplace violence. First, it is clear that the risk for workplace violence depends on the nature of one's occupation—those who work with members of the public are disproportionately more likely to experience workplace violence. For example, individuals employed in the retail (e.g., convenience stores), services (e.g., restaurants), security (protective agencies), and transportation (e.g., taxi) industries are considered to be at high risk for workplace violence and homicide due to the likelihood of robberies involving violence (e.g., Casteel & Peek-Asa, 2000; Castillo & Jenkins, 1994; Peek-Asa, Runyan, & Zwerling, 2001).

Employees who provide service, care, advice, or education can also be at increased risk for assault (e.g., Amandus et al., 1996; Canadian Centre for Occupational Health and Safety [CCOHS], 1999; see also LeBlanc & Kelloway, 2002), especially if clients, customers, inmates, or patients are experiencing frustration, insecurity, or stress (see Lamberg, 1996; National Institute for Occupational Safety and Health [NIOSH], 2002; Painter, 1987). Thus, individuals who work in health care, education, social services, and law enforcement (Casteel & Peek-Asa, 2000; Hearnden, 1988; NIOSH, 2002; Occupational Safety and Health Administration [OSHA], 2004) are at high risk for workplace violence.

LeBlanc and Kelloway (2002) and others (CCOHS, 1999; Castillo & Jenkins, 1994; Davis, 1987; Kraus, 1987; Leseleuc, 2004) have suggested that there is a list of risk factors for workplace violence that includes:

- dealing with the public,
- denying a service,
- making decisions that influence others' lives,
- supervising/disciplining others,
- security functions/physical control,
- working nights or weekends alone,
- dealing with items of value,
- working with alcohol,
- providing physical/emotional care, and
- going into peoples' homes.

It follows from these observations that individuals in occupations involving more of the risk factors are more likely to experience workplace violence. LeBlanc and Kelloway (2002) found exactly this pattern of results.

We view these risk factors as situational risks. Even within occupations, there are specific times and situations when employees are at enhanced risk. For example, when an individual is working alone, at night, with valuables, the risk of a violent robbery is increased. In the social services, whenever an employee has to deny a service or refuse a request, risk is enhanced. Managing situational risk involves recognizing the risk factors that exist in a given situation and taking steps to reduce or mitigate this risk. At least three strategies for managing situational risk are commonly discussed: workplace policies, crime reduction strategies, and employee training.

Workplace Policies

The development of policies and practices geared toward preventing workplace violence is one of the most frequently recommended strategies. Indeed, legislation and occupational health and safety regulations frequently require an anti-violence policy as part of an overall program (Kelloway & Francis, 2010). Such policies would typically express a no tolerance policy and clarify what is defined as unacceptable workplace behavior (Smith, 2000; Wassell, 2009). Policies should also outline procedures for reporting and dealing with acts of workplace violence (Smith, 2000). Finally, the policy should be communicated to employees and individuals trained in the application of the policy.

As Calnan et al. (2012) point out, policies have several limitations as a means of preventing or managing workplace violence. First, many organizations still do not have such a policy, with only 30% of U.S. organizations reporting having a formal policy pertaining to workplace violence (U.S. Department of Labor [USDL], 2006).

Second, and perhaps more importantly, workplace violence policies are primarily aimed at preventing Type III violence—the least frequently occurring form of workplace violence. It is difficult to believe that individuals committing a criminal act (i.e., a robbery or an intimate partner assault) would be dissuaded by the existence of an organizational policy. Policies may be more influential with clients but are unlikely to have any effect in high risk situations (e.g., dealing with people with dementia, prisoners in custody). Based on what we know about the prevalence of workplace violence, organizational policies alone are unlikely to be an effective deterrent of workplace violence.

As Calnan et al. (2012) note, other commonly recommended policies/practices are questionable in that they are grounded neither in experience nor empirical research. Screening or selection policies designed to "weed out" employees with violent tendencies are less than effective and run a risk of running afoul of human rights or fair employment standards (see for example Day & Catano, 2006). And of course, again, attempting to control the risk of Type III violence does not address the most prevalent forms of workplace violence.

Robbery Reduction Strategies

Given the predominance of Type I violence, preventing criminal activity will likely reduce the number of workplace homicides (see Amandus,

Hunter, James, & Hendricks, 1995). Crime prevention strategies typically involve increasing visibility, reducing the rewards, and increasing the effort associated with robbery (Desroches, 1995; Hendricks, Landsittel, Amandus, Malcan, & Bell, 1999; Mayhew, 2000a, 2000b; OSHA, 1998).

Increasing visibility. Increasing the risks for criminals frequently involves increasing visibility and ensuring that crime deterrence is in place and is visible. The use of global positioning systems that show the location of a driver in distress (OSHA, 2000), external emergency lights (Mayhew, 2000a), and in-car surveillance cameras that allow the potential identification of perpetrators (Appleby, 2000; Mayhew, 2000a) are means of increasing visibility for taxi drivers. Crimes against taxi drivers have been reduced by more than 50% since the implementation of a bylaw in Toronto, Ontario requiring taxi owners to install either security cameras or GPS in their cars (Calleja, 2002).

Most retail crimes occur late at night when there are few potential witnesses (e.g., D'Alessio & Stolzenberg, 1990). Keeping windows clear of signs (e.g., advertisements) to allow passers-by to see inside (Purpura, 1993), and locating the cash register in a location that can be seen from the outside (e.g., in the center of the store) are means of increasing visibility. Closed circuit televisions and video cameras may also deter criminal behavior by increasing would-be robbers' perceptions of risk (OSHA, 1998).

Clerk behavior can also communicate visibility. Common recommendations are that clerks should make eye contact with customers and greet them as they enter the store, thereby making would-be robbers feel conspicuous (Desroches, 1995; Gabor & Normandeau, 1989). OSHA (1998) suggests that employing two clerks during evening shifts may also reduce the incidence of robberies, although this is a controversial (see Amandus et al., 1996) recommendation. Commercial establishments should have practices in place to ensure the safety of employees who work alone (e.g., routinely check on individuals who work alone; Mayhew, 2000b).

Reducing rewards. Cash handling practices such as carrying minimal amounts of money, making frequent cash deposits (Gill, 2000), and using drop safes (see Desroches, 1995; Gill, 2000; OSHA, 1998) are effective means of reducing robberies by reducing the potential reward available to a robber. In their comparison of 400 robbed and 1201 non-robbed convenience stores, Hendricks et al. (1999) found that cash handling policy exhibited the strongest association with robberies, such that stores that were categorized as having good cash handling policies were at a significantly reduced risk for robbery.

Target hardening. Target hardening strategies focus on making it difficult to assault employees through physical design. For example, protective screens have been found to reduce the number of assaults experienced by taxi drivers (Stone & Stevens, 1999). In retail environments, strategies that reduce the ease of escape (Gill 2000), making it difficult for criminals to flee from the scene of the crime, may deter robbery (Desroches, 1995).

In addition to preventing robberies, some target hardening strategies may also reduce the likelihood that employees will be hurt during the commission of a robbery. Installation of high and wide counters, with raised floors on the employee side, to prevent robbers from jumping over counters to assault employees and provision of bullet resistant barriers (Desroches, 1995; Mayhew, 2000b) are effective means of protecting workers.

Employee Training

Employee training is also a form of target hardening that deals with the behavior of employees. Training typically focuses on both general safety precautions as well as behavior during a robbery or threatened assault. Having instructions on how to behave may give employees a sense of control of the situation and lessen the possibility that they will be injured.

In addition to providing staff with necessary knowledge and skills, training may give employees the confidence to deal with potentially dangerous situations (Health Services Advisory Committee, 1987; Levin, Hewitt, & Misner, 1998). Schat and Kelloway (2000) found that hospital workers who received training targeting workplace violence reported higher levels of perceived control compared to workers who did not receive training. In their study, perceptions of control were positively correlated with employee emotional well-being and negatively associated with employee fear of future violence.

Training initiatives can be classified across two dimensions: prevention focused versus consequence focused and target directed versus assailant directed (Schat & Kelloway, 2006). *Prevention focused training* is aimed at teaching employees how they can avoid acts of workplace aggression. *Consequence focused training* focuses on teaching employees how to respond if they have experienced workplace aggression. The majority of workplace violence training is done from a preventative standpoint (Schat & Kelloway, 2006); however, in several occupations (e.g., health care) secondary interventions are also employed and warranted (Schat & Kelloway, 2003).

Knowledge and awareness training, in particular, can help employees recognize imminent risk and respond appropriately. Violence risk training has also demonstrated improvements in employee confidence and perceptions of preparedness for future violent encounters (Beech & Leather, 2006; Ishak & Christensen, 2002; Schat & Kelloway, 2003). Specifically, a study examining training effectiveness in hospital staff indicated that those who had received training experienced higher levels of perceived control. This, in turn, translated to an increase in well-being and a reduction in fear of future violence (Schat & Kelloway, 2003). When examining occurrence rates pre- and post-training, however, results are mixed. Frequently, few, if any, reductions are noted (Wassell, 2009). This suggests that although training can have a positive effect on individual perceptions of violence, it does little to reduce the occurrence of violence.

SUMMARY: SITUATIONAL RISK

The available data suggest that there are specific tasks or work characteristics that are associated with increased risk of workplace violence. Attempts to manage these risks have largely focused on the formulation of anti-violence policies, management of the physical environment in order to reduce the probability of crime, and training employees in how to handle risky situations.

Imminent Risk

Understanding the nature of occupational and situational risks for workplace violence is helpful in alerting employees to potentially dangerous situations. However, such risks may be at such a global level that they offer little guidance to individuals who work in those occupations. For example, although taking care of others is a frequently identified risk factor, it is also the definition of health care (Calnan et al., 2012). Identifying this risk results in the recognition that health care professions are at a higher risk for workplace violence but offers little guidance as to how to reduce or mitigate risks within that occupation. Calnan et al. (2012) suggested that to be useful, risk assessments must move beyond this global level to consider more micro-level risk factors.

They focused on the notion of imminent risk, which they define as the short-term risk of violence occurring in any given situation. This type of risk is based on the notion of the assault cycle. This model outlines the cycle of escalation from standard baseline behavior (phase 1) to a physically violent act and concludes with de-escalation from the violent behavior back to the baseline. In all, the cycle comprises five phases. During the second phase, experiencing a triggering event(s), such as being denied a service or request, may agitate the individual, spurring escalation. If ignored or misinterpreted, escalation may continue until an act of violence is committed. This model is particularly relevant for a couple of reasons. It showcases the build up from baseline behavior to violence, suggesting that physical violence can stem from non-physical aggressive behavior. Moreover, it helps identify and foresee this progression, offering an opportunity to intervene before the escalation reaches its peak. Training employees who work in high risk occupations in which violence is considered imminent how to recognize triggering events and signs of escalation could substantially reduce their risk of violence.

To address this training need, Calnan et al. (2012) extend the SAV-T model to help teach individuals how to recognize escalation and, more importantly, how to intervene based on the stage of escalation. Under this version of the model, the SAV-T acronym stands for *swearing, agitation, volume,* and *threat,* each component representing a different escalation cue. By themselves, swearing, agitation, and volume are not necessarily indicative of violence; however, once an individual engages in two or more of these actions, intervention is crucial. As such, the first recommendation is to set clear, simple, and firm boundaries (Calnan et al., 2012; Caraulia & Steiger, 1997). Doing this at the first sign of escalation may help to deter further progression. Specifically, policies and tolerance for aggression and violence should be clearly communicated. If ignored, employees are encouraged to explain the consequences and to follow through with them.

If escalation persists (e.g., increased agitation and volume), employees may also choose to attempt to diffuse the situation or reduce escalation by engaging in empathetic listening (Caraulia & Steiger, 1997). To diffuse a situation, employees might use humor if appropriate, try and distract the individual, or suggest how the situation can be resolved. Empathic listening requires giving focused attention, monitoring emotions, and demonstrating understanding (Caraulia & Steiger, 1997).

In contrast to the first three escalation cues (i.e., swearing, agitation, and volume), threat poses a stronger risk that should be dealt with immediately. That is, the moment an employee is threatened, immediate action to remove that employee or the aggressor from the situation should be taken. Once a threat has been made, any effort to de-escalate the situation should stop, and assistance should be requested. Although not all threats are carried through, organizations and employees are advised to respond as if they will be. An overreaction is more favorable and goes farther in reducing workplace violence than underestimating the validity of a threat.

To increase transfer and improve practicality, the SAV-T model for situational and imminent risk is simplistic. Past research advocates for the use of clear and simple instruction for assessing and responding to risk in high stress situations (Caraulia & Steiger, 1997; Schat & Kelloway, 2005). Using a simple acronym that can be recalled quickly helps improve the speed at which risks can be assessed and further helps to facilitate actionable response (Calnan et al., 2012).

As with any intervention, it is important to consider its effectiveness as determined by empirical evaluation. To date, many of the interventions focused on reducing workplace violence and aggression have not been adequately evaluated (see also Runyan, Zakocs, & Zwerling, 2000).

Methodological constraints, among other issues, have made it difficult to determine the exact effectiveness of workplace violence interventions (see, for example, Cox, Karanika, Griffiths, & Houdmont, 2007; Randall, Griffiths, & Cox, 2005). To continue to advance our understanding of workplace violence and the extent to which interventions can aid in its reduction, methods of evaluation require more development from both academics and practitioners.

CONCLUSION

It is reasonable to expect that the occurrence of workplace violence will continue, particularly in jobs that possess the variety of risk factors (e.g., dealing with the public, denying a service, dealing with items of value, going into people's homes, etc.) reported by LeBlanc and Kelloway (2002). In the broadest sense, identifying the societal determinants and root causes of workplace violence and aggression (e.g., economic, social, environmental, etc) is certainly imperative for developing workplace violence prevention strategies and must be collectively undertaken by representatives spanning a wide range of national and international organizations.

At the organizational level, there remain inherent challenges for the impact of organizational violence policies and practices on reducing Type I violence (Calnan et al., 2012); thus, organizations must consider context specific strategies that will address the health and safety risks that millions of employees currently experience in their jobs. Given the prevalence of Type I violence (Schat et al., 2005), providing employees with training to effectively identify and assess imminent risks in the work environment should be an integral component within a comprehensive organizational prevention and management strategy.

Considering the potential benefits of employee focused training interventions, as well as the need for comprehensive organizational prevention and management approaches that include risk awareness and assessment training, we extend the SAV-T model to enable employees to identify the signs of escalation and to determine strategies for effective intervention. The benefits of employee focused training, such as the SAV-T intervention, may result in an increased perceived sense of control at work (e.g., Schat & Kelloway, 2000), as employees may feel that they are equipped with the knowledge and skills to effectively identify, assess, and respond to risk factors in their jobs. The SAV-T intervention aims to potentially reduce workplace violence and improve employee health and safety related outcomes; however, as with most workplace violence interventions, the beneficial outcomes of the SAV-T approach remain to be empirically evaluated. Overall, the SAV-T intervention provides a promising strategy.

NOTE

Preparation of this manuscript was supported by research funding from the Social Sciences and Humanities Research Council of Canada. Correspondence may be addressed to the first author at the Department of Psychology, Saint Mary's University, Halifax NS, B3H 3C3 CANADA or by email to kevin.kelloway@smu.ca or jmuleen@mta.ca.

REFERENCES

Amandus, H. E., Hunter, R. D., James, E., & Hendricks, S. (1995). Reevaluation of the effectiveness of environmental designs to reduce robbery risk in Florida convenience stores. *Journal of Occupational and Environmental Medicine, 37*, 711–717.

Amandus, H. E., Zahm, D., Friedmann, R., Ruback, R. B., Block, C., Weiss, J.,... Kessler, D. (1996). Employee injuries and convenience store robberies in selected metropolitan areas. *Journal of Occupational and Environmental Medicine, 38*, 714–720.

Anderson, C. A., & Bushman, B. J. (2002). Human aggression. *Annual Review of Psychology, 53*, 27–51.

Appleby, T. (2000, January 4). How to make the job safer for cabbies. *Globe and mail.* Retrieved March 1, 2004, from http://www.taxi-library.org/toronto02.htm

Barling, J. (1996). The prediction, experience, and consequences of workplace violence. In G. R. Vandenbos & E. Q. Bulatao (Eds.), *Violence on the job: Identifying risks and developing solutions* (pp. 29–49). Washington, DC: American Psychological Association.

Barling, J., Dupre, K., & Kelloway, E. K. (2009). Predicting workplace aggression and violence. *Annual Review Psychology, 60*, 671–692.

Baron, R. A., & Richardson, D. R. (1994). *Human aggression* (2nd ed.). New York, NY: Plenum.

Beech, B., & Leather, P. (2006). Workplace violence in the health care sector: A review of staff training and integration of training evaluation models. *Aggression and Violent Behavior, 11*, 27–43.

Berkowitz, L. (1993). *Aggression: Its causes, consequences, and control.* Philadelphia, PA: Temple University Press.

Braverman, M. (1999). *Preventing workplace violence: A guide for employers and practitioners.* Thousand Oaks, CA: Sage.

California Occupational Safety and Health Administration. (1995). *Guidelines for workplace security.* Sacramento, CA: Author.

Calleja, F. (2002, November 5). Cab hold-ups on web. *Toronto star.* Retrieved March 1, 2004, from http://www.taxi-l.org/camera04.htm

Calnan, K., Kelloway, K., & Dupre, K. (2012). Violence and aggression in the workplace; from effective prevention to necessary intervention. In C. Cooper, R. Hughes, & A. Kinder (Eds.), *International handbook of workplace trauma* (pp. 105–118). Hoboken, NJ: Wiley Blackwell.

Canadian Centre for Occupational Health and Safety. (1999). *Violence in the work-place.* Retrieved March 1, 2004, from http://www.ccohs.ca/oshanswers/psychosocial/violence.html

Caraulia, A. P., & Steiger, L. K. (1997). *Nonviolent crisis intervention: Learning to defuse explosive behavior.* Brookfield, WI: CPI Publishing.

Casteel, C., & Peek-Asa, C. (2000). Effectiveness of crime prevention through environmental design (CPTED) in reducing robberies. *American Journal of Preventive Medicine, 18,* 99–115.

Castillo, D. N., & Jenkins, E. L. (1994). Industries and occupations at high risk for work-related homicide. *Journal of Occupational Medicine, 36,* 125–132.

Cox, T., Karanika, M., Griffiths, A., & Houdmont, J. (2007). Evaluating organisational-level work stress interventions: Beyond traditional methods. *Work and Stress, 21*(4), 348–362.

D'Alessio, S., & Stolzenberg, L. (1990). A crime of convenience: The environment and convenience store robbery. *Environment and Behavior, 22,* 255–271.

Davis, H. (1987). Workplace homicides of Texas males. *American Journal of Public Health, 77,* 1290–1293.

Day, A. L., & Catano, V. M. (2006). Screening and selecting out violent employees. In E. K. Kelloway, J. Barling, & J. J. Hurrell (Eds.), *Handbook of workplace violence* (pp. 549–577). Thousand Oaks, CA: Sage.

Desroches, F. J. (1995). *Force and fear: Robbery in Canada.* Scarborough, Ontario: Nelson Canada

Duhart, D. T. (2001). *Bureau of Justice Statistics special report: Violence in the workplace, 1993–1999.* NCJ 190076. Washington, DC: U.S. Bureau of Justice Statistics.

Dupré, K. E., & Barling, J. (2006). Predicting and preventing supervisory workplace aggression. *Journal of Occupational Health Psychology, 11,* 13–26.

Gabor, T., & Normandeau, A. (1989). Preventing armed robbery through opportunity reduction: A critical analysis. *Journal of Security Administration, 12,* 3–18.

Geen, R. G. (2001). *Human aggression* (2nd ed.). Buckingham, UK: Open University Press.

Gill, M. (2000). *Commercial robbery.* Aldine Place, London: Blackstone Press Limited.

Greenberg, L., & Barling, J. (1999). Predicting employee aggression against co-workers, subordinates and supervisors: The roles of person behaviors and perceived workplace factors. *Journal of Organizational Behavior, 20,* 897–913.

Health Services Advisory Committee. (1987). *Violence to staff in the health services.* London: HMSO.

Hearnden, K. (1988). *Violence at work* [Industrial safety data file]. London: United Trade Press.

Hendricks, S. A., Landsittel, D. P., Amandus, H. E., Malcan, J., & Bell, J. (1999). A matched case-control study of convenience store robbery risk factors. *Journal of Occupational and Environmental Medicine, 41,* 995–1004.

Ishak, M., & Christensen, M. (2002). Achieving a better management for patients' aggressive behavior: Evaluation of a training program. *Journal of Occupational Health and Safety Australia and New Zealand, 18,* 231–237.

Kelloway, E. K., Barling, J., & Hurrell, J. J. (2006). *Handbook of workplace violence.* Thousand Oaks, CA: Sage.

Kelloway, E. K., & Francis, L. (2010). *Management of occupational health and safety* (5th ed.). Toronto: Nelson

Kelloway, E. K., & Teed, M. (2011). Workplace violence in small and medium sized enterprizes. In E. K. Kelloway & C. L. Cooper (Eds), *Occupational health and safety for small and medium sized enterprises* (pp. 48–68). London: Elgar.

Kraus, J. F. (1987). Homicide while at work: Persons, industries, and occupations at high risk. *American Journal of Public Health, 77*, 1285–1289.

Lamberg, L. (1996). Don't ignore patients' threats, psychiatrists told. *JAMA, 275*, 1715–1716.

LeBlanc, M. M., & Kelloway, E. K. (2002). Predictors and outcomes of workplace violence and aggression. *Journal of Applied Psychology, 87*, 444–453.

Leseleuc, S. (2004). *Criminal victimization in the workforce, 2004.* Ottawa, ON: Canadian Centre for Justice Statistics.

Levin, P. F., Hewitt, J., & Misner, T. S. (1998). Insights of nurses about assault in hospital-based emergency departments. *Image—The Journal of Nursing Scholarship, 30*, 249–254.

Mayhew, C. (2000a). Preventing assaults on taxi drivers in Australia. *Trends and Issues in Crime and Criminal Justice, 179*, 1–6.

Mayhew, C. (2000b). *Violence in the workplace—preventing armed robbery: A practical handbook.* (Series: Research and public policy series; no. 33). Canberra, ACT: Australian Institute of Criminology.

National Institute for Occupational Safety and Health. (2002). *Violence: Occupational hazards in hospitals* (DHHS Publication No. 2002–101). Retrieved March 5, 2004, from http://www.cdc.gov/niosh/2002-101.html#intro

Neuman, J. H., & Baron, R. A. (1998). Workplace violence and workplace aggression: Evidence concerning specific forms, potential causes, and preferred targets. *Journal of Management, 24*(3), 391–419.

Occupational Safety and Health Administration. (1998). Recommendations for workplace violence prevention programs in late-night retail establishments. Retrieved March 5, 2004, from http://www.osha.gov/Publications/osha3153.pdf

Occupational Safety and Health Administration. (2000). *Risk factors and protective measures for taxi and livery drivers.* Retrieved March 1, 2004, from https://www.osha.gov/OSHAFacts/taxi-livery-drivers.pdf

Occupational Safety and Health Administration. (2004). *Guidelines for preventing workplace violence for health care and social service workers.* Retrieved March 5, 2004, from http://www.osha.gov/Publications/osha3148.pdf

Painter, K. (1987). "It's part of the job": Violence at work. *Employee Relations, 9*, 30–40.

Peek-Asa, C., Runyan, C. W., & Zwerling, C. (2001). The role of surveillance and evaluation research in the reduction of violence against workers. *American Journal of Preventive Medicine, 20*, 141–148.

Peek-Asa, C., Schaffer, K. B., Kraus, J. F., & Howard, J. (1998). Surveillance of non-fatal workplace assault injuries, using police and employers' reports. *Journal of Occupational and Environmental Medicine, 40*, 707–713.

Pollack, K. M., Austin, W., & Grisso, J. A. (2010). Employee assistance programs: A workplace resource to address intimate partner violence. *Journal of Women's Health, 19*, 729–733.

Purpura, P. P. (1993). *Retail security and shrinkage protection*. Stoneham, MA: Butterworth-Heinemann.

Randall, R., Griffiths, A., & Cox, T. (2005). Evaluating organizational stress-management interventions using adapted study designs. *European Journal of Work and Organisational Psychology, 14(1)*, 23–41.

Runyan, C. W., Zakocs, R. C., & Zwerling, C. (2000). Administrative and behavioral intervention for workplace violence prevention. *American Journal of Preventive Medicine, 18*(4S), 116–127.

Schat, A. C. H., Frone, M. R., & Kelloway, E. K. (2005). Prevalence of workplace aggression in the US workforce: Findings from a national study. In E. K. Kelloway, J. Barling, & J. J. Hurrell (Eds.), *Handbook of workplace violence* (pp. 47–89). Thousand Oaks, CA: Sage.

Schat, A. C. H., & Kelloway, E. K. (2000). The effects of perceived control on the outcomes of workplace aggression and violence. *Journal of Occupational Health Psychology, 4*, 386–402.

Schat, A. C. H., & Kelloway, E. K. (2003). Reducing the adverse consequences of workplace aggression and violence: The buffering effects of organizational support. *Journal of Occupational Health Psychology, 8*, 110–122.

Schat, A. C. H., & Kelloway, E. K. (2005). Workplace violence. In J. Barling, E. K. Kelloway, & M. Frone (Eds.), *Handbook of work stress* (pp. 189–218). Thousand Oaks, CA: Sage.

Schat, A. C. H., & Kelloway, E. K. (2006). Training as a workplace aggression intervention strategy. In E. K. Kelloway, J. Barling, & J. J. Hurrell (Eds.), *Handbook of workplace violence* (pp. 579–605). Thousand Oaks, CA: Sage.

Smith, G. (2000). *Work rage: Identifying the problems, implement the solutions*. Toronto, ON: Harper Collins.

Stone, R., & Stevens, D. C. (1999). *The effectiveness of taxi partitions: The Baltimore Case* [Electronic version]. Raleigh, NC: The Southeastern Transportation Center.

Swanberg, J. E., Logan, T. K., & Marke, C. (2006). The consequences of partner violence on employment in the workplace. In E. K. Kelloway, J. Barling, & J. J. Hurrell (Eds.), *Handbook of workplace violence* (pp. 351–380). Thousand Oaks, CA: Sage.

U.S. Department of Labor. (2006). *Survey of workplace violence prevention, 2005*. USDL publication USDL 06-1860. Washington, DC: Bureau of Labor Statistics.

Wassell, J. T., (2009). Workplace violence intervention effectiveness: A systematic literature review. *Safety Science, 47*, 1049–1055.

CHAPTER 10

HOW TO ENCOURAGE CHANGES IN BEHAVIOR THROUGH INTERVENTIONS INTEGRATED INTO QUALITY OF LIFE PROGRAMS WITHIN COMPANIES

Alberto José N. Ogata
and Sâmia Aguiar Brandão Simurro

ABSTRACT

Non-communicable or chronic diseases (NCDs) are the leading cause of death worldwide and have caused high numbers of "premature" deaths, loss of quality of life, and a high degree of limitation in work and leisure activities. Additionally, they have an economic impact on families, communities, and society in general, aggravating inequity and increasing poverty. Despite the rapid growth of NCDs, their impact can be diminished through wide-ranging and cost-effective interventions that promote health by reducing risk factors and that improve health awareness, early detection, and timely treatment. A study carried out on adults in the city of São Paulo found approximately 30%

Improving Emploee Health and Well-Being, pages 153–169
Copyright © 2014 by Information Age Publishing
All rights of reproduction in any form reserved.

of participants to have mental illnesses. It is not possible to achieve significant results in improved health simply by communicating concepts and information. Understanding behavior under a broader and more comprehensive perspective makes it possible to bring about proposed interventions and effective change programs. Knowledge of behavior change models and application of this knowledge to programs and actions will help to improve results in reducing risk factors and improving quality of life.

Non-communicable or chronic diseases (NCDs) are the leading cause of death worldwide and have resulted in high numbers of "premature" deaths, loss of quality of life, and a high degree of limitation in work and leisure activities. Additionally, they have an economic impact on families, communities, and society in general, aggravating inequities and increasing poverty. Despite the rapid growth of NCDs, their impact can be diminished through wide-ranging and cost-effective interventions that promote health by reducing risk factors and that encourage health awareness, early detection, and timely treatment. In Brazil too, NCDs represent a huge health risk. They account for 72% of deaths—most notably cardiovascular diseases (31.3%), cancer (16.3%), diabetes (5.2%), and chronic respiratory disease (5.8%)—and affect people of all socio-economic backgrounds, with a higher incidence among those belonging to vulnerable groups such as the elderly and those with low income and poor education. The main risk factors for NCDs are tobacco use, eating an unhealthy diet, physical inactivity, and harmful use of alcohol. These are in large part responsible for the obesity epidemic because of the prevalence of high blood pressure and high cholesterol levels (Brasil, 2011).

Researchers Freitas and Garcia of the Brazilian Institute for Applied Economic Research (*Ipea*) carried out a recent cross-sectional study using data taken from 1998, 2003, and 2008 of the Brazilian National Household Sample Survey (Freitas & Garcia, 2012). They found that the standardized prevalence coefficient for diabetes increased in Brazil from 2.9% in 1998, to 4.3% in 2008, while for diabetes associated with high blood pressure, it increased from 1.7% to 2.8% over the same period. The authors concluded that the incidence of diabetes and associated high blood pressure is growing rapidly in Brazil. New strategies and programs should be based on identifying factors associated with risk for NCDs. Costa and Thuler (2012) analyzed the data taken from the "Household Survey of Risk Behaviours and Related Levels of Non-communicable Illness and Disease" using a representative sample from 18 Brazilian capitals. The absence of risk factors was observed in only 8.5% of the population. Excess weight (being overweight or obese) was the most common factor (48.1%). Indeed, 39.7% of the surveyed population was classified as insufficiently active (infrequently active or sedentary). Of those interviewed, 20.8% mentioned smoking cigarettes, and 7.8% had high alcohol consumption. Furthermore, 25.2% of adults confirmed they suffered from high blood pressure, 8% from diabetes, and 23.6% from hypercholesterolemia.

Evidence from the field of chronic diseases demonstrates the high incidence of neuropsychiatric diseases in the population and the way in which these diseases affect the daily lives of individuals affected, their families, and all those involved in their social entourage. This group of diseases in turn constituted risk factors for other chronic and infectious diseases. Individuals with neuropsychiatric disturbances often have a reduced capacity for self-care, making them more susceptible to a wide range of diseases (Cruz, 2012). In research drawing on a sample of 5,037 adults from the city of São Paulo, approximately 30% of participants were found to have mental disorders. This was made up of anxiety disorders (19.9%), mood swings (11%), impulse control disorders (4.3%), and substance abuse (3.6%) (Andrade et al., 2012). This information corroborates the importance of an appropriate approach to mental health as a relevant component in health care.

The report entitled *Reducing Risks, Promoting Healthy Life* (OMS, 2002) highlights the importance of promoting behaviors linked to health and the identification and prevention of risk factors. In reality, the biggest and most pressing obstacles to improved health are those individual and social behaviors associated with the expectations and culture of different groups. The choices made are determined by our potential for health or illness. The question that arises is the following: *if people prefer life and good health over death, why do they continue to put their lives in danger through behaviors that present risks to their health?*

The answer is not an easy one. Pure and simple information about a disease and prevention methods has not been sufficient for improving health-related behaviors and those linked to the individual's lifestyle. It is not possible to achieve significant results in improving a person's health, and that of a community in general, through simply communicating concepts and information. It is necessary to investigate the fact that in relation to chronic diseases, an effective approach requires radical changes to the way in which the problem is tackled, since the main factor concerns the individual's lifestyle choices, and this is without doubt the best form of intervention in gaining positive results.

The knowledge that health is fundamentally behavioral and that a healthy lifestyle could constitute an effective way of preventing many diseases has led health professionals to turn to the study and understanding of human behavior in an attempt to find effective approaches that might encourage making healthier individual and collective choices. Understanding behavior under a broader and more comprehensive perspective makes it possible to bring about proposed interventions and effective change programs. In understanding this process, it should be remembered that behaviors are multidimensional, and therefore interventions concerning change must consider more than just one specific aspect of the behavior. In order to obtain accurate and definitive results, the considerable complexity of the subject must be taken into consideration. Some theories have contributed greatly to understanding health-related behaviors.

DIFFICULTIES IN CHANGING BEHAVIOR

Personal and health-related attitudes are generated by the interactions of variable factors such as genetics, personality, environment, social and spiritual support, access to healthcare, opportunities to practice healthy habits in addition to personal well-being habits and lifestyle in general. Changing these behaviors is not a simple task. The majority of people find it difficult to change what they enjoy doing, or what they are accustomed to doing. Support is not always available, or as is sometimes the case, it is difficult to exercise control and maintain a healthy lifestyle.

An important factor in modifying behavior is the perception of the need for change. The perceived severity of the risk clearly directs the need for change. Perceived fear, urgency and vulnerability are factors that drive the action (Mcadams & St. Aubin, 1998). The level of awareness of the change is perhaps the starting point for an effective result. While it is not the only factor involved, the exchange of information constitutes part of all forms of human relations, and significant improvements to lifestyle and to peoples' health status can only be achieved based on a sufficient awareness of the need for change (Chapman, 2002). Specific situations in the life of an individual, such as illness, or a heart attack, can motivate a person to stop smoking, reduce stress levels, eat more healthily, or take up a physical activity. In these cases, experiential learning can be a powerful method of communicating information. This is all the more true if the individual can perceive the immediate benefits and value of the information (Davidson, 1989). The main challenge in changing behavior is the provision of a model that adequately attends to the mental, physical, and social needs of a person, allowing them to change.

FACTORS DETERMINING BEHAVIOR

When proposing concrete programs, what should be changed and how to obtain important information about the different elements involved in the change should both be considered. While the history of humanity demonstrates that change is inevitable, it has always been a cause for concern that emerges in an individual's thoughts and feelings and that informs peoples' responses in a new situation. Thus, promoting intentionality for change through programs involves discussing factors such as culture, legislation, social norms, values, beliefs, social status, support, personality, education, abilities, habits, motivation, needs, interests, gender, age, health status, choices, reward systems, self-perception, self-efficacy, and expectations. The following discussion aims to consider the various factors outlined, how they are related to each other, the aspects involved, and individual behaviors that are linked to health.

Personal Factors

Individual differences can be linked to social aspects such as ethnicity, age group, gender, and personality. Furthermore, attitudes, beliefs, and expectations underlie behavioral choices in general, and in terms of health, subjective expectations of life and vision of the future are determined by people's lifestyles. Perceptions and awareness of health-related vulnerability and severity, as well as awareness of auto-efficiency, influence decisions and actions linked to health. Lastly, habits and implementation of intentions are noteworthy, as in general doing something for the first time is not something we do frequently. Most daily activities are performed automatically and repeated several times. We are not conscious of them happening, meaning that we are not in complete control. Habits do not require any mental effort or deep reflection nor do they have an intentional aspect. Habits are automatic responses that lead us simply to act. Understanding these habits has gained importance among health professionals, so that they can propose interventions that facilitate behavioral changes and the acquisition of healthier habits, and so that these new habits become automatic. Past habits predict future behavior (Sheeran, 2002).

External Factors

Health is a process that concerns the body's interaction with its social and physical surroundings, and the environment has strong implications for health. Studies have demonstrated differences between groups regarding habits related to health, such as tobacco and alcohol use and practicing a physical activity (Duncan, Daly, McDonough, & Williams, 2002; Williams, 2002). Certain environmental factors should be considered in order to understand health-related behavior (Kerr, Eves, & Carrol, 2005), such as the socio-economic environment (income, physical environment, nature of the workplace, movement, pollution), psycho-social factors (social support, autonomy, control of activities), and cultural factors (beliefs and norms).

MAIN THEORIES APPLIED TO THE FIELD OF HEALTH

It has been recognized that in general, people are consistent in their pre-established thought schemes. As a result, when considering changing someone's behavior, it is important to understand what that person knows, what he or she wants, and how he or she behaves. Motivational, behavioral, and social theories contribute to an understanding of why people engage in health-related risk behaviors and, with this in mind, help to find better interventions resulting in actions that improve lifestyle and levels of well-being. Some of the factors and theories that form an important base for developing effective interventions to improve health are considered here.

Health Belief Model

The health belief model (HBM) has been used widely in studies within the field of health. It was developed in the 1950s by social psychologists at the U.S. Public Health Service in an attempt to explain the causes for a generalized failure of disease prevention programs (Rosenstock, 1974). According to this model, the decision to carry out a healthy behavior fundamentally derives from four psychological variables:

- *Perceived susceptibility*: the individual's belief that this disease could affect them;
- *Perceived severity*: the belief that this disease might have serious consequences;
- *Perceived benefits*: the belief that this disease could be prevented by action; and
- *Perceived barriers*: the belief that this action might involve negative aspects or obstacles.

Heightened levels of perceived susceptibility and severity of the situation must exist in order for a person to feel at risk. This model suggests that the greater the threat, the more motivated a person will be to engage in a lifestyle change. However it is not simply a motivation to reduce the threat, or indeed the degree of risk, that will successfully lead a person to adopt a new behavior (stop smoking, go on a diet, take up physical exercise). This theory suggests that individuals weigh up the costs and benefits, and if the perceived threat is high, the costs of adopting a positive behavior are acceptable. The benefits of actions are evaluated in terms of perceived barriers to successful completion.

According to this model, in order for a behavior change program or health promotion program to succeed, it is fundamental that the strategy is devised in such a way that each individual can perceive their degree of susceptibility; in other words they can identify their own risk factors, the severity of the situation, as well as their limitations, inabilities, suffering and quality of life. Equally this strategy must also include an understanding of the benefits that positive actions bring to the individual, allowing the person to overcome the identified or foreseeable barriers. The reinforcement provided by making progress motivates the individual to transcend these barriers, thereby increasing chances of successfully changing behavior.

The model suggests that interventions should follow some initial steps:

1. Define in detail the characteristics of the target population of the intervention.
2. Where appropriate, use a scale to determine the degree of influence of characteristics such as locus of control, attributions, and auto-efficiency.
3. Begin health-related communication actions with general information about the population's risk factors and basic information about the importance of effort and personal resources for improvement.
4. Clearly present the short-term benefits of health-enhancing activities related to improvement and control of risk factors.
5. Show that the decision to engage in healthy behaviors can be difficult. Provide information that is consistent and has a scientific base.
6. Describe in detail examples of others who have been successful in engaging in healthier behaviors and actions and the effort and personal resources they required.
7. Explain the threat to health in detail, and the susceptibility of the population.
8. Describe situations where other people from this population have taken up healthy behavior independent of risk factors. Demonstrate ways in which people from this population acquired the resources and effort necessary for committing to healthy behaviors.

The Rational Action Theory and the Theory of Planned Behavior

The rational action theory—the aim of this theory is not simply to understand, but also to predict a given behavior. According to this model, health behaviors can be influenced by attitudes and habits, as well as by values and feelings. Attitude is an important construct within this theory, which has merited much attention from various researchers in the field of human behavior. It is defined as a predisposition, or mental and neural state of readiness to respond in a favorable or unfavorable way to an object, person, institution, or event. This readiness is based on affective, behavioral, and cognitive experiences, and, consequently, the authors believe it impossible to evaluate attitude purely through direct observation (Ajzein & Fishbein, 1980; Fishbein & Ajzein, 1975). Attitudes can only be evaluated through measurable answers with three basic components: the cognitive component (involving thoughts and beliefs), the affective component (feelings and emotions), and the behavioral component (essentially the reactions of individuals).

The theory of planned behavior—an extension and reformulation of the rational action theory (Ajzein & Fishbein, 1980). This theory includes the concept of "perceived control" over the performance of a given behavior as determining intention and behavior. The inclusion of this concept is based on the assumption that a greater degree of perceived control corresponds to a greater likelihood that the performance of the behavior will be successful. This theory makes significant contributions both in terms of feasibility of educational campaigns that are aimed at minimizing health-related risk behaviors and in terms of defining public policies with respect to these variables.

Protection Motivation Theory

Protection motivation theory was originally developed by Dr. R. W. Rogers in 1975, in order better understand the influence of fear and how people dealt with it. Based on the health belief model, the theory evolved into a more general approach to persuasive communication (Rogers, 1983). The theory indicates two appraisal processes:

1. Threat-appraisal process stems from perceptions of severity and vulnerability of the situation. It is centered on the source of the threat and the factors that increase or decrease the probability of adaptive behaviors. Severity refers to the degree of harm from the health-related risk behavior, and vulnerability refers to the likelihood of this harm occurring.
2. Coping-appraisal process concerns the effective responses by the recommended behavior in removing or preventing harm and the self-efficacy that refers to the belief that one can indeed successfully perform the recommended behavior. Thus, the capacity for coping is the combined ability of response efficacy with self-efficacy, in addition to the capacity to cope with or avert the threat, minus any physical or psychological harm that results from the adoption of the recommended preventive action.

The model proposes that motivation and the intention to protect derive from four factors: (1) the perceived severity of the threat, (2) perceived vulnerability, (3) perceived self-efficacy in adopting this behavior, and (4) perceived efficacy of the behavior (benefits x barriers). According to the protection motivation theory, there are two possible sources of information that influence the intentionality of behavior and promote a coping response, which can be adaptive (the intention of improving health) or maladaptive (denying or avoiding the situation). The first of these sources is environmental, concerning factors such as verbal persuasion and observational learning, and the second is intrapersonal, involving, for example, previous experience. This theory is implicated in various educational health campaigns such as anti-smoking and AIDS prevention.

Social Cognitive Theory

Developed by Albert Bandura in 1971, social cognitive theory suggests that intentionality is a fundamental human characteristic. Intentions involve plans and strategies for action. Another characteristic is the pursuit of goals and the prediction of likely results, which instigate and motivate efforts in the present, as a cognitive representation of a future result is constructed in the present. According to this theory, behavior is governed by social beliefs and expected results. Bandura suggests that it is the mechanisms for thought that make behavior worthy of further study, and he intended to create a theory that could be applied and that could provide modifiable determinants. This theory proposes that the beliefs people hold about their own efficacy in controlling the events that affect their lives influence the attitudes they hold regarding their aspirations, efforts, perseverance, resistance to problems, vulnerability to stress, depression, and performance. It is based on the fact that if people do not believe their actions can lead them to produce the desired results, they tend to have little incentive for action or for perseverance when faced with difficulties. Many studies on the effects of perceived effectiveness have been developed since then (Bandura, 1977).

The assumption arises that health behaviors are planned and regulated by things such as self-efficacy and outcome expectations (Bandura, 1977). Self-efficacy is associated with personal beliefs or the extent to which the individual believes him/herself capable of successfully performing a given action that is necessary for achieving the expected result. Health behaviors are directly influenced by expectations of self-efficacy. For example, the more a person believes him or herself to be capable of eating at least five servings of fruit and vegetables a day, the more likely he or she is to actually do so. Health behaviors are also influenced by outcome expectations; for example, if I eat at least five servings of fruit and vegetables a day, I will feel better and improve my health. Self-efficacy does not refer to the individuals' actual abilities, but instead to their perception of these abilities. This theory forms part of the theoretical base for building awareness strategies for a healthier lifestyle. It points to the individual's ability to give significance to behavior, to learn through observing others, to self-determine, and to self-regulate behavior. It considers the individual able to critically analyze and reflect on an experience and determine if this behavior will or will not occur in a particular situation (Bandura, 1971).

Increasing the individual's expectations of self-efficacy is an important aspect to be considered in interventions for changing health behaviors. One way of achieving this is through increasing the individual's capacity to influence these expectations. In turn, promoting the acquisition of personal capabilities increases the possibility of self-efficacy. In relation to healthy behaviors, it is essential that some capacities should be developed, such as cognitive restructuring (for a more realistic perception of the situation) and balancing emotions (so that they are positive and motivational). There are some effective problem-solving techniques:

a. Identifying the problem
b. Appreciative inquiry
c. Selecting objectives (goals and subgoals)
d. Alternative solutions (as many as possible)
e. Decision-making (pros, cons, and possible flaws)
f. Implementing actions for the selected solution
g. Evaluation of results

Transtheoretical Model

The transtheoretical model was proposed by James Prochaska (Prochaska, Norcross, & Diclemente, 1995). This model was developed using comparative analysis of more than 29 psychotherapeutic theories, focusing on the process of change. Prochaska concluded that all the theories have their limitations and that none of them could explain the process that motivates individuals to make change. This model, therefore, attempts to develop a theory and a model for intervention that promote personal change. For Prochaska, DiClemente, and Norcross (1992), successfully changing behavior depends on the application of the right strategies (or processes) at the appropriate time (or stage). The transtheoretical model focuses on intentional change, or the individual's decision-making. It is based on the premise that behavior change occurs via a process that involves progression through different levels (or stages) of motivation for the change. The stages of change correspond to implicit or explicit activities, in which people engage in changing their thoughts, affection, behavior, or relationships linked to the behavior. In this context, any activity intended to change behavior, feelings, or way of thinking is a process of change.

The stages of awareness can be classified as follows:

Precontemplation: no intention of making changes in the foreseeable future (over the next six months). People may be uninformed, unmotivated, or disbelieving of the possibility of change. They may have tried and been unsuccessful on occasions in the past. They might underestimate the gains, or overestimate the costs. Consequently, unhealthy or risk behaviors are taken up, and denial is the greatest obstacle in this phase.

Contemplation: The individual is considering the possibility of change within the next six months and demonstrates thought for and a clear evaluation of the pros and cons of making the change. Ambivalence is the prevalent characteristic of individuals at this stage. While they have a strong desire to effect change, they also feel doubt and anxiety. "Chronic contemplators" can remain in this phase for years, without taking any action.

Preparation: This is where transition to the action stage begins. In this phase there are two specific changes, namely focusing on the solution to problems and thinking that is directed to the future and not to the past as before. This phase involves a heightened awareness on the part of the individual and is characterized by planning of action. It is important that the individual communicates publicly about their intentions for change so that they are involved in an external commitment. At this point, there is not yet any concrete action for change, as in general the feeling of ambivalence has not yet been totally resolved.

Action: The individual is aware of the need for change and that a significant amount of energy and dedication will be needed in order for it to happen. In this stage, a person makes a clear effort to modify their lifestyle over the next six months. Changes that take place at this stage are much more noticeable than those that take place during other stages. According to this model, action is just one of the stages of change and is followed by the maintenance stage, which is fundamental.

Maintenance: This is an extremely important phase, as the change is not realized simply through the action itself. Maintenance is the greatest challenge in the change process, as it leads to the behavior becoming stabilized. The task here is to consolidate the gains made thanks to the change and prevent possible relapses.

Termination: This is the final objective for those who achieved the change. In this stage, no effort is needed to maintain the behavior, and it is has already become a habit. Individuals are confident they can cope without fear of relapse. There is some cause for debate, as some professionals believe that certain problems never cease to exist and will always require maintenance.

Relapse is a normal and important part of the process, allowing the individual to benefit from taking time to reflect more deeply and learn until a definitive and long-term change can be achieved.

The Health Action Process Approach (HAPA)

Put forward by Schwarzer (1992), the HAPA considered two factors in developing theories. The first was the inclusion of a temporal element in understanding beliefs and behaviors, and the second was distinguishing between the decisional and motivation stages of action. There is a pre-intentional motivational process, which precedes developing the behavioral intention, and a post-intentional process, which determines current behavior. This model can be applied to all health-compromising or health-improvement behaviors, where different attitudes and expectations in the two stages can be observed. At the motivational stage, the person develops the intention to act (Schwarzer, 2001). The model attempts to combine elements of the health belief model, the transtheoretical model for change, and the theory of planned behavior. According to Schwarzer (1992), self-efficacy has always been the best indication of intention and of behavior change for a variety of behaviors linked to protecting and maintaining health. This includes examples such as: flossing, breast self-examination, participating in programs to stop smoking, weight loss programs, doing physical exercise, and so on.

INTERVENTION STRATEGIES

Some models and approaches can act as useful resources for facilitating behavior change in the contexts of health, well-being, and quality of life. Change involves adopting interventions and strategies at different levels (individual, family, community, and social), and additional tools are needed if the change is to be successful. Understanding human behavior is undoubtedly a complex question, as it is determined on a reciprocal basis by a multitude of internal and external influences resulting from the interaction of the individual with the environment in which he or she lives. Despite this, some models can be very useful for developing interventions.

Motivational Interviewing

Motivational interviewing is a style of collaborative counseling that is client-centered and that aims to direct and strengthen motivation for change

(Miller & Rollnick, 2002). Using this technique, the professional aims to promote a space that offers up the conditions necessary for making a change in a non-directive way. Instead of imposing a change on the individual, or attempting to convince them to change, this technique allows them to find reasons within themselves for making the change. Motivational interviewing (MI) draws on techniques from various approaches to psychological interventions, such as brief psychotherapies, cognitive therapy, systemic therapy, and even the social psychology of persuasion. Sessions are particularly similar to the client-centered therapeutic techniques of Carl Rogers, in which empathy and reflective listening constitute fundamental tools in the process. MI recognizes that in pre-contemplation, the change is not considered—resistance and denial prevail over an awareness of the need to change. Contemplation marks the beginning of the process in which ambivalence prevails, and resolving and working on ambivalence is part of this phase and will allow the person to progress on to the following stages.

Self-Efficacy

Self-efficacy is a concept that arose from cognitive social psychology. It refers to a belief that the person holds about his or her ability to produce a given level of performance in an activity. This is linked to the individual's perception of his or her ability to reach the defined objective. Self-efficacy determines how people feel, think, motivate themselves, and behave (Bandura, 1994). While self-efficacy and self-esteem are different concepts, they are, however, related. Self-efficacy concerns an individual's perception of his or her ability to reach a goal, while self-esteem relates to the feeling the person has about him or herself.

CHALLENGES IN DESIGNING INNOVATIVE QUALITY OF LIFE PROGRAMS

Implementation of programs to improve quality of life in companies is a major challenge. It is essential that the conceptual framework of the program be defined in order to establish the basis of planning. Programs often primarily aim to improve the organization's climate through motivational actions, in order to promote health (with subsequent maintenance of health status and control of healthcare costs) and to improve human productivity.

International studies analyzing absenteeism (being away from work) and presenteeism (being at work but being unproductive), healthcare costs, accidents at work, and early retirement due to occupational problems show that interventions in the work environment are effective and that they reduce these indicators. Companies have faced serious problems with increasing healthcare costs. In Brazil, the claim rate for medical, hospital, and laboratory costs has increased systematically above inflation, and managers in turn have used various tools to seek to control this expense. Lifestyle of employees is therefore of great importance.

The epidemiological profile of the Brazilian population points to a trend towards an ageing population and an increase in the rate of chronic diseases (cardiovascular diseases, diabetes, and cancer) associated with lifestyle. Fries (2002) proposes that longer life expectancy increases morbidity and that there is a reduced quality of life in older individuals. This requires additional effort in attempting to reach morbidity compression. According to this model, the time-span of physical and mental disability can be reduced, by compressing this phase into the shortest possible time, considering that the date of death is fixed. As life expectancy increases, so too will costs related to healthcare, if morbidity and disability are not reduced.

A healthy and motivated workforce makes a big difference to an organization. Well-being is necessary for individuals to complete tasks and contribute to the group and to business. The workplace can provide easy access to initiatives, and when appropriately addressed there is a good chance of successfully influencing individuals to make changes for healthier lifestyle choices. The implementation of quality of life programs is often motivated by a manager's concern over medical costs, absenteeism, accidents at work, absenteeism due to illness, and decreasing productivity.

A quality of life program allows participants to benefit in various ways, such as improving lifestyle, reducing risk factors, increasing their ability to take control of their own health, managing personal and professional stress factors more positively, improving relationships, and increasing motivation for work and for life in general.

There are significant challenges to overcome in ensuring the success of a program. Indeed many are narrow in scope and are often focused on a single risk factor or element (high blood pressure, stress, relationships, healthy-eating, or physical exercise, for example), thereby substantially reducing their potential impact. Others have a limited duration and finish before the desired results can be obtained. In general, programs have low levels of participation and are criticized for carrying out strategies that do not reach the majority of workers or that do not raise awareness of those in at risk groups. Perhaps the propagation of activities restricted to dissemination of information (lectures, leaflets, posters, websites, etc.) is the main reason for poor results that do not produce sustainable behavior changes and the aggravation of risk factors related to chronic diseases.

It is recognized that a significant part of the global burden of disease is associated with behaviors such as over-eating, smoking, excessive alcohol consumption, and physical inactivity. Despite people recognizing that these behaviors can be harmful to health, they do not change their behavior even when there are unwanted consequences. Today, it is still the case that many interventions designed to change such behaviors disseminate information and attempt to encourage people to change. However, these approaches are very often ineffective, and it is known that an important factor in human behavior is the observation of people acting in an automatic way, through environmental stimuli, resulting in actions that are, for the most part, not accompanied by conscious reflection. It is now necessary to look for specific interventions and suggest ways of determining how interventions that aim to encourage automatic processes can increase overall efforts to prevent disease (Marteau, Hollands, & Fletcher, 2012).

Knowledge of behavior change models and application of this knowledge to programs and actions will help to improve results in reducing risk factors and improving quality of life. Within this context, the current challenge is to devise effective and innovative programs and actions that are founded on scientific evidence and that will improve the health and wellbeing of the population.

Various authors have shown that the most feasible alternative for maximizing the results of health-related actions and quality of life is the construction of care networks. These overarching organizations are made up of a collection of health services linked by a single mission, common objectives, and by cooperative and interdependent action. This enables them to offer sustained and comprehensive care to the population at the right time, place, and price, in a humane, safe, and fair manner. They take on responsibilities for participants and give value to this population, be it a company, community, or city (Mendes, 2012).

This vision leads to the achievement of more effective results that are not restricted to localized or one-off actions and that stem from a perspective of innovation that does not end in the search for innovation but aims to introduce and maintain a positive impact on the quality of life and health of the population.

REFERENCES

Ajzein, I., & Fishbein, M. (1980). *Understanding attitudes and predicting social behavior*. Englewood Cliffs, NJ: Prentice-Hall.

Andrade, L. H., Wang, Y. –P., Andreoni, S., Silveira, C. M., Alexandrino-Silva, C., Siu, E. R., . . . Viana, M. C. (2012). Mental disorders in megacities: Findings from the São Paulo Megacity Mental Health Survey, Brazil. *PlosOne, 7*, 1–11.

Bandura, A. (1971). *Social learning theory*. Morristown, NJ: General Learning Press.

Bandura, A. (1977). Self-efficacy: Towards a unifying theory of behavior change. *Psychological Review, 84*, 191–215.

Bandura, A. (1994). Self Efficacy. In V. S. Ramachaudran (Ed.), *Encyclopedia of human behaviour* (pp. 71–81). New York: Academic Press. http://www.des.emory.edu/mfp/BanEncy.html

Chapman, L. (2002). Awareness strategies. In M. P. O'Donnell (Ed.), *Health Promotion in The Workplace* (3rd ed., pp. 163–181). Albany, NY: Delmar Thomson Learning.

Costa, L. C., & Thuler, L. C. S. (2012). Fatores associados ao risco para doenças não transmissíveis em adultos brasileiros—estudo transversal de base populacional. *Revista Brasileira de Estudos da População, 29*(1), 133–145.

Cruz, F. O. (Fiocruz). (2012). A saúde no Brasil em 2030: Diretrizes para a prospecção estratégica do sistema de saúde brasileiro. / *Fundação Oswaldo Cruz [et al.]*. Rio de Janeiro: Fiocruz/Ipea/Ministério da Saúde/Secretaria de Assuntos Estratégicos da Presidência da República, p.323.

Davidson, C. (1989). Employee benefits communication. *Employee Benefits Basics* (Fourth Quarter). Brookfield, WI: International Foundation of Employee Benefit Plans.

Duncan, G. J., Daly, M. C., McDonough, P., & Williams, D. R. (2002). Optimal indicators of socioeconomic status for health research. *American Journal of Public Health, 92*, 1151–1157.

Fishbein, M., & Ajzen, I. (1975). *Belief, attitude, intention, and behavior: An introduction to theory and research*. New York, NY: Addison-Wesley.

Freitas, L. R. S., & Garcia, L. P. (2012). Evolução da prevalência do diabetes e deste associado à hipertensão arterial no Brasil: Análise da Pesquisa Nacional por Amostra de Domicílios, 1998, 2003 e 2008. *Epidemiologia e Serviços de Saúde, 21*(7), 7–19.

Fries, J. (2002). Aging, natural death and the compression of morbidity. *New England Journal of Medicine, 303*, 130–135.

Kerr, J., Eves, F., & Carrol, D. (2005). Six-month observational study of prompted stair climbing. *Preventive Medicine, 33*, 422–427.

Marteau, T. M., Hollands, G. J., & Fletcher, P. C. (2012). Targeting automatic processes changing human behavior to prevent disease: The importance of targeting automatic processes. *Science, 337*, 1492–1494.

Mcadams, D. P., & St. Aubin, E. (1998). Generativity and adult development: How and why we care for the next generation. Washington, DC: American Psychological Association.

Mendes, E. V. (2012). O cuidado das condições crônicas na atenção primária à saúde: o imperativo da consolidação da estratégia da saúde da família. *Brasília: Organização Pan-Americana da Saúde*.

Miller, W. R., & Rollnick, S. (2002). *Motivational interviewing, 2nd edition: Preparing people for change*. New York, NY: Guilford Press.

Organização Mundial da Saúde (OMS). (2002). Relatório sobre a Saúde Mundial, *Reduzindo Riscos e Promovendo uma Vida Saudável*, Genebra.

Prochaska, J. O., Diclemente, C. C., & Norcross, J. C. (1992). In search of how people change: Applications to the addictive behaviors. *American Psychologist, 47*, 1102–1114.

Prochaska, J. O., Norcross, J. C., & Diclemente, C. C. (1995). *Changing for good*. New York, NY: Avon Books.

Rogers, R. W. (1975). A protection motivation theory of fear appeals and attitude change. *Journal of Psychology, 91,* 93–114.

Rogers, R. W. (1983). Cognitive and physiological processes in fear appeals and attitude change: A revised theory of protection motivation. In J. T. Cacioppo & R. E. Petty (Eds.), *Social psychophysiology: A sourcebook* (pp. 153–176). New York, NY: Guilford Press.

Rosenstock, I. (1974). The HBM and preventive health behavior. *Health Education Monographs, 2,* 354–386.

Schwarzer, R. (1992). *Self-efficacy: Thought control of action.* Washington, DC: Hemisphere Publishing Corp.

Schwarzer, R. (2001). Social-cognitive factors in changing health-related behavior. *Current Directions in Psychological Science, 10,* 47–51.

Sheeran, P. (2002). Intention-behavior relations: a conceptual and empirical review. *European Review of Social Psychology, 12*(1), 1–36.

Williams, D. R. (2002). Racial/ethnic variations in women's health: The social embeddedness of health. *Public Health Matters, 92*(4), 588–597.

CHAPTER 11

QUALITY OF LIFE
AND SELF-CARE
IN CIVIL SERVANTS

Prevention and Intervention

Dulce Helena C. Hatzenberger
and Mary Sandra Carlotto

ABSTRACT

This is an observational study with a cross-sectional analytical design aimed at assessing the quality of life and its relationship with self-care in a representative sample of 535 state civil servants in the city of Porto Alegre, Rio Grande do Sul State, Brazil. An instrument designed to collect socio-demographic and labor-related variables was used, the *World Health Organization Quality of Life*, brief version (WHOQOL-bref), to assess quality of life, and the health and lifestyle questionnaire, based on the *Appraisal of Self-Care Agency Scale* (ASA) for the assessment of self-care. Results were analyzed using Student's t-test, showing that workers who perform self-care actions without actually being ill or without being at risk of becoming ill have a better quality of life in all assessed domains. Results show actions designed to encourage adequate health habits, physical, and leisure activities and provide greater access to health related information.

Improving Emploee Health and Well-Being, pages 171–185
Copyright © 2014 by Information Age Publishing

INTRODUCTION

Most people today try to achieve the ideal of a healthy life, being increasingly concerned with their own health (Mendonça & Menandro, 2010) and, therefore, with their quality of life (QoL). The increasing concern with QoL issues comes with a greater awareness that goes beyond simply controlling symptoms, decreasing mortality, or extending life expectancy (Almeida & Gutierrez, 2010).

QoL is a multidisciplinary field, including not only various sciences and popular knowledge, but also concepts that permeate people's lives as whole. In this regard, it relates to several elements of people's day-to-day activities, from subjective perceptions and expectations towards life to more deterministic issues such as clinical action taken when facing diseases and illnesses (Almeida, Gutierrez & Marques, 2012).

The World Health Organization (WHO) defines health as a state of complete physical, mental, and social well-being and not merely the absence of disease or infirmity. This state of well-being is found when individuals use their own skills, are able to cope with the ordinary stressors of life, are able to produce and enjoy their work, and contribute to their community. The concept of health is related to the concept of well-being people have at the society level and also to the personal interpretation of every individual regarding his or her physical and mental state. This concept encompasses two dimensions: a subjective dimension and an objective or social dimension (Férnandez & Fórnes, 1991). This extended concept requires the use of subjective instruments that include self-perception and self-assessment of all factors involved in examining well-being (Bowling, 2005). Significant progress has been made over the years in the field that assesses the relationship between health and QoL as a formal discipline, with theoretical frameworks, consistent methods, and applicability (Terwee, Dekker, Wiersinga, Prummel & Bossuyt, 2003).

The Ottawa Charter, a document of intentions designed to contribute to health policies in all countries in an equal and universal fashion, presented at the First International Conference on Health Promotion highlighted the role of organizations, systems, and communities in valuing individual behaviors and skills, such as self-care and generating possibilities and opportunities to promote health and the development of different groups and populations. In this regard, it shows that it is important to educate the community in order to improve their QoL and health, emphasizing that health promotion should not be limited to health care but rather should be everyone's responsibility (WHO, 1986).

According to the WHO (1995), QoL is the perception individuals have of their position in life, in the context of the culture and value systems under which they live, and of their objectives, expectations, standards, and concerns. The concept highlights subjectivity by considering perception individuals have of their health status and non-medical aspects of their life context. Therefore, according to a current perspective, QoL should be assessed by the individual him/herself (Seidl & Zannon, 2004).

QoL is the perception individuals have of their position in the context of the culture and value systems under which they live and of their objectives, expectations, standards, and concerns, including the ethical and political dimension (Almeida & Gutierrez, 2010). It is a dynamic state that is subjectively perceived; at the institutional level it is the framework that allows social and individual foundations to be laid that will help individuals search for their subjective ways of performing self-care (Tozetti et al., 2010). Self-care refers to the knowledge, skills, and experiences people must get to care for themselves, being also influenced by basic conditioning factors, being an important tool to help individuals start and perform activities in their own benefit with the purpose of keeping life, health, and QoL (Orem, 2001).

Quality of working life (QoWL) encompasses improving the quality of health conditions at the workplace, trying to identify issues with the active participation of the individuals engaged in the work process in order to redesign it in a broad process of negotiation (Laurell & Noriega, 1989). Therefore, it assumes changing habits and routines, in other words, changing the organizational culture itself and making progress in human development policies (Régis Filho & Lopes, 2001).

In order to approach this issue today, we must adopt a pluralistic conception regarding work, since individuals operate in a broad social context. Likewise, the social representation of the activity performed impacts their lives and well-being, which may result in varying levels of burnout among different workers. Therefore, QoWL encompasses both objective and subjective aspects of work as a result of the interpretation made by every individual (Paiva & Avelar, 2011). Considering this, the actions taken by companies and workers to achieve bio-psychosocial integration and the control of factors related to occupational risk are related to QoWL management. However, we should point out that when dealing with QoL, there is a thin line between work life issues and issues related to family and community life, because in every case the purpose is to ensure and promote people's overall well-being (Oliveira & Limongi-França, 2005).

The experiences at the workplace impact workers' daily life, their professional, family and social context, thus interfering with their QoL. Promoting QoL goes beyond promoting health, because QoL is understood as all environmental, socio-economic, educational, psychosocial, and political conditions that are required for people to live well, and the experiences workers have in their workplace impact their day-to-day lives (Silveira & Monteiro, 2010). At the organizational level, workers today are challenged every day to constantly interact with others, achieve goals, and follow the values advocated by their supervisors, even if they disagree with everything that is imposed on them (Belo & Moraes, 2011).

We find three key concepts in the frameworks used to define QoWL: humanization of work, participation in management decisions, and well-being (Ferreira, Alves, & Tostes, 2009). Fernandes (1996) highlights its dynamic and contingent nature that includes the organization's physical, psychosocial, and technological factors, since they all affect the organizational culture and climate, reflecting on workers' well-being and on the productivity of organizations. Today, new aspects have been included, and its definition and focus of interest are being extended. QoWL is concerned with new technologies and their impact on the health, environment, salaries, incentives, and profit-sharing schemes of the organizations, on the creativity, autonomy, degree of control, and power workers have on the work process (Laurell & Noriega, 1989).

Due to the complexity of the subject, attention should be given to the inadequate use of the term QoWL, sometimes used to refer exclusively to programs related to marketing policies or programs designed to improve the extrinsic conditions of the work. Even though these efforts are essential for the workers' well-being, they are not enough because they neglect responsibility sharing, autonomy, and other factors that are necessary for a good QoL of those who work (Sant'anna, Kilimnik, & Moraes, 2011).

Scientific production on QoL in Brazil is relatively recent and has been growing each year, not being restricted to a given social group. However, for the most part studies have been conducted with adults who are selected for already being affected by some type of condition, thus reflecting the interest to know how these conditions are compromising the life of individuals, focusing the analysis on health-related QoL. This type of research design has been the target of criticism because although the health status is rather important for people's lives, not every aspect of human life is related to medical or health issues (Almeida & Gutierrez, 2010). Therefore, it is also important to expand research to assumedly "healthy" populations, in other words, those without any previous conditions that characterize them as a study group. An example of this is the study on QoWL conducted with judges from the Brazilian state of Minas Gerais that highlights a unique feature in addition to the need to constantly interact with others and follow the values of the organization: their work involves decisions on rights and duties, which are not always easy to distinguish, and construal of laws, which often times are not explicit. Additionally, with the enactment of the new Brazilian Constitution in 1988, the doors of the judiciary were opened to a large number of citizens who were eager to guarantee their rights, but the judiciary did not have the adequate material or human resources in place to keep up with the growing demand (Belo & Moraes, 2011). Therefore, although the population in this study is not the same as in the above mentioned study, we can consider that there are similarities between them if we think that any activity in a state court of justice involves responsibilities with deadlines and actions that will ensure that decisions that impact people's lives are actually enforced, which can have an impact on the QoWL of those working in the judiciary. As such, research that analyzes socio-professional categories can serve as a basis for supra-organizational efforts to promote QoWL.

Although the public sector does not aim at profit, its management model is concerned with achieving targets and results, demanding from their organizations and agencies more regular and more careful performance appraisals and the commitment of healthy and productive workers (Nogueira & Frota, 2011).

Considering the close relationship between QoL and self-care and the importance of this relationship for QoWL, this observational study with a cross-sectional analytical design aimed at looking at QoL and its relationship with self-care in civil servants working at the judiciary of the Brazilian state of Rio Grande do Sul.

METHOD

Study Population and Target Population

The study population comprised 8,185 workers who were part of the headcount in 2011 who worked in 164 cities in the State of Rio Grande do Sul, out of which 536 workers were interviewed. The sample was calculated considering a confidence interval of 95%, a margin of error of 5% to 10% for possible losses. The calculation resulted in a sample of 627 subjects, with a response rate of 85.3%, corresponding to 535 workers. The majority of the sample was female (65.4%), age group from 31 to 50 years (70.9%), had children (68.8%), was in a marital relationship (71.2%), and had a college degree (80%).

Instruments

1. The self-administered socio-demographic questionnaire with socio-demographic (gender, age, marital status, marital relationship, children, education) and labor-related questions (time at the job, job location).
2. *World Health Organization Quality of Life*, brief version (WHOQOL-bref). This instrument is used to assess QoL in adults. The instrument is made of 26 items, out of which 24 are distributed in four different domains: physical health, psychological health, social

relationships, and environment. Every domain is represented by facets, and their questions are framed in a Likert-type of scale, with an intensity scale (never–always) and assessment (very dissatisfied–very satisfied; very poor–very good) (Fleck et al., 2000).

3. Health and lifestyle questionnaire based on the *Appraisal of Self-Care Agency Scale* (ASA; Evers, 1989), an instrument used to assess self-care in adult patients with varying health status, with a focus on overall and development requirements. The answer scale is dichotomous (yes/no).

Procedures

Data collection was performed using an online assessment made available in the organization's intranet. The enrolled workers got an individual code/password to access the system for a period of one week.

Data were entered into the database and later analyzed using SPSS—Statistical Package for Social Sciences (version 17.0). Descriptive analyses were first made in order to assess in the database the distribution of the items, missing cases, identification of outliers, and typing errors. Later, a descriptive analysis was used to calculate averages, standard deviations, frequency, and percentage of answers. Finally, an inferential analysis was made using Student's t-test complemented by Cohen's d to calculate the effect size.

RESULTS

QoL results show that the dimension with the highest average was Social QoL, and the one with the lowest average was Environmental QoL, as shown in Figure 11.1.

Regarding issues involving self-care, we can see that the most commonly found behavior was seeking information on health problems (84.9%), followed by the difficulty to take care of oneself (71.1%), and try to keep healthy, changing one's routine if necessary (70.1%).

The analysis of the association between self-care and QoL shows that civil servants who change their routine to stay healthy, sleep enough to feel rested, eat properly to preserve their health, find time to take care of themselves in their daily lives, have some kind of hobby, and do some physical activity have a better QoL in all four domains. Workers who regularly undergo health checks and search for information for their health problems have a better psychological, social, and environmental QoL. Workers who are not undergoing medical or psychological treatment have better physical and

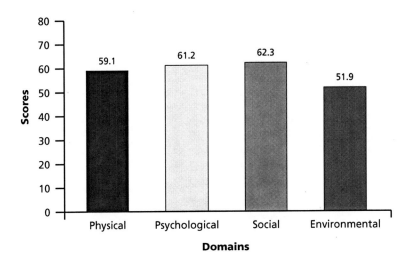

Figure 11.1 Distribution of the group according to the quality of life.

TABLE 11.1 Frequency and Percentage of the Self-Care Items

	Yes		No	
Items	n	%	n	%
1. Trying to keep healthy	376	70.1	160	29.9
2. Having enough sleep to feel rested	225	42.0	311	58.0
3. Eating properly	370	69.0	166	31.0
4. Finding time to take care of oneself	155	28.9	381	71.1
5. Seeking information on health problems	455	84.9	81	15.1
6. Undergoing regular health checks	359	67.0	177	33.0
7. Receiving some medical treatment	246	46.2	287	53.8
8. Being on some type of medication	258	48.2	277	51.8
9. Receiving some psychological/psychiatric treatment	108	20.2	427	79.8
10. Doing some physical activity	263	49.1	273	50.9
11. Having a leisure activity/hobby	221	41.4	313	58.6

psychological QoL, and those who are not on any type of medication have better physical, psychological, and social QoL (Table 11.2).

DISCUSSION

This study, which aimed at assessing QoL and its relationship to self-care in civil servants who work at the judiciary, showed that the domain with

TABLE 11.2 Association between QoL and Self-Care

QV	AC	n	M	DP	t	p	d
1. Trying to keep healthy							
Physical QoL	yes	375	62.49	18.04	6.524	0.001*	0.617
	no	160	51.44	17.72			
Psychological QoL	yes	373	64.36	15.23	7.170	0.001*	0.673
	no	159	53.87	15.92			
Social QoL	yes	375	65.93	18.47	6.520	0.001*	0.604
	no	159	54.17	20.41			
Environment QoL	yes	376	54.24	14.86	5.436	0.001*	0.512
	no	159	46.57	15.06			
2. Having enough sleep to feel rested							
Physical QoL	yes	224	68.71	15.73	11.133	0.001*	0.984
	no	311	52.32	17.52			
Psychological QoL	yes	223	67.92	13.05	8.998	0.001*	0.775
	no	309	56.39	16.47			
Social QoL	yes	224	68.73	16.86	6.696	0.001*	0.577
	no	310	57.88	20.53			
Environment QoL	yes	225	57.94	13.57	8.138	0.001*	0.718
	no	310	47.63	15.07			
3. Eating properly to keep one's health							
Physical QoL	yes	369	62.64	18.33	6.651	0.001*	0.630
	no	166	51.50	16.97			
Psychological QoL	yes	367	64.45	14.90	7.193	0.001*	0.659
	no	165	54.05	16.58			
Social QoL	yes	368	66.17	18.22	6.450	0.001*	0.617
	no	166	54.14	20.68			
Environment QoL	yes	370	55.34	14.22	8.093	0.001*	0.749
	no	165	44.38	15.01			
4. Finding time to take care of oneself							
Physical QoL	yes	154	70.79	16.15	9.967	0.001*	0.968
	no	381	54.49	17.49			
Psychological QoL	yes	153	70.98	11.16	11.154	0.001*	0.984
	no	379	57.29	16.20			
Social QoL	yes	155	72.15	15.33	8.532	0.001*	0.767
	no	379	58.45	20.06			
Environment QoL	yes	155	61.23	12.67	10.298	0.001*	0.950
	no	380	48.19	14.69			
5. Having a physical activity							
Physical QoL	yes	263	62.84	18.44	4.547	0.001*	0.392
	no	272	55.65	18.15			

(continued)

TABLE 11.2 Association between QoL and Self-Care (continued)

QV	AC	n	M	DP	t	p	d
Psychological QoL	yes	259	64.75	14.82	5.005	0.001*	0.435
	no	273	57.88	16.69			
Social QoL	yes	262	66.05	17.99	4.219	0.001*	0.364
	no	272	58.95	20.84			
Environment QoL	yes	263	54.72	14.12	4.169	0.001*	0.360
	no	272	49.29	15.97			
6. Having a leisure activity/hobby							
Physical QoL	yes	220	65.45	17.14	6.794	0.001*	0.601
	no	313	54.74	18.44			
Psychological QoL	yes	218	67.39	13.55	8.029	0.001*	0.696
	no	312	56.88	16.48			
Social QoL	yes	221	68.02	17.70	5.633	0.001*	0.501
	no	311	58.47	20.33			
Environment QoL	yes	221	57.32	14.03	7.118	0.001*	0.630
	no	312	48.13	15.11			
7. Undergoing regular health checks							
Physical QoL	yes	358	59.67	18.63	0.857	0.392	0.078
	no	177	58.20	18.63			
Psychological QoL	yes	357	62.27	16.31	2.131	0.034*	0.198
	no	175	59.10	15.68			
Social QoL	yes	358	63.99	19.04	2.611	0.009*	0.236
	no	176	59.26	20.96			
Environment QoL	yes	358	53.34	15.25	2.973	0.003*	0.273
	no	177	49.18	15.12			
8. Receiving some medical treatment							
Physical QoL	yes	246	53.08	17.96	−7.281	0.001*	0.632
	no	286	64.35	17.66			
Psychological QoL	yes	244	58.06	16.86	−4.231	0.001*	0.370
	no	285	63.98	15.02			
Social QoL	yes	245	61.21	19.46	−1.361	0.174	0,118
	no	286	63.55	20.03			
Environment QoL	yes	245	50.79	15.43	−1.719	0.086	0,149
	no	287	53.06	15.03			
9. Being on some type of medication							
Physical QoL	yes	258	54.48	17.45	−5.800	0.001*	0.502
	no	276	63.57	18.69			
Psychological QoL	yes	256	58.66	16.29	−3.568	0.001	0.309
	no	275	63.61	15.71			
Social QoL	yes	257	60.36	19.05	−2.346	0.019*	0.203
	no	276	64.37	20.35			

(continued)

TABLE 11.2   Association between QoL and Self-Care (continued)

QV	AC	n	M	DP	t	p	d
Environment QoL	yes	257	51.10	15.21	−1.246	0.213	0.107
	no	277	52.75	15.43			
10. Undergoing some psychological treatment							
Physical QoL	yes	108	52.66	17.98	−4.143	0.001*	0.450
	no	426	60.86	18.46			
Psychological QoL	yes	108	56.17	15.56	−3.658	0.001*	0.398
	no	423	62.47	16.07			
Social QoL	yes	108	59.22	19.01	−1.894	0.059	0.206
	no	425	63.25	19.95			
Environment QoL	yes	108	50.71	15.45	−0.963	0.336	0.103
	no	426	52.30	15.30			
11. Searching for health-related information							
Physical QoL	yes	454	59.33	18.76	0.427	0.670	0.052
	no	81	58.37	17.96			
Psychological QoL	yes	451	61.98	16.24	2.559	0.011*	0.316
	no	81	57.02	15.13			
Social QoL	yes	454	64.37	18.98	5.550	0.001*	0.650
	no	80	51.41	20.84			
Environment QoL	yes	454	53.18	15.09	4.428	0.001*	0.536
	no	81	45.14	14.88			

* $p < 0.05$

the highest average was the social domain, and the one with the lowest average was the environment domain. A similar result was found in a study conducted with workers by Dávila, Casagrande, and Pereira (2011). The work setting comprises interpersonal, internal, and external relationships, which often translate into out of work relationships. The environment domain showed the greatest impact because workers may not have the time available for leisure and to be with their families, in addition to being more affected by things like traffic, transportation, pollution, and noise.

Regarding self-care, seeking information on health problems was the most commonly found behavior in this group (84.9%). This result could be related to the sample profile in terms of age and the high educational level of the civil servants. Education has been linked to a greater ability to take care of oneself, according to Baquedano, Santos, Teixeira, Martins, and Zanetti (2010). Additionally, a significant number of civil servants (71.1%) had difficulties finding time to take care of themselves, which might be related to the characteristics of the sample because the majority was married and had children, which involves the performance of social roles that require care and attention to others. The recent changes in families and the labor market have worsened the capacity families have to deal with the conflicting requirements of work and family (Sorj, Fontes, & Machado, 2007). According to Dickson, Howe, Deal, and McCarthy (2012), the work-life balance demands can impact self-care demands. This results in greater investment in terms of time and energy to manage this conflict, thus making individual needs and care be placed at a second level, thus remaining, in practice, unattended.

The analysis of the association between self-care and QoL showed that those who perform actions designed to change their routine in order to stay healthy, sleep enough to feel rested, eat properly to preserve their health, find some time to take care of themselves in their day-to-day, have a hobby, and practice physical activities have a better QoL in all four domains. Therefore, we could think that workers who perform self-care actions in order not to get ill have a better QoL. A study conducted by Myint et al. (2011) with a population considered healthy found that changes in habits and lifestyle (eating habits, alcohol and tobacco use, and physical activity) were linked to better health outcomes. Health behaviors are directly connected to health expectation and not only to life expectancy. Although QoL is impacted by the needs to find a livelihood, public policies, and living conditions, which are all political-organizational factors determined by society, individual practices (lifestyle) have a greater direct influence when they are made possible by socio-economic factors and the way and conditions in which people live (Almeida, Gutierrez, & Marques, 2012).

When self-care actions are taken when some risk or illness is already involved, connections take place only in some domains. Workers who undergo regular health checks and search for information on their health problems have a better psychological, social, and environmental QoL. This outcome can be related to the fact that the participant has a health issue, realizing that he has worse QoL, and thus when he takes actions to improve his condition, the result is a better outcome in other QoL domains.

Workers who are undergoing medical or psychological treatment have a worse physical and psychological QoL, and those who are on medications have worse physical, psychological, and social QoL. A study carried out by Dickson, Howe, Deal, and McCarthy (2012) found that subjects who worked and were on some type of medication had less self-care behaviors, claiming that they had to meet their job demands and had less time to engage in self-care. The combination of high demands and low control over their work makes it difficult for workers who already have some type of condition to comply with their treatment and healthcare, thus resulting in lower QoL scores. Patients who engage in self-care actions have fewer symptoms and better physical performance and overall well-being (Finch & Sneed, 2003).

CONCLUSION

Contemporary society defines and establishes life standards to be followed through processes of renewal and cultural transmission that become part of people's perception and expectations to life. The concern with QoL is an issue that affects not only the individual, but society as whole, because it is linked to conditions of survival and comfort of the subjects who are part of it. Thus, it is a social issue that includes actions to be taken at different levels, from the state to the adoption of healthy practices by individuals (Almeida, Gutierrez, & Marques, 2012).

QoL is the result of the relationship between the various facets of our daily life that are influenced by external factors. The identification of the factors that compromise QoL can help to develop measures that contribute to improve it. However, these factors are often hard to identify due to their complexity and interdependence, particularly when groups of workers with different characteristics are followed (Santos, Scandelari, Carvalho, Vaz, & Santos, 2009).

Although the study used the self-care construct to explain QoL, it should be stressed that this is not an individual responsibility. Actually, considering that the study looked at successful self-care strategies, it has the potential to provide information to organization-wide actions that extend these results to other workers. Placing the responsibility only on the individual would mean to adopt a reductionist view following the capitalist logic, disregarding the interaction that is also established from the conditions in which the work is carried out.

According to Gonçalves (2004), this logic, which is characterized by democratism in individual actions, promotes the idea that health and QoL can improve directly with the adoption of healthy lifestyles, and this becomes a strategy for social control. This is the case because not always are the conditions that enable individuals to adopt healthy habits in place. The idea is spread that in order to improve life, some practices should be followed, as if this depended solely on an individual's will, even in work settings that discourage these practices or render them unfeasible, either due to overload or pressure to perform tasks. Rendering people responsible for their own QoL is based on the assumption of "blaming the victim," a way of not rendering authorities accountable for the actions that provide actual improvements in life conditions. Things like the level of control over tasks performed by workers and a match between the management leadership style and the expectations of the team members, for example, could be analyzed in organizational settings in order to improve objective conditions that favor a better QoL.

Therefore, it is key that managers and organizations develop actions designed to identify the factors that impact QoL so that healthy practices can be jointly implemented inside and outside the organizations by managers and workers.

REFERENCES

Almeida, M. A. B., & Gutierrez, G. L. (2010). Qualidade de vida: Discussões contemporâneas In R. Vilarta, G. L. Gutierrez, & M. I. Monteiro (Orgs.), *Qualidade de vida: evolução dos conceitos e práticas no século XX* (pp.151–160). Campinas: Ipes.

Almeida, M. A. B., Gutierrez, G. L., & Marques, R. (2012). Qualidade de vida: Definição, conceitos e interfaces com outras áreas de pesquisa. São Paulo: Escola de Artes, Ciências e Humanidades—EACH/USP.

Baquedano, I. R., Santos, M. A., Teixeira, C. R. S., Martins, T. A., & Zanetti, M. L. (2010). Fatores relacionados ao autocuidado de pessoas com diabetes mellitus atendidas em Serviço de Urgência no México. *Revista da Escola de Enfermagem da USP, 44*(4), 1017–1023. doi: 10.1590/S0080-62342010000400023

Belo, I. F., & Moraes, L. F. R. (2011). Qualidade de vida no trabalho de magistrados. In A. S. Sant'anna & Z. M. Kilimnik (Orgs.), *Qualidade de vida no trabalho: Abordagens e fundamentos* (pp. 31–43). Rio de Janeiro: Elsevier.

Bowling, A. (2005). Mode of questionnaire administration can have serious effects on data quality. *Journal of Public Health, 27*(3), 281–291. doi:10.1093/pubmed/fdi031

Dávila, M. H. X., Casagrande, R. J. T., & Pereira, V. C. G. (2011). Qualidade de vida do trabalhador de uma instituição de ensino. *Cadernos da Escola de Saúde, 4*(1), 110–126.

Dickson, V. V., Howe, A., Deal, J., & Mccarthy, M. M. (2012). The relationship of work, self-care, and quality of life in a sample of older working adults with cardiovascular disease. *Heart & Lung: The Journal of Acute and Critical, 41*(1), 5–14. doi: 10.1016/j.hrtlng.2011.09.012

Evers, G. C. M. (1989). *Appraisal of self-care agency: ASA-scale.* Maastricht: Van Corcum.

Fernandes, E. C. (1996). *Qualidade de vida no trabalho: Como medir para melhorar* (5th ed.). Salvador: Casa da Qualidade.

Fernández, B. C., & Fórnez, J. V. (1991). *Educación y salud.* Palma: Universitat de lês IllesBalears.

Ferreira, M., Alves, L., & Tostes, N. (2009). Gestão de qualidade de vida no trabalho no serviço público federal: O descompasso entre problemas e práticas gerenciais. *Psicologia: Teoria e Pesquisa, 25*(3), 319–327. doi: 10.1590/S0102-37722009000300005

Finch, N., & Sneed, N. (2003). Quality of life when living with heart failure. *Critical Care Nursing Clinics of North America, 15*, 511–517. doi: 10.1016/S0899-5885(02)00093-X

Fleck, M. P. A., Louzada, S., Xavier, M., Chachamovich, M. E., Vieira, G., Santos, L., & Pinzon, V. (2000). Aplicação da versão em português do instrumento abreviado de avaliação da qualidade de vida "WHOQOL-bref." *Revista de Saúde Pública, 34*(2), 178–183. doi: 10.1590/S0034-89102000000200012

Gonçalves, A. (2004). Em busca do diálogo do controle social sobre o estilo de vida. In R. Vilarta (Org.), *Qualidade de vida e políticas públicas: Saúde, lazer e atividade física* (pp. 17–26). Campinas, IPES.

Laurell, A. C., & Noriega, M. (1989). *Processo de produção e saúde.* São Paulo: Hucitec.

Mendonça, V. S., & Menandro, M. C. S. (2010). O cuidado com a própria saúde: Representações e práticas de futuros profissionais da saúde. *Revista Electrónica de Psicología Política, 8*(22), 116–127.

Myint, P. K., Smith, R. D., Luben, R. N., Surtees, P. G., Wainwright, N. W. J., Wareham, N. J., & Khaw, K.-T. (2011). Lifestyle behaviours and quality-adjusted life years in middle and older age. *Age Ageing, 40*(5), 589–595. doi: 10.1093/ageing/afr058

Nogueira, C. V., & Frota, F. H. S. (2011). Qualidade de vida no trabalho: Percepções sobre sua importância como Política de Valorização no Serviço Público. *Revista Conhecer: Debate Entre o Público e o Privado, Fortaleza, 1*(3), 31–58.

Oliveira, P. M., & Limongi-Franca, A. C. (2005). Avaliação da gestão de programas de qualidade de vida no trabalho. *RAE, 4*(1). Retrieved on December 1, 2012 from http://www.scielo.br/scielo.php?script=sci_arttext&pid=S1676-56482005000100005&lng=en&nrm=iso doi: 10.1590/S1676-56482005000100005

Orem, D. E. (2001). *Nursing concepts of practice* (6th ed.). Boston, MA: Mosby.

Paiva, K. C. M., & Avelar, V. L. L. M. (2011). Qualidade de vida e estresse ocupacional em central de regulação médica de serviço de atendimento móvel de urgência In A. S. Sant'anna & Z. M. Kilimnik (Orgs.), *Qualidade de vida no trabalho: Abordagens e fundamentos* (pp. 222–258). Rio de Janeiro: Elsevier.

Régis Filho, G. I., & Lopes, M. C. (2001). Qualidade de vida no trabalho: A empresa holística e a ecologia empresarial. *Revista de Administração, 36*(3), 95–99.

Sant'anna, A. S., Kilimnik, Z. M., & Moraes, L. F. R. (2011). Antecedentes, origens e evolução do movimento em torno da qualidade de vida no trabalho In A. S. Sant'anna & Z. M. Kilimnik (Orgs.), *Qualidade de vida no trabalho: Abordagens e fundamentos* (pp. 3–30). Rio de Janeiro: Elsevier.

Santos, C. B., Scandelari, L., Carvalho, D. R., Vaz, M. S. M. G., & Santos, M. G. P. (2009). Aquisição de conhecimento implícito de indicadores de qualidade de vida. *Revista Brasileira de Qualidade de Vida, 1*(1), 35–37. doi: 10.3895/S2175-08582009000100004

Seidl, F. M. E., & Zannon C. L. M. C. (2004). Qualidade de vida e saúde, aspectos conceituais e metodológicos. *Caderno de Saúde Pública, 20*(2), 580–588. doi: 10.1590/S0102-311X2004000200027

Silveira, V. A., & Monteiro, M. I. (2010). Qualidade de vida de trabalhadores de enfermagem de uma unidade de terapia intensiva. In R. Vilarta, G. L. Gutierrez, & M. I. Monteiro (Orgs.), *Qualidade de vida: evolução dos conceitos e práticas no século XX* (pp. 161–168). Campinas: Ipes.

Sorj, B., Fontes, A., & Machado, D. C. (2007). Políticas e práticas de conciliação entre família e trabalho no Brasil. *Cadernos de Pesquisa, 37*(132), 573–594. doi: 10.1590/S0100-15742007000300004

Terwee, C. B., Dekker, F. W., Wiersinga, W. M., Prummel, M. F., & Bossuyt, P. M. (2003). On assessing responsiveness of health-related quality of life instruments: Guidelines for instrument evaluation. *Quality of Life Research, 12*(4), 349–362. doi: 10.1023/A:1023499322593

Tozetti, E. D., Rocha, M. do R. A., Barros, A. de S., Paraizo, C. R., Aquino, M. das G. F., Carvalho, T. H. P. F. de, & Coentro, V. (2010). Pesquisa das condições de saúde do trabalhador da Universidade Estadual de Campinas como revelação de mecanismos de avaliação para atuação sistêmica em qualidade de vida institucional. In R. Vilarta, G. L. Gutierrez, & M. I. Monteiro (Orgs.), *Qualidade de vida: evolução dos conceitos e práticas no século XX* (pp. 65–72). Campinas: Ipes.

World Health Organization. (1986). Carta de Ottawa. In Ministério da Saúde/Fiocruz, *Promoção da Saúde: Cartas de Ottawa, Adelaide, Sundsvall e Santa Fé de Bogotá* (pp. 11–18). Brasília: Ministério da Saúde/IEC.

World Health Organization. (1995). The World Health Organization quality of life assessment (WHOQOL): Position paper from the World Health Organization. *Social Science and Medicine, 10,* 1403–1409.

CHAPTER 12

JOB STRESS PREVENTION

An Overview of Approaches

Joseph J. Hurrell, Jr.
and Steven L. Sauter[1]

ABSTRACT

There is keen interest in the topic of job stress prevention among researchers, practitioners, organizations, and governments. However, the research literature on the topic is enormously complex. This complexity serves as an impediment to understanding and applying knowledge gained from studies on the topic. In this chapter we provide a framework for understanding the job stress prevention literature and an overview of the growing body of research in the arena. We describe prevention studies and efforts that have focused on individual workers, jobs, organizations, and national and international populations. Where possible, we provide information about the efficacy of approaches and tools to aid both researchers and practitioners in developing job stress prevention studies and applied job stress prevention efforts. We conclude the chapter by drawing attention to a new, comprehensive prevention approach to occupational health and safety problems that we believe holds promise for job stress prevention.

Improving Emploee Health and Well-Being, pages 187–206
Copyright © 2014 by Information Age Publishing

Over the past 50 years, knowledge of the causes of work-related illnesses and injuries has grown dramatically. Yet our understanding of how to best utilize this knowledge for prevention and intervention purposes remains stubbornly limited. This situation is especially alarming given not only the enormous human toll of work-related illnesses and injuries but their massive drain on national economies. As acknowledged nearly 40 years ago in a prescient report commissioned by the U.S Secretary of Health Education and Welfare entitled *Work in America* (1973), both workers and society bear the cost of health problems that have their origins in the workplace, and these costs could be greatly reduced by preventative measures. Indeed, work remains a relatively unutilized institutional tool that could be used to improve the health of workers and thereby help reduce the staggering and ever escalating costs of health care. In addition, workplace investments in worker health (including stress prevention efforts) have the potential to enhance productivity and increase organizational profitability (Goetzel & Ozminkowski, 2008).

As witnessed by a proliferation of works examining the topic of job stress prevention (see, e.g., Biron, Karanika-Murray, & Cooper, 2012; Hurrell, 2005; LaMontagne, Keegle, Louie, Ostry, Landsbergis, 2007; Sauter & Murphy, 2004; Semmer, 2006), interest in the topic is keen. The purpose of this chapter is to provide a framework for understanding this literature and an overview of the growing body of research on the topic. We will describe the nature of different approaches and, where available, provide information on their prevalence and efficacy and tools to aid in their application.

PREVENTION CLASSIFICATION

A major challenge to understanding and drawing meaningful conclusions from the job stress prevention literature involves the diverse, and at times confusing, terminology found in the literature (Hurrell, 2005) and the resulting difficulty of being able to describe and discreetly classify prevention efforts. Indeed, the term "prevention" itself has different meanings for different people and different meanings in different fields of health. Historically, reviews of the job stress prevention literature have relied heavily upon adaptations of a long standing public health prevention classification system (see Commission on Chronic Illness, 1957) to characterize efforts in the area. In this system, prevention is viewed as an effort aimed at reducing the likelihood of an illness (or, more generally, something harmful) from occurring or minimizing its effects. Three "levels" are recognized that reflect *when* the prevention efforts occur with respect to the degree (or "stage") of illness progression: primary prevention, secondary prevention, and tertiary prevention. The goal of primary prevention (which occurs when both illness and their risk factors are absent) is preventing the occurrence of illness. The goal of secondary prevention (which occurs when risk factors are present, and early stage illness may be evident) is to avert the occurrence of frank illness by eliminating the risk factors. Tertiary prevention (which occurs when both illness and their risk factors are present) is focused on minimizing the impact of existing illnesses (i.e., preventing the progression of the illness, decreasing the amount of disability, and restoring function) and restoring health and wellness. Considerable confusion results when this model is utilized in the job stress prevention arena where stress-related illnesses are not widely considered as principal targets of intervention, the concept of job stress can lack specificity, and the etiological relationship between risk factors and particular stress-related illnesses are unclear.

As job stress prevention can be targeted to individuals, job incumbents, departments, organizations, industries, and the institution of work as a whole, terminology used in the literature to describe the focus of intervention efforts (and often described in the literature in terms of intervention "levels"), or *where* it occurs, further confounds job stress prevention approach classification and understanding. Finally, prevention efforts, regardless of where they occur, are often complex and multifaceted and difficult to succinctly and accurately classify. While various taxonomies for classifying job stress prevention efforts can be found in the literature (e.g., Parkes & Sparkes, 1998; Sauter & Murphy, 2004), in the hope of minimizing confusion, we will focus our discussion using the categories described in Table 12.1. The reader should recognize at the outset that not all job stress prevention efforts that occur in workplaces fit uniquely in these categories and that some types of prevention may occur at multiple levels. Subsumed in this table is a model of job stress in which job stressors (aversive job conditions) serve as risk factors for job stress (psychological and physiological responses to adverse job conditions), and stress-related illnesses (such as

TABLE 12.1 Types of Workplace Job Stress Prevention Efforts

Focus (or Level) of Prevention Effort (Where)	Occurrence of Prevention Effort Relative to Problem Onset (When)		
	Job Stressors, Job Stress, and Illness Absent	Job Stressors and/or Job Stress Present, Illness Absent	Job Stressors, Job Stress, and Illness Present
Individual	Health Promotion	Stress Management	Treatment
Job	Job Design	Job Redesign and Training	Job Redesign
Organization	Culture and Leadership	Work-Life Balance Enhancement	Accommodation
Supra-Organization	Prevention Regulation	Prevention Standards	Disability

psychological disorders and cardiovascular disease) are thought to be consequences of prolonged experience of job stress.

INDIVIDUAL LEVEL PREVENTION

Health Promotion

Worksite health promotion (WHP) is generally aimed at enhancing individual strengths in order to reduce the risk of later problematic health outcomes and, in this sense, tends to be seen as situated toward the primary prevention end of the prevention spectrum. WHP activities involve promoting healthy lifestyles (e.g., exercise, healthy eating, and smoking cessation) by means of worker health education and counseling or coaching, and through workplace ecological interventions such as the provision of fitness programs, cafeterias that foster healthy eating, and changes in the built environment to encourage exercise. Notably, however, the content and boundaries of WHP are not well demarcated. Screening for the early detection of disease (e.g., breast cancer and hypertension) is a nearly ubiquitous element of WHP, and employee assistance, stress management, and disease management programs are sometimes included within the framework of WHP (Linnan et al., 2008). In this regard, WHP interventions can cover the range of primary, secondary and tertiary prevention and, in many respects, are similar to what are called workplace "wellness" programs.

WHP activities are quite common among organizations, and, as might be expected, their prevalence increases with organizational size. The 2004 National Worksite Health Promotion Survey found that, on average, WHP elements such as smoking cessation, physical activity, nutrition, and weight management programs were available in roughly 20 percent of establishments, but these prevalence rates were tripled in organizations with greater than 750 employees (Linnan et al., 2008).

Although the results of WHP intervention studies are somewhat uneven, the weight of the evidence suggests positive, albeit not dramatic, effects of WHP on unhealthy behaviors such as tobacco use and improvement in health indicators such as reduced blood pressure, reduced health care utilization, and reduced sickness absenteeism (CDC, 2007; Parks & Steelman, 2008; Pelletier, 2011). Of related interest, accumulating evidence shows that these health improvements translate to sizable economic returns to organizations. A recent meta-analysis of WHP interventions by Baicker, Cutler, and Song (2010), for example, showed a return on investment of $3.27 for medical cost savings and $2.73 for reduced absenteeism.

Despite the fact that WHP targets many health outcomes associated with occupational disease, including job stress, WHP historically has not been not been integrated into the occupational safety and health field nor, except for stress management, discussed widely in the context of job stress prevention. This situation, however, is changing, and in the final section of this chapter we describe a new a new prevention strategy that features the integration of WHP with occupational safety and health programs and other organizational functions that may influence stress, health, and safety in the workplace.

Stress Management

The term stress management is most often used to characterize efforts aimed at altering the ways in which individuals respond to job stressors and, in this regard, represents a form of secondary prevention. These approaches seek to educate workers about the causes and consequences of stress and to teach them relaxation and coping skills for managing the psychological and physiological symptoms of stress (Murphy, Hurrell, Sauter, & Keita, 1995). The most common types of stress management efforts are progressive muscle relaxation, cognitive-behavioral skills training (sometimes referred to as cognitive behavioral therapy or CBT), meditation, and multimodal approaches.

Stress management programs began to be seen in worksites in the 1980s, often as part of WHP initiatives (Murphy, 1988). Stress management remains the most commonly used type of stress prevention effort found in organizations today. Data from the 2010 General Social Survey suggest that more than one-third of workers in the U.S. have access to workplace stress management programs (Smith, Marsden, Hout, & Jibum, 2011), and the 2004 National Worksite Health Promotion Survey found that one-fourth of organizations in the U.S. reported that stress management programs were offered to their employees and their families (Linnan et al., 2008). As with WHP programs in general, this survey found that the prevalence of stress management programs increased as a function of organization size, growing to over 50% of organizations with more than 750 employees.

The effectiveness of stress management programs has been the subject of a growing number of both systematic narrative and meta-analytic reviews (e.g., Bhui, Dinos, Stansfeld, & White, 2012; Murphy, 1988, 1996; Richardson & Rothstein, 2008; van der Hek & Plomp, 1997; van der Klink, Blonk, Schene, & van Dijk, 2001) that date back to the 1970s (e.g., Newman & Beehr, 1979). A number of general conclusions can be drawn from these reviews. As previously noted by Sauter and Murphy (2004), stress management training is more often than not associated with benefits to workers with respect to reduced feelings of distress and physiological arousal and fewer somatic complaints. Of the various stress management techniques, cognitive-behavioral skills training seems to be most effective with respect to improving individual psychological outcomes. Moreover, a recent study (Flaxman & Bond, 2010) suggests that cognitive-behavioral skill training can produce clinically significant results, but the effects observed in many studies may have been significantly moderated by the initial level of distress (i.e., stronger effects with higher levels of distress). Despite previous suggestions to do so (e.g., Hurrell & Murphy, 1996; Murphy, Dubois and Hurrell, 1986), very few stress management studies have included organizational level outcome measures (such as absenteeism and accident rates) in their designs, and the results from the few that have provide little evidence that these types of prevention efforts by themselves impact organizationally relevant outcomes. A further limitation noted by a number of reviews of the stress management literature (e.g., Murphy, 1996; Richardson & Rothstein, 2008) is that long-term follow up is uncommon, but when such follow up is present, salutary effects of stress management do not seem to persist.

Not generally discussed in the context of stress management are various commonly found forms of training offered to employees (such as time management and conflict resolution). However, such training may have a "secondary" effect of reducing perceived levels of job stress (Sauter & Murphy, 2004) by enhancing workers' abilities to affect job stressors (such as workload and interpersonal conflict).

Treatment

Workplace treatment of job-stress related illnesses (whether or not identified as such) has traditionally occurred through company occupational health services and/or employee assistance programs (EAPs). In general, occupational health programs are not structured to provide extensive or long-term care for stress-related illnesses, and they must rely on making referrals to other health care providers. Job stress-related psychological disorders can present challenges to occupational health programs, which are generally not prepared to deal with them or make referrals (Kahn, 1993).

EAPs grew out of occupational alcohol programs (Wrich, 1984) in the 1940s. EAPs evolved dramatically since the 1940s and now offer a wide range of assistance for personal problems including legal, family, and substance abuse problems. In some sense, the basic service of EAPs is to provide access to individual counseling (Kelloway, Hurrell & Day, 2008), and most EAPs offer limited workplace counseling (brief psychological therapy). Reviews of the evidence of the effectiveness of workplace counseling (Kirk & Brown, 2003; McLeod, 2001, 2010) are not fully supportive but seem to suggest that counseling is perceived by employees as beneficial, is generally effective in alleviating psychological problems, can alter sickness absence, and is moderately effective in improving attitudes toward work. However, it should be noted that the quality of the studies that support such evidence has been questioned, as has the clinical significance of the reported psychological benefits (see McLeod & Henderson, 2003).

JOB LEVEL PREVENTION

Job Design

The importance of job (and component task) design, sometimes termed work organization, in preventing the occurrence of job stress and stress-related illness has long been recognized. Indeed, job design recommendations are an integral part of the U.S. National Strategy for Preventing Work-Related Psychological Disorders proposed by the U.S. National Institute for Occupational Safety and Health (NIOSH) (Sauter, Murphy & Hurrell, 1990). Seven design elements are recognized:

1. Demands (both physical and mental) should be commensurate with the capabilities and resources of individuals, avoiding overload as well as underload.
2. Work schedules should be compatible with demands and responsibilities outside of the job.
3. Roles and job responsibilities should be well defined.
4. Ambiguity should not exist in matters of job security and opportunities for career development.
5. Jobs should provide opportunities for personal interaction, both for purposes of emotional support and for actual help as needed in accomplishing tasks.
6. Jobs should be designed to provide meaningful stimulation and the opportunity to use skills.
7. Individuals should be given the opportunity to have input on decisions or actions that affect their jobs and performance of their tasks.

Very similar recommendations regarding the design of jobs and work are also inherent in the risk management approach to job stress recommended by both the Health Services Executive (HSE) in Great Britain (HSE, 2011) and the European Agency for Safety and Health at Work (EU-OSHA, 2012a).

Although the importance of many of these design elements has been widely investigated and acknowledged, the extent to which they are reflected in actual practice is uncertain. Results from the 2009 EU-OSHA European Agency for Safety and Health at Work (ESENER) (EU-OSHA, 2012b) provide a rather optimistic picture of the prevalence of worksite efforts to reduce job stress risks through work redesign. This telephone survey collected information on the way workplace health and safety risks are managed from 36,000 managers and worker representatives in organizations with 10 or more employees in 31 European countries. Twenty-five percent of survey respondents reported that their establishments had procedures in place to deal with work-related stress. Forty percent reported that, within the last three years, their establishments had made "changes to the way work is organized" to "deal with psychosocial risks." Of interest with respect to the prevalence of individual approaches, only 32 percent of organizations engaged in confidential counseling for employees. A slightly smaller proportion reported that changes had been made in working time arrangements.

Information of this nature from the U.S. is unavailable. A recent survey of 282 U.S. human resource and/or health benefit managers in organizations with at least 1,000 employees found that 21% to 34% reported that their firms were taking action to reduce stress related to structural aspects of work design, such as excessive workload, long work hours, lack of work-life balance, inadequate staffing, and unclear or conflicting job expectations (National Business Group on Health, 2010). However, the extent to which these actions involved work redesign or a combination of interventions since the study did not specify the types of action taken.

Job Redesign

Intervention efforts aimed at redesigning jobs and/or their component tasks to eliminate the causes of job stress (job stressors or risk factors for job stress) are becoming more common in the job stress literature. The largest numbers of such studies are based upon the principles of participatory action research (PAR). In general, PAR involves researchers and workers collaborating in a process of data-guided problem solving for the dual purposes of improving the organization's ability to provide workers with desired outcomes and engaging in research to contribute to scientific knowledge (see, Schurman & Israel, 1995). These PAR interventions have involved two distinct approaches: those focusing on defining problems at the workplace and developing interventions to improve health and well-being, and those that focus more exclusively on job redesign (Hurrell, 2005). While both approaches have shown limited evidence for the efficacy of PAR interventions in terms of self-reported measures of affect and perceived job satisfaction (Parkes & Sparkes, 1998; Hurrell, 2005), those that have focused more exclusively on job redesign have tended to show more consistent positive results (Hurrell, 2005). Importantly, a recent study (Nielsen & Randall, 2012) clearly suggests that both worker participation in the intervention process and actual changes in jobs and work procedures are strongly related to intervention success.

A smaller number of job redesign intervention efforts found in the literature have involved making changes in objective working conditions (e.g., workloads, work schedules, work processes, and work procedures) but did not involve employee-employer or employee-employer-researcher collaboration (see Hurrell, 2005). While small in number, taken as a whole, these studies provide rather consistent evidence for the effectiveness of the intervention.

Training

Training provided to both employees and supervisors can serve to reduce job stress by addressing the job context. For example, in addition to teaching stress coping skills, stress management programs may contain components that serve to educate workers on job stressor recognition with the implicit understanding that by recognizing the causes of job stress, workers will be in a better position to deal with them. A number of studies have also suggested that job stress training for supervisors and managers may have beneficial effects that extend beyond the supervisors and managers themselves (Hurrell, 2005). This seems to suggest that training supervisors and managers on how to provide support to workers who are experiencing job stress may lessen the effects of stressors in the work environment. If this is the case, such training might represent a potentially effective and seemingly cost efficient approach to prevention. Notably, of all forms of workplace intervention for job stress reported in the ESENER (EU-OSHA, 2012a), training interventions were the most common (acknowledged by nearly 60 percent of respondents).

ORGANIZATION LEVEL PREVENTION

Culture

The concepts of organizational culture and climate are quite different from one another, and they are frequently confused. In general terms, organizational culture refers to the basic values that guide life in organizations, while organizational climate refers to the meanings that people attach to interrelated experiences they have at work (Schneider, Ehrhart, & Macy, in press). Although research directly linking organizational culture and climate to job stress is surprisingly scarce in the job stress literature, both culture and climate are thought to be integrally related to the experience of job stress within organizations.

Very recent analysis of the ESENER data examined the role of organizational culture in relation to practices that are associated with effective management of psychosocial risks (i.e., job stressors) within organizations (EU-OSHA, 2012c). The results indicated that while *organizational culture* was reported to be a barrier to effective management of job stressors by around 20% of the organizations surveyed, it was not significantly associated with having in place procedures for work related stress (or bullying/harassment and violence) or measures taken to deal with psychosocial risks. By contrast, having a good *occupational health and safety (OHS) culture* was strongly associated with psychosocial risk management within an organization. Indeed, a key finding of the analysis was that organizations reporting a higher implementation of OHS management practices more often also reported having in place procedures to manage psychosocial risks. These practices, indicative of a strong OHS culture, included: the existence of an OHS policy, an established OHS management system, regular undertaking of risk assessments, being informed of developments in OHS knowledge development, management involvement in OHS management, formal employee involvement in OHS management processes, use of OHS services either external or internal, and routine analysis of causes of sickness absence and measures to support return to work of employees following long-term sickness absence.

Leadership

Leaders in organizations are granted the power to influence many of the conditions (i.e., job stressors) that influence job stress. As noted by Kelloway, Sivanathan, Francis, and Barling (2005), poor leaders contribute to the experience of stress in two major ways. First, poor leadership by itself is likely to be stressful for subordinates, and, secondly, poor leaders are likely to create work environments and conditions where job stressors are present. While there is some evidence of a relationship between leadership and employee job satisfaction, job well-being, sickness absence, and work related disability (see, Kuoppala, Lamminpaa, Liira, & Vainio, 2008), there is surprisingly little research examining the specific nature of these relationships. However, a recent longitudinal study of Danish government employees (Nielsen, Raymond, Yarker, & Brenner, 2008) offers some intriguing evidence regarding how one form of leadership (transformational leadership) might impact follower well-being. In particular, the study found that followers' perceptions of work characteristics (job stressors such as role clarity, meaningfulness of work, and opportunities for growth) mediated the relationship between transformational leadership style and self-report-ed well-being. Only limited evidence for a direct relationship between lead-ership behavior and follower well-being was observed. More specifically, the study suggests that exerting behaviors associated with the transformational leadership style (e.g., encouraging followers to engage in decision mak-ing and problem solving, providing a clear vision, mentoring, etc.) may increase the well-being of followers but only if these behaviors alter their followers' perceptions of work characteristics. In addition, the study found evidence for a feedback loop whereby the followers' level of well-being also influences the reporting of transformational leadership behavior. As noted by the authors, these findings have important implications for interven-tions efforts. They suggest, for example, that training supervisors in trans-formational leadership may have effects that are similar to wide-ranging job design changes to eliminate job stressors.

Work/Life Balance

The nature of the relationship between work and family life is multi-di-mensional, multi-directional and complex. For example, work can interfere and with family life (and vice versa), and work can enrich family life (and vice versa). While research examining the complex relationship between these two life domains is still in its infancy, it clearly suggests that an imbal-ance between them can result in negative consequences for the worker, the worker's family, and the organization.

To address the potential organizational consequences of imbalance, many companies have instituted initiatives to increase workplace flexibility (Galin-ski, Bond, & Sakai, 2008). They include policies and practices such as flexible work schedules, job sharing, telecommuting, family leave, and child or elder care assistance. Flexibility programs are widely viewed by employers as impor-tant with respect to employee retention, recruitment, and productivity. While unequivocal research support for the individual and organizational benefits of the components of these programs is lacking, the presence of workplace flexibility seems to have important benefits for both. For example, a recent report by the Families and Work Institute (Matos & Galinski, 2011) based upon a nationally representative survey found that flexibility programs ben-efit organizations of all sizes and industries, resulting in increased employee job satisfaction, lower turnover, and lower insurance costs.

The most common type of workplace flexibility available to employees is flexible work scheduling. Understanding whether and how work schedul-ing flexibility is beneficial to employees and employers is complicated by the diverse nature of this flexibility. Indeed, a large variety of flexible work schedules exist that permit employees control over when they work, where they work, how much they work, and the continuity of their work (Kossek & Michel, 2011). However, a large scale prospective study, conducted by the Work Family and Health Network, is currently underway (www.kpchr.org/ workfamilyhealthnetwork/public/default.aspx) that will assess the utility of increased work schedule flexibility as an intervention to improve worker health and productivity and should shed light on these issues.

Accommodation

While often not discussed in a job stress context, organizations utilize a variety of approaches to accommodate the needs of individuals with disabilities (including a number of disabling conditions that can be job and job stress related). According to the provisions of the he United States Americans with Disability Act (ADA; Americans with Disabilities Amendment Act, 2008), employers are required to make reasonable accommodations to known physical and mental limitations of employees with disabilities. The ADA defines a covered disability as "a physical or mental impairment that substantially limits a major life activity," and decisions on whether or not a particular condition is considered as a disability are made on a case by case basis. A variety of psychological disorders (whether or not job stress related) can substantially limit major life activity and therefore result in some form of accommodation. Post traumatic stress disorder (PTSD) is one such disorder that is almost universally recognized as a qualifying condition under the act and therefore requires employer accommodation (Equal Employment Opportunity Commission Regulations to Implement ADA, 2011). PTSD is a condition that can occur after exposure to terrifying events where grave physical harm occurred or was threatened (DSM-IV; American Psychiatric Association, 2000) and is commonly found in occupations where the potential for such exposure is high (nurses, firefighters, police officers, paramedics, prison guards, etc). Harassment and bullying are examples of stressful workplace exposures that are increasingly recognized as risk factors for PTSD (Nielsen & Einarsen, 2012).

SUPRA-ORGANIZATION LEVEL PREVENTION

Prevention Regulation

While there are no laws that are specific to work-related stress as an outcome in the U.S., there are laws that protect workers from undue exposure to known stressors such as discrimination and harassment and occupation specific stressors such as long work hours in transportation. In Europe, national legislation specific to job stress is limited but exists in some countries (Llorens & Ortiz de Villacian, 2001). However, work-related stress is implicitly acknowledged in the EU Framework Health and Safety Directive (89/391/EEC) that mandates an employer obligation for "developing a coherent overall prevention policy which covers technology, organization of work, working conditions, social relationships and the influence of factors related to the working environment" (see Council of European Communities, 1989).

Prevention Standards

A number of national and international initiatives to prevent job stress have been attempted that focus on entire populations. These efforts rely on providing standardized guidance for prevention that is based upon rigorous scientific evidence. One of the earliest of these was the aforementioned U.S. National Strategy for the Prevention of Work-related Psychological Disorders proposed by NIOSH (see Sauter et al., 1990). This strategy identified roles for industry, labor, government, and academia and, in particular, described steps to be taken to improve stressful working conditions. While the efficacy of this strategy has not been evaluated, the strategy itself has been widely cited in the job stress prevention literature over the past 22 years.

In 2000, the British Health and Safety Commission (responsible for health and safety in Great Britain) set targets for the reduction of the burden of occupational health (including the contribution of work related stress) and developed a 10-year priority program to meet the targets. The program utilizes a population approach with action to be taken across Great Britain industries. As a part of this program, a series of job stress "management standards" were developed by the Health and Safety Executive (HSE) that would allow organizations to gauge performance and to facilitate continuous improvement (see Mackay, Cousins, Kelly, Lee, & McCaig, 2004). Notably, a Canadian national standard for psychological health and safety in the workplace modeled, in part, after the HSE standards is under development, with publication anticipated in early 2013 (Mental Health Commission of Canada, 2012).

The HSE standards cover six key job stressor areas (demands, control, support, relationships, work role, and change) that if not properly managed are thought to result in poor health and well-being, increased sickness absence, and lower productivity. Along with these standards, the HSE provides a variety of tools to assist organizations in assessing the key job stressor risks, comparing their results to suggested long term targets, and implementing change to management-identified risks (see, www.hse.gov.uk/stress). Practical guidance and tools of this nature have also been issued by other national and international institutes (e.g., British Standards Institution, 2011; International Labor Office, 2012; NIOSH, 1999).

Evidence for the overall efficacy of this approach is the subject of a recent analysis (see Mackay, Palferman, Saul, Webster, & Packham, 2012) and appears to be mixed. For example, national surveillance data indicate no significant changes in stressful working conditions six years after the implementation of the standard for the number of workers who report having discussed stress with their supervisor. There was, however, some improvement in perceived managerial and peer support. As noted by the authors, changes to working conditions may require a longer "gestation period."

As might be expected, given the global nature of the economy in the 21st century, concern regarding job stress is not restricted to individual countries, and preventing it in a global economy may require macro-level attention. Indeed, a recent European Union survey of 35,000 people, sponsored by EU-OSHA found that 82% of the respondents felt that job-related stress will increase over the next five years, with 52% of them believing that it will " increase a lot" (EU-OSHA, 2012d). Preventing job stress across Europe is part of the responsibility of EU-OSHA. Set up in 1996 by the European Union, this agency researches, develops, and distributes reliable safety and health information and organizes Pan-European awareness campaigns. In 2009, this agency carried out the first Europe-wide survey on health and safety at the workplace (the ESENER survey described above). The agency is planning an awareness raising campaign for 2014 that will highlight practical solutions for psychosocial risks and promote the use of various tools and methods to manage them.

Disability

In the United States, workers are eligible for compensation resulting from work- related disability under two separate insurance programs: Social Security disability and workers' compensation. Social Security disability insurance (SSDI) is a payroll tax-funded federal insurance program. SSDI, which was established in 1954, is designed to provide workers with income if they are unable to work due to a disability or until their condition improves and guarantees income if the condition does not improve. The program pays only for total disability, and no benefits are available for partial disability or for short-term disability. Workers are generally considered disabled if they cannot do work that they did previously, cannot adjust to other work because of their condition(s), and their disability has lasted or is expected to last for one year or result in death (Raphael & Del Regno, 2001). Psychiatric illness constitutes a recognized disability within the system and, according to a survey by the Council for Disability Awareness (http://www.disabilitycanhappen.org/

research/CDA_LTD_Claims_Survey_2011.asp), mental and psychiatric disorders represented 9.1% of all new claims in 2010.

Workers' compensation generally refers to a type of insurance that provides medical benefits and wage replacement to workers injured on the job and can be found in numerous countries. In the United States, employers are required to have this insurance, and compensation is administered on a state-by-state basis. While the protections offered people who are injured on the job vary greatly by jurisdiction, in most states workplace stress claims are compensable under workers' compensation, and benefits for temporary disability, medical treatment, and permanent disability are available (Workers' Comp and Safety News, 2007). These claims include physical-mental claims (where a physical injury leads to a mental disability), mental-physical claims (where mental stress leads to a physical illness or condition), and mental-mental claims (where mental stress leads to a mental condition or disability). However, in the last two decades worker compensation law has been increasingly amended across states to deny compensation for mental claims.

New Directions in the Prevention of Job Stress

Our discussion of approaches to the prevention of job stress and stress-related illnesses and disorders has focused thus far on the description of discrete and conceptually distinct types of interventions that, for the most part, have been implemented in piecemeal fashion. We conclude this discussion by drawing attention to a new, more comprehensive approach for prevention of occupational illness and injury that holds promise for the prevention of job stress and stress-related disorders. The central feature of this new approach, which is discussed in depth in reports by NIOSH (2012) and the Institute of Medicine (2005), is the integration of interventions targeting the individual (health promotion), the conditions of work (health protection), and all levels of intervention (primary through tertiary).

Over the last decade this concept of integration has gained steady traction as efficacy data emerge and as the occupational safety and health field comes to further appreciate the totality of factors affecting the health of workers and the limitations of conventional, fragmented approaches to prevention. Beginning in 2010, NIOSH intensified its programmatic efforts, under the moniker Total Worker Health™ (TWH), to advance research and practice involving integrative prevention strategies (http://www.cdc.gov/niosh/TWH/default.html). More recently, the American College of Occupational and Environmental Medicine issued a guidance statement on the importance of integrating workplace health promotion and health protection activities (Hymel et al., 2011). Other important developments include the recent publication of practice guidelines for designing integrated programs by Harvard University (http://centerforworkhealth.sph.harvard.edu/images/stories/SafeWellPracticeGuidelinesFeb2012_final_facingpages.pdf) and by the California Department of Industrial Relations (http://www.dir.ca.gov/chswc/WOSHTEP/Publications/WOSHTEP_TheWholeWorker.pdf).

The promise of a more integrative approach to the prevention of job stress and stress-related disorders is illustrated in a 2007 review of the job stress intervention evaluation literature by LaMontagne and colleagues (LaMontagne et al., 2007). Most notably, the review found that job stress interventions focused on secondary prevention (e.g., progressive muscle relaxation, meditation, cognitive-behavioral skill training) were quite effective in producing near term reductions in somatic and/or psychological symptoms of stress (85% of studies), an effect observed in other reviews as we previously noted. Also consistent with prior findings, positive effects on organizational outcomes, such as absenteeism, turnover, injury rates, and productivity, were far less common (31% of studies). Of special interest, however, studies investigating secondary interventions in combination with primary interventions (mainly directed toward the organization of work) more consistently showed gains at the organizational level, such as reduced absenteeism and sickness absence (97% of studies), and more sustained health effects at the individual level. Studies integrating WHP and organizational interventions were too few to draw conclusions, but findings for the combination of primary and secondary intervention suggest a similar, if not amplified, pattern of effects could be expected. Clearly the emergence of integrative approaches to the prevention of occupational illness and injury represents an exciting new framework for the investigation and practice of ways to prevent stress at work.

NOTE

1. The findings and conclusions in this report are those of the author(s) and do not necessarily represent the views of the National Institute for Occupational Safety and Health.

REFERENCES

Americans With Disability Amendment Act of 2008, Pub. L. No. 110-325. 122 Stat. 3553(codified at 42 U.S.C., && 1210, 12103, 12205a [Supp. II 209]).

American Psychiatric Association (APA). (2000). *Diagnostic and statistical manual of mental disorders* (4th ed.). Washington, DC: Author.

Baicker, K., Cutler, D., & Song, Z. (2010). Workplace wellness programs can generate savings. *Health Affairs, 29,* 304–311.

Bhui, K. S., Dinos, S., Stansfeld, S. A., & White, P. D. (2012). A synthesis of the evidence for managing stress at work: A review of the reviews reporting on anxiety, depression, and absenteeism. *Journal of Environmental and Public Health, 2012.* doi: 10.1155/2012/515874 Retrieved from http://www.hindawi.com/journals/jeph/2012/515874/

Biron, C., Karanika-Murray, M., & Cooper, C. L. (Eds.). (2012). *Improving organizational interventions for stress and well-being.* London: Routledge.

British Standards Institution. (2011, February). *PAS1010, guidance on the management of psychosocial hazards in the workplace.* London, UK: Author

Centers for Disease Control (CDC). (2007). *Community preventive services task force report: Assessment of health risks with feedback to change employees' health.* Retrieved from http://www.thecommunityguide.org/worksite/ahrf.html

Commission on Chronic Illness. (1957). *Chronic illness in the United States.* (Vol.1. Published for the Commonwealth Fund). Cambridge, MA: Harvard University Press.

Council of European Communities. (1989). European framework directive (89/391/EEC). Retrieved from http://eur-lex.europa.eu/LexUriServ/LexUriServ.do?uri=CELEX:31989L0391:en:HTML

European Agency for Safety and Health at Work (EU-OSHA). (2012a). *Management of psychosocial risks at work: An analysis of findings of the European survey of enterprises on new and emerging risks (ESENER).* Retrieved from http://osha.europa.eu/en/publications/reports/management-psychosocial-risks-esener

European Agency for Safety and Health at Work (EU-OSHA). (2012b). *(ESENER) European survey of enterprises on new and emerging risks—Summary.* Retrieved from http://osha.europa.eu/en/publications/reports/en_esener1-summary.pdf

European Agency for Safety and Health at Work (EU-OSHA). (2012c). *Drivers and barriers: An analysis of findings of the European survey of enterprises on new and emerging risks (ESENER).* Retrieved from https://osha.europa.eu/en/publications/reports/drivers-barriers- psychosocial-risk-management-esener

European Agency for Safety and Health at Work (EU-OSHA). (2012d). *Stress in the workplace to rise, say 8 out of 10 in major pan-European opinion poll.* News Release, March 27, 2012. Retrieved from http://osha.europa.eu/en/press/press- releases/stress_workplace_to_rise_say_8_out_of_10_in_major_pan- european_opinion_poll

EEOC Regulations to Implement the Equal Employment Provisions of the Americans With Disabilities Act, as Amended, 76 Fed Reg. 16,987, 1699 (March 25, 2011) (Codified as 29 CFR pt. 1630).

Flaxman, P. E., & Bond, F. (2010). Worksite stress management training: Moderated effects and clinical significance. *Journal of Occupational Health Psychology, 15,* 347–357.

Galinski, E., Bond, J., & Sakai, K. (2008). *National survey of employers.* Retrieved from http://familiesandwork.org/site/research/reports/2008nse.pdf

Goetzel, R. Z., & Ozminkowski, R. J. (2008). The health and cost benefits of work site health- promotion programs. *Annual Rev Public Health, 29,* 303–323.

Health and Safety Executive. (2011). *Management standards.* Retrieved from http://www.hse.gov.uk/stress/standards/index.htm

Hurrell, J. J., Jr. (2005). Organizational stress interventions. In J. Barling, E. K. Kelloway & M. R. Frone (Eds.), *Handbook of work stress* (pp. 623–646). Thousand Oaks, CA: Sage Publications.

Hurrell, J. J., Jr., & Murphy, L. R. (1996). Occupational stress intervention. *American Journal of Industrial Medicine, 29,* 338–341.

Hymel, P. A., Loeppke, R. R., Baase, C. M., Burton, W. M., Hartenbaum, M. P., Hudson, T. W., . . . Larson, P.W. (2011). Workplace health protection and promotion: A new pathway for a healthier—and safer—workforce. *Journal of Occupational and Environmental Medicine, 53,* 695–702.

Institute of Medicine. (2005). *Integrating employee health: A model program for NASA.* Retrieved from http://www.cdc.gov/niosh/docs/2012-146/

International Labour Office. (2012). *Stress prevention at work checkpoints.* Geneva: Author.

Kahn, J. P. (1993). *Mental health in the workplace: A practical psychiatric guide.* New York, NY: Van Nostrand Reinhold.

Kelloway, E. K., Hurrell, J. J., Jr., & Day, A. L. (2008). Workplace interventions for occupational stress. In K. Näswall, M. Sverke, & J. Hellgren (Eds.), *The individual in the changing working life* (pp. 419–442). Cambridge: Cambridge University Press.

Kelloway, E. K., Sivanathan, N., Francis, L., & Barling, J. (2005). Poor leadership. In J. Barling, E. K. Kelloway, & M. R. Frone (Eds.), *Handbook of work stress* (pp. 89–112). Thousand Oaks, CA: Sage Publications.

Kirk, A. K., & Brown, D. F. (2003). Employee assistance programs: A review of the management of stress and wellbeing through workplace counselling and consulting. *Australian Psychologist, 38,* 138–143.

Kossek, E., & Michel, J. (2011). Flexible work schedules. In S. Zedek (Ed.), *APA handbook of industrial and organizational psychology* (pp. 535–572) Washington, DC: American Psychological Association.

Kuoppala, J., Lamminpaa, A., Liira, J., & Vainio, H. (2008). Leadership, job well-being, and health effects—A systematic review and a meta-analysis. *Journal of Occupational & Environmental Medicine, 50,* 904–915 doi: 10.1097/JOM.0b013e31817e918d

LaMontagne, A. D., Keegle, T., Louie, A. M., Ostry, A., & Landsbergis, P.A. (2007). A systematic review of the job stress intervention evaluation literature: 1990–2005. *International Journal of Occupational and Environmental Health, 13,* 268–280.

Linnan, L., Bowling, M., Childress, J., Lindsay, G., Blakey, C., Pronk, S., Wieker., & Royall, P. (2008). Results of the 2004 National Worksite Health Promotion Survey. *American Journal of Public Health, 98,* 1503–1509.

Llorens, C., & Ortiz deVillacian, D. (2001). Work-related stress and industrial relations. *European industrial relations on-line.* Retrieved from http://www.eurofound.europa.eu/eiro/2001/11/study/tn0111109s.htm

Mackay, C. J. Cousins, R., Kelly, P. J., Lee, S., & McCaig, R. H. (2004). Management standards and work-related stress in the UK: Policy background and science. *Work and Stress, 18,* 91–112.

MacKay, C. J., Palferman, D., Saul, H., Webster, S., & Packham, C. (2012). Implementation of the management standards for work-related stress in Great Britian. In C. Biron, M. Karanika-Murray, & C. L. Cooper (Eds.), *Improving organizational interventions for job stress and well-being* (pp. 313–332). London: Routledge.

Matos, K., & Galinski, E. (2011). *Workplace flexibility in the United States: A status report.* Families and Work Institute. Retrieved from http://familiesandwork.org/site/research/reports/www_us_workflex.pdf

McLeod, J. (2001). *Counselling in the workplace: The facts. A systematic study of the research evidence.* Rugby: British Association for Counseling and Psychotherapy.

McLeod J. (2010). The effectiveness of workplace counseling: A systematic review. *Counselling and Psychotherapy Research, 10,* 238–248.

McLeod, J., & Henderson, M. (2003). Does workplace counseling work? *The British Journal of Psychiatry, 182,* 103–104.

Mental Health Commission of Canada. (2012). *The national standard on psychological health and safety in the workplace and technical committee activities: September 2012 update.* Retrieved from http://www.mentalhealthcommission.ca/SiteCollection Documents/Workforce/Workforce_PHSW_Update_September2012_ENG.pdf

Murphy, L. R. (1988). Workplace interventions for stress reduction and prevention. In C. L. Cooper & R. Payne (Eds.), *Causes consequences and coping with stress at work* (pp. 301–331) Chichester: John Wiley & Sons.

Murphy, L. R. (1996). Stress management in work settings: A critical review of the health effects. *American Journal of Health Promotion, 11,* 112–135.

Murphy, L. R. DuBois, D., & Hurrell J. J., Jr. (1986). Accident reduction through stress management. *Journal of Business Psychology, 1,* 5–18. doi: 10.1007/BF01014163

Murphy, L. R., Hurrell, J. J., Jr., Sauter, S. L., & Keita, G. P. (1995). *Job stress interventions.* Washington, DC: American Psychological Association. doi: 10.1037/10183-000

Newman, J.D ., & Beehr, T. (1979). Personal and organizational strategies for handling job stress: A review of research and opinion. *Personnel Psychology, 32,* 1–43.

National Business Group on Health. (2010). *The health and productivity advantage. 2009/2010 staying@work report.* Washington, DC: Author.

National Institute for Institutional Safety and Health (NIOSH). (1999). *Stress at work.* Retrieved Dec. 11, 2012 from http://www.cdc.gov/niosh/docs/99-101/

National Institute for Institutional Safety and Health (NIOSH). (2012). *The NIOSH Total Worker Health™ Program: Seminal research papers 2012.* Retrieved from http://www.cdc.gov/niosh/docs/2012-146/

Nielsen, K., & Randall, R. (2012). The importance of employee participation and perceptions of changes in procedures in a teamworking intervention. *Work and Stress, 26,* 91–111. doi: 10.1080/02678373.2012.682721

Nielsen, K., Raymond, R., Yarker, J., & Brenner, S. (2008). The effects of transformational leadership on followers' perceived work characteristics and psychological well-being: A longitudinal study. *Work & Stress, 22,* 16–32. doi: 10.1080/02678370801979430

Nielsen, M. B., & Einarsen, S. (2012). Outcomes of workplace bullying: A meta-analytic review. *Work and Stress, 26,* 309–332.

Parkes, K. M., & Sparkes, T. J. (1998). *Organizational interventions to reduce work stress: Are they effective? A review of the literature.* (Contract Report No. 193/198). Oxford, UK: Health and Safety Executive, University of Oxford.

Parks, K. M., & Steelman, L. A. (2008). Organizational wellness programs: A meta-analysis. *Journal of Occupational Health Psychology, 13*, 58–68.

Pelletier, K. R. (2011). A review and analysis of clinical and cost-effectiveness studies of comprehensive health promotion and disease management programs at the worksite: Update VIII 2008–2010. *Journal of Occupational and Environmental Medicine, 53*, 1310–1331.

Raphael, J. L., & Del Regno, P. (2001). Social security claims of psychiatric disability: Elements of case adjudication and role of primary care physicians. *The Primary Care Companion to the Journal of Clinical Psychiatry, 3*, 255–262. Retrieved from http://www.ncbi.nlm.nih.gov/pmc/articles/PMC181194/

Richardson, K. M., & Rothstein, H. R. (2008). Effects of occupational stress management intervention programs: A meta-analysis. *Journal of Occupational Health Psychology, 13*, 69–93.

Sauter, S. L., & Murphy, L. R (2004). Work organization interventions: State of the art knowledge and future directions. *Social and Preventive Medicine, 49*, 79–86. doi: 10,1007/s00038-004-3085-z

Sauter, S. L., Murphy, L. R., & Hurrell, J. J., Jr. (1990). Prevention of work-related psychological disorders: A national strategy proposed by the National Institute for Occupational Safety and Health (NIOSH). *American Psychologist, 45*, 1146–1158.

Schneider, B., Ehrhart, M. G., & Macy, W. H. (in press). Organizational climate and culture. *Annual Review of Psychology, 64*. doi: 10.1146/annurev-psych-113011-143809

Schurman, S. J., & Israel. B. A. (1995). Redesigning work systems to reduce stress: A participatory action research approach to creating change. In L. R. Murphy, J. J. Hurrell, Jr., S. L. Sauter, & G. P. Keita (Eds.), *Job stress interventions* (pp. 235–236). Washington, DC: American Psychological Association. doi: 10.1037/10183-000

Semmer, N. K. (2006). Job stress interventions and the organization of work. *Scandinavian Journal or Work, Environment & Health, 32*, 515–527.

Smith, T. W., Marsden, P. V., Hout, M., & Jibum, K. (2011, March). *General social surveys, 1972–2010: Cumulative codebook.* Chicago, IL: National Opinion Research Center.

van der Hek, H., & Plomp, N. H. (1997). Occupational stress management programs: A practical overview of published studies. *Occupational Medicine, 47*, 133–141.

van der Klink, J. J. L., Blonk, R. W. B., Schene, A. H., & van Dijk, F. J. (2001). Benefits of intervention for work-related stress. *American Journal of Public Health, 91*, 279–276.

Work and Health (1973). *Report of a Special Task Force to the Secretary of Health, Education and Welfare*, pp. 74–278, MIT Press: Cambridge, MA.

Workers Comp and Safety News. (2007). Stress and workers' compensation. *Workers Comp and Safety News, 5*, 104. Retrieved from www.campinsurancepro.com/resources/WCSN0706.pdf

Wrich, J. (1984). *The employee assistance program.* Minneapolis, MN: Hazelden Educational Foundation.

ABOUT THE EDITORS

Ana Maria Rossi, PhD, is president of the International Stress Management Association in Brazil (ISMA-BR) and a Brazilian representative for the Occupational Health Section of the World Psychiatric Association (WPA). She is the director of the Clínica de Stress & Biofeedback, in Porto Alegre. She has written many books and papers published in professional journals and has worked in the field of stress management for 30 years. She is the pioneer of self-control and biofeedback techniques in Brazil. She is a Fellow of The American Institute of Stress (AIS).

James A. Meurs, PhD, is an assistant professor of human resources and organizational dynamics in the Haskayne School of Business at the University of Calgary. He has research interests in occupational stress, political skill, personality, and socio-economic status. He serves on the Editorial Review Board of the *Journal of Occupational Health Psychology*. He has published in journals such as *Journal of Management, Journal of Organizational Behavior, Jornal of Occupational Health Psychology, Journal of Vocational Behavior, Journal of Managerial Psychology, Human Performance,* and the *International Journal of Human Resource Management.*

Pamela L. Perrewé, PhD, is the Haywood and Betty Taylor Eminent Scholar of Business Administration and Distinguished Research Professor at Florida State University. She has focused her research interests in the areas of job stress, coping, organizational politics, emotion, and personality. Dr. Perrewé has published over 30 book chapters and over 100 journal articles in journals such as *Academy of Management Journal, Journal of Management,*

Improving Emploee Health and Well-Being, pages 207–208
Copyright © 2014 by Information Age Publishing
All rights of reproduction in any form reserved.

Journal of Applied Psychology, Organizational Behavior and Human Decision Processes, Journal of Organizational Behavior and *Personnel Psychology*. She has fellow status with Southern Management Association, the Society for Industrial and Organizational Psychology, and the American Psychological Association. Finally, she is the co-editor of an annual series entitled *Research in Occupational Stress and Well-Being* published by Emerald Publishing.

ABOUT THE CONTRIBUTORS

Chapter 1: Workplace Politics and Well-Being:
An Allostatic Load Perspective

Christopher C. Rosen is an associate professor of management in the Sam M. Walton College of Business at the University of Arkansas. Professor Rosen's research interests include organizational politics, measurement and modeling of personality, employee-organization exchange relationships, and work stress and well-being. His work has been published in journals such as *Academy of Management Journal, Journal of Applied Psychology, Organizational Behavior and Human Decision Processes*, and *Personnel Psychology*. Professor Rosen currently serves on the editorial review boards of *Journal of Business and Psychology, Journal of Occupational and Organizational Psychology, Journal of Organizational Behavior*, and *Organizational Behavior and Human Decision Processes*.

Daniel C. Ganster (PhD, Purdue University) is the senior associate dean for administration for the College of Business at Colorado State University. His research broadly concerns the impact of work life experiences on the mental and physical well-being of organizational members. He is on the editorial review boards of the *Academy of Management Journal, Journal of Applied Psychology, Journal of Management*, and the *Journal of Occupational Health Psychology*. He previously served on the boards of *Organizational Behavior and Human Decision Processes, Journal of Organizational Behavior* and *Stress and Health*.

Improving Emploee Health and Well-Being, pages 209–215
Copyright © 2014 by Information Age Publishing

Chapter 2: Occupational Demands, Environmental Resources, and Personal Resources Effects on Presenteeism and Health

Lois E. Tetrick (PhD) is the director of the industrial and organizational psychology program at George Mason University. She is a past editor of the *Journal of Occupational Health Psychology* and co-edited the *Handbook of Occupational Health Psychology* (1st and 2nd editions) with James C. Quick. Dr. Tetrick is a fellow of the European Academy of Occupational Health Psychology, the American Psychological Association, the Society for Industrial and Organizational Psychology, and the Association for Psychological Science. Dr. Tetrick's research interests are in the areas of occupational health psychology and understanding the employee-organization relationship.

Clifford R. Haimann is a third year industrial and organizational psychology PhD student at George Mason University. He conducts empirical research on presenteeism and is interested in other topics such as the work/life balance. He also studies the legal aspects of IO psychology. Clifford has presented multiple times at the Annual Conference of Industrial and Organizational Psychology and has published on the Americans with Disabilities Act.

Chapter 3: Quality of Working Life: Meaning and Sense for Companies and Employees

Raphael Henrique C. Di Lascio is a psychologist from Universidade Tuiuti do Paraná, MSc from Universidade Federal de Santa Catarina. He is a specialist in human resources planning and organization, business administration, and work psychology. He also is a professor in undergraduate and graduate programs and coordinator of the psychology program at Universidade Positivo-Paraná. He has thirty-two years working in the field of psychology, and he has won the awards of "City of Curitiba 2011" and "Paul J. Rosch" from ISMA-BR in 2002.

Chapter 4: Assessing Stress in Nursing Students—Analysis Standardization

Rodrigo Marques da Silva is a nurse with a degree from Universidade Federal de Santa Maria, PET-Enfermagem, Pibic-CNPQ and Social Programs scholarships recipient. He is a member of the research group "Work, Health, Education and Nursing" researching stress, coping, and burnout, and is he currently a master's student at the nursing graduate program at Universidade Federal de Santa Maria.

Carolina Tonini Goulart is a nurse, MSc in rural extension from Universidade Federal de Santa Maria. She is a master's student in the nursing graduate program at Universidade Federal de Santa Maria.

Luis Felipe Dias Lopes has a PhD in production engineering and is a specialist in statistics and quantitative modeling. He is associate professor in the business administration department, Universidade Federal de Santa Maria.

Ana Lucia Siqueira Costa is a nurse, with a degree from the department of nursing, Universidade Estadual de Campinas. She also has a PhD and MSc in nursing from the School of Nursing, Universidade de São Paulo. She is a specialist in operating room nursing from the School of Nursing (USP), professor in the Department of Medical-Surgical Nursing at the School of Nursing (USP), and leader of the research group in stress, coping, and work.

Laura de Azevedo Guido is a nurse, specializing in operating room nursing, anesthetic recovery, and material and sterilization center, from Escola de Enfermagem da Universidade de São Paulo. She has an MSc in nursing from Universidade Federal de Santa Catarina and PhD in nursing (EEUSP). She is associate professor (retired) from Universidade Federal de Santa Maria and coordinator of the following lines of research: stress, coping, and burnout in adults in critical life situations.

Chapter 5: Building Resilience to Improve Employee Well-Being

Matthew R. Leon is a doctoral student in the department of management and marketing in the Culverhouse College of Commerce and Business Administration at the University of Alabama. He received his MA in industrial/organizational psychology from the University of West Florida and his BA in psychology from Auburn University. His research experiences include time with the Naval Aerospace Medical Research Laboratory studying cognitive and biological correlates of hardiness, and he has publications in *Experimental and Clinical Psychopharmacology* and *The Journal of Behavioral Medicine.*

Jonathon R. B. Halbesleben is the HealthSouth chair of health care management and associate professor in the department of management and marketing in the Culverhouse College of Commerce and Business Administration at the University of Alabama. He received his PhD in industrial/organizational psychology from the University of Oklahoma. His research concerning employee well-being and coworker helping behavior has been published in the *Journal of Applied Psychology, Journal of Management,* and *Journal of Organizational Behavior,* among others. He is editor of the *Journal of Occupational and Organizational Psychology* and series co-editor for *Research in Occupational Stress and Well-Being.*

Chapter 6: The "Right" Tools: Stress Response Lessons from the Opposite Sex

Faye K. Cocchiara is an associate professor of management at Arkansas State University. Cocchiara received her PhD in organizational behavior and human resource management from the University of Texas at Arlington. She is a former human resource manager, responsible for diversity management programs including designing and implementing corporate diversity training. Cocchiara's research interests focus on performance stereotypes, fairness in employment selection, and gender-related stress antecedents and effects. Her research appears in the *Handbook of Work and Health Psychology, Journal of Organizational Behavior, Organizational Behavior and Human Decision Processes, Human Resource Management*, and the *Academy of Management Learning & Education*.

Dr. David Gavin is an assistant professor of management at Marist College. Dr. Gavin received his doctorate from University at Albany in 2010. He teaches courses in strategic management and entrepreneurship. His research focus is governance, leadership, CEO and board power, and he has articles appearing in *The International Journal of Organization Theory and Behavior* and the *International Journal of Humanities and Social Science*. Dr. Gavin's most recent work is the forthcoming book *Live Your Dreams: Change the World*. Prior to obtaining his doctorate, Dr. Gavin spent twenty-five years leading organizations in the foodservice, software technology, publishing, and manufacturing/retail industries.

Dr. Joanne H. Gavin is associate professor of organizational behavior and chair of the department of management at Marist College. Her research interest is in the area of personal character and executive health. She is co-author of articles appearing in *Academy of Management Executive, Applied Psychology: International Review, Academy of Management Journal, Business and Society*, and *Organizational Dynamics*. Dr. Gavin is also co-author of several chapters in books such as *Organizational Behavior: The State of the Science, International Review of Industrial and Organizational Psychology*, and *Psychology Builds a Healthy World*. She is also co-author of the *Financial Times Guide to Executive Health* and *Managing Executive Health*.

Dr. James Campbell (Jim) Quick is John and Judy Goolsby–Jacqualyn A. Fouse Endowed Chair, Goolsby Leadership Academy at The University of Texas at Arlington and honorary professor, Lancaster University Management School, UK. His books include the second edition of *Preventive Stress Management* (American Psychological Association, 2013) and the second edition of the *Handbook of Occupational Health Psychology* (American Psychological Association, 2011). Jim is a fellow of the Society for Industrial and Organizational Psychology, American Psychological Association, and American Institute of Stress. The University of Texas at Arlington honored Jim with a 2009 university award for Distinguished Record of Research. Jim is married to the former Sheri Grimes Schember.

Chapter 7: When Dealing with Quality of Working Life, It Is Impossible to Forget: Regrettably, Taylor Is Still Alive and Kicking!

José Vieira Leite is a post-doc in human sciences from Pontifícia Universidade Católica do Rio de Janeiro, and he has a PhD in production engineering and MSc in sociology and anthropology from Universidade Federal do Rio de Janeiro. He is a researcher with ErgoPublic at Universidade de Brasília. He is the coordinator of the 5th National Meeting on QoL at Public Services of ISMA-BR and QWL at the Brazilian Central Bank Workers' Union. He is author of the book *A Questão do Sentido no Trabalho Contemporâneo* (The Issue of Meaning in Contemporary Work), five chapters in books, and several articles.

Chapter 8: Socio-environmental Responsibility in Public Administration

Marcos Weiss Bliacheris is an attorney with the federal government of Brazil. He is a specialist in state law and coordinator of the book *Sustentabilidade na Administração Pública: Valores e Práticas de Gestão Socioambiental* (Sustainability in Public Administration: Values and Practices of Socio-environmental Management). He is author of several articles on environmental and administrative law and a speaker in the area of environmental management in public administration and sustainable tenders.

Chapter 9: SAV-T First: A Risk Management Approach to Workplace Violence

E. Kevin Kelloway is the Canada Research Chair in occupational health psychology at Saint Mary's University, where he also holds appointments as professor of psychology and management and director of the CN Centre for Occupational Health and Safety. A prolific researcher, he is a fellow of the Society for Industrial/Organizational Psychology, the Association for Psychological Science, and the Canadian Psychological Association. His research focuses on occupational health psychology, including the effect of leadership on employee health and safety and the study of occupational stress. Most recently, he has focused on the application of positive psychology to occupational health.

Kate Calnan is a PhD candidate and part time professor of occupational health psychology at Saint Mary's University, Halifax, NS, Canada. Kate has been awarded many research grants, including a doctoral scholarship from the Social Sciences and Humanities Research Council. Kate is also a member of the CN Centre for Occupational Health and Safety, where she maintains an active role in research and consulting projects. Her current research interests focus on organizational functioning and employee well-being, with specialized focus on workplace violence, conflict, and positive occupational health psychology. Kate has presented her research at several conferences and has contributed to several edited books.

Jane Mullen is an associate professor of organizational behavior/human resource management in the Ron Joyce Center for Business Studies at Mount Allison University. Her research interests include occupational health and safety, with a primary focus on young workers, leadership, and workplace aggression. She has published in the *Journal of Occupational Health Psychology*, *Work and Stress*, and the *Journal of Occupational and Organizational Psychology*.

Mike Teed is a professor at the Williams School of Business at Bishop's University. He is currently in the final stages of completing his PhD in industrial/ organizational psychology at Saint Mary's University in Halifax, Nova Scotia. Mike has consulted in both private and public organizations, working on a variety of projects including personal selection, organizational assessments, stress interventions, personnel selection, and performance evaluations. His research has been published in academic journals including *International Journal of Workplace Health Management* and *Basic and Applied Social Psychology*, and he has also presented at numerous international conferences.

Chapter 10: How to Encourage Changes in Behavior through Interventions Integrated into Quality of Life Programs within Companies

Alberto José N. Ogata is a physician, MSc in medicine and health economics from Universidade Federal de São Paulo, member of the international committee of the International Association for Worksite Health Promotion, and coordinator of the MBA in management of health promotion programs at the Centro Universitário São Camilo. He is author of the books *Wellness*, *Guia Prático de Qualidade de Vida* (Practical Quality of Life Guide), and *Profissionais Saudáveis—Empresas Produtivas* (Healthy Workers—Productive Companies) and is president of the Brazilian Association of Quality of Life (ABQV).

Sâmia Aguiar Brandão Simurro is a psychologist, with an MSc in psychology from Universidade de São Paulo. She is a specialist in psychosomatics, stress, health care, and hospital psychology and has international certification in wellness coaching and management of health promotion programs. She is author and co-author of books and vice-president of the Brazilian Association of Quality of Life (ABQV).

Chapter 11: Quality of Life and Self-Care in Civil Servants: Prevention and Intervention

Dulce Helena C. Hatzenberger has a psychology degree, specialization in organizational psychology, and an MSc and PhD in education from Pontifícia

Universidade Católica do Rio Grande do Sul. She is currently associate professor at PUCRS, coordinator of the department of social, work and health psychology at the School of Psychology at PUCRS, health expert at the Rio Grande do Sul State Department of Health, and volunteer psychologist at the charity *Casa da Criança Auxiliadora.*

Mary Sandra Carlotto has a psychology degree from UNISINOS, specialization in human resources management (Universidade Cândido Mendes), an MSc in collective health from Universidade Luterana do Brasil, and a PhD in social psychology (Universidad de Santiago de Compostela). She is currently professor at the School of Psychology at Pontifícia Universidade Católica do Rio Grande do Sul. She is a member of the Unidad de Investigación Psicosocial de la Conducta Organizacional (Universidad de Valencia) and a member of the investigation team at the Psychosocial Rehabilitation Laboratory at Universidade do Porto (Portugal).

Chapter 12: Job Stress Prevention: An Overview of Approaches

Joseph J. Hurrell, Jr. is the current editor of the *Journal of Occupational Health Psychology (JOHP)* and was previously affiliated with the National Institute for Occupational Safety and Health (NIOSH) where, for many years, he conducted both basic and applied research on the topic of occupational stress. He is a founding member of the Society for Occupational Health Psychology.

Steven L. Sauter is a member of the Associate Graduate Faculty at Northern Kentucky University, and a consultant to the National Institute for Occupational Safety and Health where he formerly served as Coordinator of the NIOSH Program on Work Organization and Stress.

CPSIA information can be obtained at www.ICGtesting.com
Printed in the USA
LVOW10s1937060514

384652LV00007B/173/P